Perspectives on Modern Literature

# PERSPECTIVES

# ON

# MODERN

# LITERATURE

*edited, and with an introduction by*

Frederick J. Hoffman
*University of California*
*Riverside*

ROW, PETERSON AND COMPANY

Evanston, Illinois                    Elmsford, New York

# ACKNOWLEDGMENTS

The editor wishes to express his thanks to the following publishers and individuals for granting permission to reprint the selections listed below:

"The Mood of Three Generations" by Daniel Bell. From *The End of Ideology,* The Free Press, 1960. Reprinted by permission of the author and the publishers. (Part A originally appeared in the *New Leader* [April 1, 1957]; Part B in the *Saturday Review* [March 21, 1955]; Part C in the *New Leader* [December 9, 1957]; Part D in *Encounter* [September, 1959].)

Excerpt from *The History of a Literary Radical* by Randolph Bourne. Reprinted by courtesy of S. A. Russell, Publishers.

"Revolutionary Symbolism in America" by Kenneth Burke. From *American Writers' Congress,* International Publishers, 1935. Reprinted by permission of the author.

"D. H. Lawrence" by Christopher Caudwell. Reprinted by permission of Dodd, Mead & Company from *Studies in a Dying Culture* by Christopher Caudwell.

"General Aims and Theories" by Hart Crane, as reprinted in Philip Horton's *Hart Crane,* W. W. Norton & Company, 1939. Reprinted by permission of Samuel Loveman, executor of the Crane estate.

"Baudelaire" from *Selected Essays* by T. S. Eliot, copyright, 1932, 1936, 1950, by Harcourt, Brace & World, Inc.; copyright, 1960, by T. S. Eliot. Reprinted by permission of the publishers.

"The Stockholm Address" by William Faulkner, delivered in Stockholm, Sweden, when Faulkner received the Nobel Prize for Literature, November, 1950.

Part II of "Humanism in the Twentieth Century" by Norman Foerster. From *Toward Standards,* Farrar & Rinehart, 1930. Reprinted by permission of the author.

"Wilder: Prophet of the Genteel Christ" by Michael Gold. From *Proletarian Literature in the United States,* International Publishers, 1935. Reprinted by permission of International Publishers. (Originally

# PREFACE

Just how may a collection of this kind prove useful? There are many anthologies of modern criticism, and if *Perspectives on Modern Literature* were just another one of these, it would have no real reason for being. I base my justification for this book on the manner in which it proves its title. The student of modern literature needs more than its texts if he is to see it in any depth at all. College libraries simply cannot accommodate present large enrollments; there are not enough books. Other collections are limited to criticism and are based on the assumption that criticism is another art, to be judged in and of itself, with only occasional glances at its subject.

I have tried to reprint essays here from several areas and levels of discourse in twentieth-century British and American writing. Some of them are avowedly pieces of journalism; others are reactions to cultural and intellectual situations of peculiar and special interest to the time of publication. There are critical essays as well, but I have chosen these because they are above all another kind of "perspective."

Let me speculate on the uses of this book. Suppose students in modern literature were asked to read a paperback reprint of a novel or play or poem. The text itself will of course yield much; but there is a time in any course when the student needs to see the text from one or two or three perspectives that are available only to risky inference or vague speculation. *Perspectives on Modern Literature* contains several perspectives on any one text that may be selected. Once having settled upon the values within the literature itself, the student can help himself immensely by reviewing it in terms of these perspectives. The conditions—intellectual, cultural, ideological—in which a literary text is created vary considerably in intensity and relevance. Without these perspectives, the student must rely upon various secondary sources (histories of ideas, popular exploitations of social manners like F. L. Allen's *Only Yesterday*, etc.) of indifferent value and dependability. With the aid of *Perspectives*, he has a much better chance to test any literary or intellectual history against his own experience in reading, not just *about* but *in* the period.

As I have suggested in the Introduction, *Perspectives* offers evidences of both ideological and moral tensions in modern literature. These tensions are especially complex in our time, because systems of belief, approaches to knowledge, even the qualities of knowledge, change radically and quickly and often. I believe *Perspectives* to be an indispensable register of these changes. As such, it can be very useful to students in any course that is not altogether satisfied with the limits of pure textual analysis.

FREDERICK J. HOFFMAN

University of California
Riverside

# TABLE OF CONTENTS

## 3 Poetry and Belief

PART II    THE 1930's

## 4 The Survival Values of Tradition

## 5 The Leftist Imperative

x

# INTRODUCTION

## I

A word is perhaps needed in explanation of the kind of book *Perspectives on Modern Literature* is. It is designed as a supplement to paperbacked selections used in surveys of modern literature. For the most part, this book contains critical and/or journalistic pieces that are not otherwise easily available to such courses. Frequently the lecturer in modern literature finds himself talking about a text which is not easily available to the student; and, enrollments being what they are, the college library cannot accommodate him.

This supplementary role is indispensable to the task of giving a complete account of modern literature. But an additional comment should help to explain the word *Perspectives* of the title. These essays are *not* the literature of the twentieth century; they are, instead, a wide variety of lights thrown upon that literature, from a number of directions, ideological, moral, political, and sometimes merely topical. They are, in short, "documents" which help to give modern literature a setting, to suggest characteristics of *milieu:* a common fund of intellectual circumstances to which modern literature often refers and from which it frequently has had its beginnings.

The quarrel over what is the most useful approach to literature has now been going on for four decades. In its modern context, the debate is concerned with three major questions: Should a literary text be examined exclusively in formal terms? Is scholarship relevant to the study of literature? Are documentary matters, drawn from the setting of a literature, at all relevant to the study of it? I have collected this group of essays in the assumption that formalist analysis is very important but not exclusively so. A literature has a cultural relevance, just as a culture has a bearing on the full meaning of a literature. Literary taste is formed both in the awareness of what a text is and as a consequence of shifting and changing standards concerning its vitality and meaning. The most rigorously formal criticism has a moral foundation in the critic's valuation of language and form and in his earnest concern over the issues of communication.

Even a cursory examination of the essays in this volume will reward the reader with a number of suggestions as to the interaction of literature with both contemporary and universal concerns. A philosophy—naturalism, for example—affects the core of formal representations. A sense of cultural urgency stimulates re-examinations of the value and strength of art. Contemporary social absurdities incite critics or journalists

1

to caricatural or satirical attacks, and these in turn affect literary representations of the times. Most important of all, what is apparently an intensely formalist judgment of literature is inspired by the most literal of moral concerns; that it concentrates on intrinsic rather than extrinsic matters may be a clue to the dissolution (whether temporary or permanent) of extrinsic guides.

These essays offer *perspectives*, therefore, in the sense that they help to explain the peculiarities of modern literature as formal responses to the special circumstances of modern culture. I should like to think of a *milieu* as a composite of the following elements, each of which may affect the writer deliberately or insidiously:

1. Theories of reality, or intellectual dispositions toward it.
2. Social forms, or manners, what Lionel Trilling has called "a culture's hum and buzz of implication." [1]
3. Moral forms, or the formal risks an artist takes with the morality of his time, whether he adapts it to his work or uses his work to express his rebellion against it.
4. Conventions, or what the imagination does to the moral and social forms by way of adjusting them to formal requirements.
5. Emotional tonality: that is, the degree of emotional intensity, or sentimentality, with which a writer applies himself to the moral and intellectual circumstances of his time.
6. Forms and qualities of knowledge, as these exist in the philosophical, scientific, and cultural worlds a writer inhabits.

All of these conditions act to exert pressure upon a writer's conception of human reality. Reality is what an artist, acting within and because of them, formally makes of it. The language he uses, the forms he selects, the kinds of image and metaphor we find in his work are all affected by his receptiveness to contemporary intellectual persuasions and pressures. One may argue that these qualities are found in the literature itself and that the narrowest kind of scrutiny of the literature is the best way of realizing them; but there are many occasions when an awareness of the special nature of a culture and its bearing upon it help to enrich the study of literature.

There is an old, tired cliché to the effect that "literature does not exist in a vacuum." It means, of course, that a writer responds to many social and cultural pressures. It would be better to say that many perspectives play upon the literature itself, that a close look at these perspectives, as they appear in critical, editorial, and other types of document, will help to make us realize what has gone into literature. The key terms are psychological, moral, and ideological; these describe circumstances which must affect the creative talent as they describe the struggle between extremes of individual and impersonal pressures upon it.

---

[1] "Manners, Morals, and the Novel" (1947), in *The Liberal Imagination* (New York: The Viking Press, 1950), p. 206.

Far from distorting the intrinsic nature of a literature, a study of the perspectives given in these essays will help us to determine the conditions in which it was created. They should bring us closer to it and to the special problems with which modern creativity has had to contend.

## II

What are these perspectives, and how may they conveniently be described? No organization of them is wholly satisfactory, because modern culture is extraordinarily complex. The broadest kind of definition must include these characteristics: a great self-consciousness, a continuous effort to define and redefine social morality, a preoccupation with the problem of communicating values through words and forms, and a reappraisal—along the lines of personal relevance—of the significance of Christianity. Ideological pressures, whether religious or secular, are the most important facts of modern culture. I define an ideology as any effectively systematic description of the human condition and its relation to impersonal or suprapersonal causes. Naturalism is an ideology in that sense, as are Christianity, communism, and fascism. The modern writer is suspicious of ideologies; and a common enough occupation is to act as though he were free of their pressures. But this apparent rejection of ideologies is actually a response to them; he wishes either to act unsystematically (on the grounds that to act in accordance with an imposed system will destroy his individuality), or to redefine himself in the terms of literature itself, giving an extraordinary importance to the *particulars* of the literary experience. But these acts of denial are in themselves acts of ideological reconstruction. Again and again in the essays included in this volume, the writer is seen in the act of showing his hand, of betraying his anxious concern over extra-literary meaning. It is not so much that the writer in modern culture despises ideology, but that the conditions of our time make for a confusion of ideologies, so that he frequently senses the need to improvise on his own. The impression these essays give is of many personal ideological maneuvers, which come out of a distrust of conventional interpretations of the world, and lead to a restatement of "faith," whether in the past as personally viewed, or in the present as seen within the limits of the form and word of literature itself.

If we take the years 1915 to 1930, for example, we can discern three major perspectives upon them: a national self-consciousness, conspicuous among American writers because they sense themselves (for the first time as they think) obligated beyond merely provincial responsibilities; an urgent sense of the need to redefine literature itself, to concentrate upon its specific formal values; a struggle to differentiate scientific knowledge from poetic, and to explore the consequences of science for human belief.

As for the first of these, we have many explorations of the American present, and correspondingly of the American past, for the purpose of trying to find out how we came to be what we are now. The critics of the *Seven Arts* magazine (1916–1917), of the *Freeman* (1920–1924), and in a different sense of the old *Masses* (1911–1917) reveal a strong drive toward national self-knowledge, which is accompanied by much self-criticism and a vigorous reordering of the historical sense. The list includes Van Wyck Brooks, Lewis Mumford, Randolph Bourne, Paul Rosenfeld, Waldo Frank. Each of them examines the intellectual scene, finds it lacking in many of the purposes and graces that a mature culture should have, then moves back in time, in a desire to explain the lack. There is a curious mixture in these essays of embarrassment and pride, a sense of importance and a sense of failure. The Puritans, Emerson, Thoreau, Whitman, are named again and again; the split between materialism and idealism is invoked by way of explanation; a proud sense of the land's extent and promise is met by an anguished realization of our having fallen short of expectations. Henry James's *The American Scene* (1907) is the model of such criticism, generally much more acute and penetrating than those that followed.

When we turn to the second of these perspectives, the drive toward critical redefinition, we note no lessening of moral fervor or concern, only a withdrawal from larger issues into what are apparently more minute ones, a concentration upon the particulars of literary experience. T. E. Hulme, Ezra Pound, and T. S. Eliot all ask for a clearer literary focus; the tendency is to be wary of generalities, to respect and even worship the image, the word; they want clarity, freedom from what Pound called "a pentametric echo of the sociological dogma printed in last year's magazines." [2] Yet they do not write an unideological criticism, but are as much revisionists as are the critics of the first group. They wish to judge and to form and re-form ideas in terms of the special qualities of their art. This is only apparently a reductive measure; perspectives are rescued or regained as these critics move beyond the explication of central matters to areas of philosophical and moral speculation and to literary history.

The core idea is that of the union or fusion of the particulars of literature with the universals of meaning. The expression of this unity is in the language itself, which ranges from basic simplicity to ultimate complexity and paradox. Not that these critics wish to discard universals, but that the universals should reside within the details of language and metaphor. While the writers of the first group generally look at literature from "the outside" (that is, they stand at a distance away from it and ask what it should mean), those of the second look at culture from "the inside," from the contained work and from the specific nature of its containment. The honorific terms are "precision," "integrity," "exactness"; the ideally adjusted intellectual is the person whose mind and feeling collaborate in his reaction to the phenomena of his world and to

---

[2] Letter to Harriet Monroe, August 18, 1912. In *Letters,* edited by D. D. Paige (New York: Harcourt, Brace, 1950), p. 9.

their meaning. Variations of this ideal are the person who feels but does not think, the person who thinks but feels insufficiently, and the person who does both but not precisely or at the same time. The mind should register feeling; the sensibility ought concretely to react to the mind's ideas.

These concerns are related to history and to society by the very nature of integrity's demands. Since language is a means of communication, all critics of this group ascribe great moral significance to the "hardness" and what Hulme calls the "dryness" (as distinguished from Romantic "dampness") of language uses. A highly selective revision of literary history results; the historical perspective of Pound and Eliot is as startlingly original and unorthodox as the conventional histories of literature were undiscriminating and "catholic." The crucial turning point for Eliot was the seventeenth century, in the latter half of which a "dissociation of sensibility" (as he called it) set in.[3] For Pound there is not only one but several points of literary crisis; his view of their history is closely linked to his definition of the role of literature in communicating truth. Literature is an indispensable part of the whole society. That is why it is so important that the artist communicate and not "lie" or be guilty of dishonest literary methods. Literature is the clue to the health of a society.[4]

We find that the perspectives offered by critics of the second group are no less valuable than those of the first; their manner of approaching literature is very different, we may almost say antithetic. Yet there is much "moral fervor" in each, much concern over self-definition and over the proper means of arriving at it. Ideologies are only apparently held in abeyance in either case.

The third group of writers may be said to be preoccupied with the effects of new knowledges, or half-knowledges, upon ideologies. At the one extreme, naturalism led to a kind of romantic pessimism, as is obvious in the excerpt published here from J. W. Krutch's *The Modern Temper* (1929). On the one hand, scientific terminologies and conclusions led to strange alterations of conventional beliefs; on the other, they contributed to a *faute de mieux* desperation, that left the question of moral sanctions for human conduct largely unanswered or ignored altogether.

Such critics as Eliot and I. A. Richards were more concerned with the poetics and linguistics of belief than with the metaphysics of disbelief. Eliot debated not so much the intrinsic value of Christianity but its failure in history, more specifically in nineteenth- and twentieth-century history. Thus it is that, in his essay on "Baudelaire," he regards any suggestion of deep moral feeling an encouragement to the survival of Christianity. As all of us know who have read Eliot's work of the

[3] See "The Metaphysical Poets," in *Selected Essays* (New York: Harcourt, Brace, 1950), pp. 241–50. First printed in 1921.
[4] See "The Serious Artist," in *The Literary Essays* (New York: New Directions, 1954), pp. 41–57. First printed in 1913.

twenties, the way of the Christian believer is hard indeed. Implicit in his description of these states of unbelief is a profound disturbance over the dominance of hard naturalism and empty materialism in the modern scene. Richards is preoccupied, with something of the same intensity, with the language and psychology of this situation. He differentiates between verifiable (scientific) reference and "pseudo statement," or aesthetic statement. The very serious question he raises has to do with the apparent mutual exclusiveness of the two. One comes eventually to the conclusion that Richards does not wish to disparage "pseudo statement," but that he is nevertheless disturbed by the quite forbidding hostility between the two forms of communication, which spells the defeat of an earlier confidence, when poetic and other forms of discourse were less far apart, indeed managed together to communicate a richly endowed truth.

These are additional perspectives upon the modern ideological struggle. If poetic discourse does not communicate "truth" (that is, if it can make only "pseudo statements"), then how can we serve ourselves from the despair which Krutch rhetorically describes and Richards analyzes? Eliot would have us think that we need to "redeem the time," [5] to hold on to what powers of belief we do possess, and, in short, to survive an age of disbelief; the expectation is that the Christian ideology is universally valid, but that the "Word" is temporarily "unheard" and not understood.

### III

There were many other views. In fact, we may say that were it not for Eliot's distinction as a poet and critic, he would have been discovered at the height of his fame to hold a minority view, or to demonstrate one among several reactions to the problems of ideological confusion in the postwar world. The most frequently asserted points of view were secular, dependent upon a neoclassical view of human psychology or a purely secular world view. The period of 1929–39 was not exclusively a time of "leftist" or "proletarian" criticism; in fact, as we gain more and more perspective upon that decade, the suspicion grows that leftist critical strategies were not so important as some others, which did not make nearly so much noise nor speak with such an ideological confidence of their monopoly over future expectations. The Humanist point of view was an older one, which had been in process of development for some decades, at the hands of Paul Elmer More and Irving Babbitt. In fact, it may be said that 1930 marked a point of crisis in its history, signalized by the publication of two symposia, *Humanism in America* (edited by Norman Foerster) and the anti-Humanist volume, *The Critique of Humanism* (edited by C. Hartley Grattan).

[5] A phrase used both in the poem "Ash-Wednesday" (1930) and in the last paragraph of the essay, "Thoughts After Lambeth" (1931).

Another perspective upon the ideological struggle was the Southern or "Agrarian" position, represented here by the introduction to *I'll Take My Stand* by "Twelve Southerners" (also published in 1930). The point of view was very complex, but in general we can say that its sponsors held to a philosophy of tradition and "the land," an agrarian world in which values might be preserved by being "lived" through generations of persons who appreciated the "special yield" [6] of tradition; all of these they opposed to an industrial, mechanized, materialistic, restless, progressive, "Northern" culture, which they admitted had gained ascendancy after the Civil War and was engaged in overwhelming all that was left of American culture.

Both the "Agrarians" and the Humanists valued the past, but their perspectives upon it were radically different. For the "Agrarians," it was a landed tradition, a rescue of legitimate moments of experience and their preservation from the destructive mobilities of a hostile society. The Humanists believed in literary values—that is, moral values that had been captured in literature; and they jealously guarded these and the "purity" of their occasions. They did not often analyze literature, but instead assumed that the values in it could be intuited and their psychological effects readily assimilated by the man of "good taste" and moral sense.

Indeed, Yvor Winters' major criticism of them was that they were not critics but merely moralists, so that they never defined what they were after or how it might be discerned. Winters offered instead a "moralist" criticism that was closely tied to the assumption that literary form and rational control were indispensably related. As a consequence of this relationship, the critic might discover both the quality and the degree of any writer's "control" through investigating the soundness of his forms and his diction. Winters above all maintained that critical evaluation was not only possible but necessary. One could not be satisfied with an eclectic choice of morally edifying passages, but must assert on both moral and aesthetic grounds (they were after all the same) what was good literature and what was bad. The values that made literature were moral values, as they were for the Humanists, but for Winters they were necessarily linked to formal and analytic powers and discriminations, about which the Humanists were at best vague. Despite his obstinacy and his occasional exaggerations of value in literature (he made mistakes, as did any other critic), Winters has proved to be a focal point of moralism in criticism, if only because his judgments were often supraliterary without necessarily being nonliterary.

However important these judgments of tradition and morality in literature have come to be, there can be no doubt that the most popular, and the noisiest, type of criticism in the thirties was prompted by Marxist ideology and by current stresses and strains in the world economy.

---

[6] See Ransom's poem, "Antique Harvesters," Stanza 3. Originally published in *Two Gentlemen in Bonds* (New York: Alfred A. Knopf, 1927).

This anthology presents as wide a variety of leftist criticism as its space permits: from the worst (Mike Gold) to the best (Christopher Caudwell). The earnestness with which leftist critics debated the functional values of literature is nowhere better manifested than in the several Writers' Congresses and their equivalent in Britain. Much of the talk in these meetings was naïvely activist and narrowly pragmatic, but occasionally a sharp thrust of intelligence is noticeable, as in the piece of Kenneth Burke's that is reprinted here. Burke was to go on, to become one of the most distinguished and complex of modern critics; but the basic interest in the psychology of motives for saying and writing has persisted, however subtle and clever its more recent manifestations have become. Caudwell (Christopher St. John Sprigg) demonstrates the ranges of Marxist criticism: its grasp of history, its curious rhetoric, its sense of urgent arbitrariness (the insistence that things "must be this way," to prove the validity of developmental strategies).

There is no doubt that the leftist perspectives on modern literature were gained in a time of frantic and often violent events; history was happening quickly. Most significant of all the features of this decade were the frequent occasions on which ideological commitment was tested against the fact of violence. The question of whether language can match an increasing violence of disruptive event and fact is one of the most important of our time. Shortly before the so-called "leftist" decade began, the two Massachusetts anarchists, Sacco and Vanzetti, were executed (in August of 1927) for a crime that most historians have agreed they did not commit. This was an example of ideologically motivated violence; but it was a single event and readily comprehensible; and it was possible to be sentimental, or angry, or to feel outraged over it, without feeling that its quality of violence was too much for any kind of conviction to accommodate.

Our recent history has proved more and more clearly the difficulty that ideologically supported convictions have in grasping violence; it is *too* destructive for one to "take sides" with confidence. The specific questions of guilt and complicity all but go unanswered. That is why the Spanish Civil War (1936–39) is so important to students of modern literature. Much more violently explosive and destructive than the execution of two anarchists or any police "atrocity" of the thirties could have been, it was still only a minor prelude to catastrophes to come. Because it was a civil war, it was bitterly fought, and with passions at white heat. Because it was an ideological struggle, it drew to it all of the conflicting passions and commitments that had been growing in the decade.

Perhaps above all, the Spanish war was an early demonstration of the growing distance between ideology and impersonal event. Again and again, the experience of violence is proved too great to be explained adequately on ideological grounds. George Orwell (Eric Blair) offered an important perspective upon the decade in the best book on the Spanish Civil War (*Homage to Catalonia*, 1938). He was in an especially good position to observe both the dissolution of ideological "faith" into many conflicting loyalties and expedients and the actual experiencing of violence and disorder and its effect upon the motives of the struggle.

The perspectives of the thirties raised many questions that are still being asked, though not satisfactorily answered. To the general mistrust of large schemata of explanation that we can observe in the twenties, we can add the condition which Daniel Bell was to call "the end of ideology." One critic has pointed out the great attractiveness of Marxism to the modern intellectual,[7] its apparently persuasive simplicity and the extent of its doctrinal readiness to explain everything systematically and even logically. Like other forms of modern ideology, Marxism has suffered severely from the events to which the war of 1936–39 in Spain served as an introduction.

## IV

In general, the "verities" of which William Faulkner spoke so eloquently in 1950 have had a hard time of it since his Stockholm address. Not that verities are in themselves no longer available to the modern sensibility, but that the peculiarities of Faulkner's rhetoric, while powerful enough in its insistence that it be attended to, was "old fashioned" even in 1950. Perspectives upon the literature since then are hard to come by, and harder to evaluate. Much of our literature is angry or uncomfortably sententious, or rather naïvely charismatic. Its one distinguishing feature is that it is nonideological, that the disciplines it advocates are either wholly (and even joyfully) destructive, or plainly conducive to an almost total separation from society and its "issues." Daniel Bell explains these conditions in the excerpt from *The End of Ideology* that is reprinted here.

There is a complex of reasons. One of them, discussed above, is the shock of violence, too great to be accounted for by any arrangement of "verities" or in terms of simple motivations. Not that the war wasn't clearly explained; its objectives were much more clearly seen than those of World War I. Rather, the shock of war has led to a dissociation of feeling from thought more violent than any discovered by Eliot or his contemporaries. Reasons no longer convince; the intellect does not persuade; and the sensibility retreats from the fact of an awkward divorce of fact from universal.

In many respects, the attitudes of the fifties were compulsively hostile to a "business-as-usual" postwar philosophy. The manner of preparing for a corporative or an organizational or an institutional life was less and less credibly associated with the "whole man" of whom the *Seven Arts* critics had spoken, or with the "trained sensibility" of Eliot and Richards, or even of the ideological saint of the thirties. Mr. Faulkner urged his

---

[7] Victor Brombert, *The Intellectual Hero* (Philadelphia: J. B. Lippincott, 1961), pp. 149–50.

verities upon the postwar world in much the same romantically compulsive way as Bertrand Russell used in 1918 (*Mysticism and Logic*), when he said that the pessimistic conclusions of scientific naturalism ought to be "heroically" accepted. But neither kind of heroism was available to the generation of the fifties, or desired by it. Instead that decade displayed an unideological anger or scorn of both verities and institutions.

In the case of Norman Mailer and many of his contemporaries, they expressed a vigorous hostility to convention, an attempt somehow to match the impersonal violence of the war with as strong an expression of inner, personal violence as possible, to "murder and create" outside the bounds of either conventional or ideological proprieties. The so-called "Beats" made a virtue of passivity, though their literature (and especially their poetry) showed a sufficiently lively and satirical interest in the ludicrous imbalances present in conventional society.[8] Like them, the contemporaries of John Wain were "marginal personalities," though the literature of the so-called "Angry Young Men" was as conventional (both in its satires and in its "domestic comedies") as some examples of Anthony Trollope and other Victorian novelists. They were, in short, within the tradition; however angry their protests against society were, they were made within the social and literary conventions of the past. One had really to cross the Channel, to France, to find a genuinely untraditional literary manner and mood. Perhaps only Colin Wilson, among the young British writers, behaved as though he were a genuine and an articulate outsider; and Colin Wilson's talent was regrettably small.

All of this suggests that the generation of the fifties was an "interim generation." To what it would prove to be a transition, it is surely hard to determine: perhaps, to World War III; less likely, to a new conservatism or expedient convention; scarcely at all, to the conversion of the "squares" to its way of life and its mood of revolt. Meanwhile, though there may be little or no conventional moral strength, there is a demonstrable literary vitality, perhaps because this generation has so skillfully and expertly aimed at so obvious a target.

## V

*Perspectives on Modern Literature* is designed to nourish and to enrich the study of modern literature. Its major purpose is to enable the student to look at it from several vantage points beyond those offered by an exclusive scrutiny of the texts. Without wishing in any way to give the essays included here an independent, "nonliterary" value, I am convinced that the convenience and the understanding are served by means of providing as many perspectives upon literature as are available within

---

[8] See my anthology, *Marginal Manners* (Evanston, Illinois: Row, Peterson and Co., 1962).

a *milieu*. These essays are admittedly supplementary. They should often prove more than useful, at stages in a literature course, where the nature of the text cries out for references beyond itself. They are in this sense a necessary check upon a too narrow or a too simple-mindedly concentrated attention to "pure literature." The impulses behind these essays are predominantly moral: they are a moral commentary upon conditions that inspire or force the creation of a literature to answer them.

# PART I

# 1915–1930

# CULTURE AND THE INTELLECTUAL

*RANDOLPH BOURNE*

*from*

## THE HISTORY OF A LITERARY RADICAL

Randolph Bourne (1886–1918) was one of the great, promising young men of the World War I generation. His untimely death cut off what might have been a distinguished career as critic of American culture. He was associated with Brooks, Rosenfeld, and others of the *Seven Arts* group, and spent much of his time criticizing what he thought were serious weaknesses in the transmission of culture to his generation. Miro, his "literary radical," reflects this discontent and points to the impulse toward a fresh interest in contemporary American literature and culture, that "certain hopeful vision of a 'young world,'" as Bourne called it. This interest, expressed especially in the last paragraphs of the following essay, links him to Brooks, Mumford, Rosenfeld, and the other members of his generation.

*F*or a man of culture, my friend Miro began his literary career in a singularly unpromising way. Potential statesmen in log-cabins might miraculously come in touch with all the great books of the world, but the days of Miro's young school life were passed in innocence of Homer or Dante or Shakespeare, or any of the other traditional mind-formers of the race. What Miro had for his nourishment, outside the Bible, which was a magical book that you must not drop on the floor, or his

15

schoolreaders, which were like lightning flashes of unintelligible scenes, was the literature that his playmates lent him—exploits of British soldiers in Spain and the Crimea, the death-defying adventures of young fili-busters in Cuba and Nicaragua. Miro gave them a languid perusing, and did not criticize their literary style. Huckleberry Finn and Tom Sawyer somehow eluded him until he had finished college, and no fresher tale of adventure drifted into his complacent home until the era of "Richard Carvel" and "Janice Meredith" sharpened his wits and gave him a vague feeling that there was such a thing as literary art. The classics were stiffly enshrined behind glass doors that were very hard to open— at least Hawthorne and Irving and Thackeray were there, and Tenny-son's and Scott's poems—but nobody ever discussed them or looked at them. Miro's busy elders were taken up with the weekly *Outlook* and *Independent* and *Christian Work*, and felt they were doing much for Miro when they provided him and his sister with *St. Nicholas* and *The Youth's Companion*. It was only that Miro saw the black books looking at him accusingly from the case, and a rudimentary conscience, slipping easily over from Calvinism to culture, forced him solemnly to grapple with "The Scarlet Letter" or "Marmion." All he remembers is that the writers of these books he browsed among used a great many words and made a great fuss over shadowy offenses and conflicts and passions that did not even stimulate his imagination with sufficient force to cause him to ask his elders what it was all about. Certainly the filibusters were easier.

At school Miro was early impressed with the vast dignity of the lit-erary works and names he was compelled to learn. Shakespeare and Goethe and Dante lifted their plaster heads frowningly above the teach-er's, as they perched on shelves about the room. Much was said of the greatness of literature. But the art of phonetics and the complications of grammar swamped Miro's early school years. It was not until he reached the High School that literature began really to assume that sacredness which he had heretofore felt only for Holy Scripture. His initiation into culture was made almost a religious mystery by the con-scientious and harassed teacher. As the Deadwood Boys and Henty and David Harum slipped away from Miro's soul in the presence of Milton's "Comus" and Burke "On Conciliation," a cultural devoutness was en-gendered in him that never really died. At first it did not take Miro beyond the stage where your conscience is strong enough to make you uncomfortable, but not strong enough to make you do anything about it. Miro did not actually become an omnivorous reader of great books. But he was filled with a rich grief that the millions pursued cheap and vulgar fiction instead of the best that has been thought and said in the world. Miro indiscriminately bought cheap editions of the English clas-sics and read them with a certain patient incomprehension.

As for the dead classics, they came to Miro from the hands of his teachers with a prestige even vaster than the books of his native tongue. No doubt ever entered his head that four years of Latin and three years of Greek, an hour a day, were the important preparation he needed for his future as an American citizen. No doubt ever hurt him that the world into which he would pass would be a world where, as his teacher said, Latin and Greek were a solace to the aged, a quickener of taste, a refreshment after manual labor, and a clue to the general knowledge of all human things. Miro would as soon have doubted the rising of the sun as have doubted the wisdom of these serious, puckered women who had the precious manipulation of his cultural upbringing in their charge. Miro was a bright, if a rather vague, little boy, and a fusion of brightness and docility gave him high marks in the school where we went together.

No one ever doubted that these marks expressed Miro's assimilation of the books we pored over. But he told me later that he had never really known what he was studying. Caesar, Virgil, Cicero, Xenophon, Homer, were veiled and misty experiences to him. His mind was a moving present, obliterating each day what it had read the day before, and piercing into a no more comprehended future. He could at no time have given any intelligible account of Aeneas's wanderings or what Cicero was really inveighing against. The Iliad was even more obscure. The only thing which impressed him deeply was an expurgated passage, which he looked up somewhere else and found to be about Mars and Venus caught in the golden bed. Caesar seemed to be at war, and Xenophon wandering somewhere in Asia Minor, with about the same lengthiness and hardship as Miro suffered in reading him. The trouble, Miro thought afterwards, was that these books were to his mind flickering lights in a vast jungle of ignorance. He does not remember marvelling at the excessive dullness of the stories themselves. He plodded his faithful way, using them as his conscientious teachers did, as exercises in language. He looked on Virgil and Cicero as essentially problems in disentangling words which had unaccountably gotten into a bizarre order, and in recognizing certain rather amusing and ingenious combinations, known as "constructions." Why these words took so irritating an order Miro never knew, but he always connected the problem with those algebraic puzzles he had elsewhere to unravel. Virgil's words were further complicated by being arranged in lines which one had to "scan." Miro was pleased with the rhythm, and there were stanzas that had a roll of their own. But the inexorable translating that had to go on tore all this fabric of poetry to pieces. His translations were impeccable, but, as he never wrote them down, he had never before his eyes the consecutive story.

Translations Miro never saw. He knew that they were implements of deadly sin that boys used to cheat with. His horror of them was such as a saint might feel towards a parody of the Bible. Just before Miro left school, his sister in a younger class began to read a prose translation of the Odyssey, and Miro remembers the scorn with which he looked down on so sneaking an entrance into the temple of light. He knew that not everyone could study Latin and Greek, and he learned to be proud of his knowledge. When at last he had passed his examinations for college—his Latin composition and grammar, his syntax and his sight-reading, and his Greek composition and grammar, his Greek syntax and sight-reading, and his translation of Gallic battles and Anabatic frosts, and Dido's farewell and Cicero's objurgations—his zealous rage did not abate. He even insisted on reading the Bucolics, while he was away on his vacation, and a book or two in the Odyssey. His family was a little chilled by his studiousness, but he knew well that he was laying up cultural treasures in heaven, where moth and rust do not corrupt, neither do thieves break in and steal.

Arrived at college, Miro expanded his cultural interests on the approved lines. He read Horace and Plato, Lysias and Terence, impartially, with faithful conscience. Horace was the most exciting because of the parodies that were beginning to appear in the cleverer newspapers. Miro scarcely knew whether to be amused or shocked at "Odi Persicos" or "Integer Vitæ" done into current slang. The professors, mild-mannered men who knew their place and kept it, never mentioned these impudent adventures, but for Miro it was the first crack in his Ptolemaic system of reverences. There came a time when his mind began to feel replete, when this heavy pushing through the opaque medium of dead language began to fatigue him. He should have been able to read fluently, but there were always turning up new styles, new constructions, to plague him. Latin became to him like a constant diet of beefsteak, and Greek like a constant diet of fine wheaten bread. They lost their taste. These witty poets and ostentatious orators—what were they all about? What was their background? Where did they fit into Miro's life? The professors knew some history, but what did that history mean? Miro found himself surfeited and dissatisfied. He began to look furtively at translations to get some better English than he was able to provide. The hair-splittings of Plato began to bore him when he saw them in crystal-clear English, and not muffled in the original Greek. His apostasy had begun.

It was not much better in his study of English literature. Miro was given a huge anthology, a sort of press-clipping bureau of *belles-lettres*, from Chaucer to Arthur Symons. Under the direction of a professor who was laying out a career for himself as poet—or "modern singer," as he expressed it—the class went briskly through the centuries sampling their genius and tasting the various literary flavors. The enterprise reminded Miro of those books of woollen samples which one looks through when one is to have a suit of clothes made. But in this case, the student did not even have the pleasure of seeing the suit of clothes. All that was expected of him, apparently, was that he should become familiar, from these microscopic pieces, with the different textures and patterns. The great writers passed before his mind like figures in a crowded street. There was no time for preferences. Indeed the professor strove diligently to give each writer his just due. How was one to appreciate the great thoughts and the great styles if one began to choose violently between

them, or attempt any discrimination on grounds of their peculiar con-
geniality for one's own soul? Criticism had to spurn such subjectivity,
scholarship could not be wilful. The neatly arranged book of "readings,"
with its medicinal doses of inspiration, became the symbol of Miro's
education.

These early years of college did not deprive Miro of his cultural loyalty, but they deadened his appetite. Although almost inconceivably
docile, he found himself being bored. He had come from school a serious boy, with more than a touch of priggishness in him, and a vague
aspiration to be a "man of letters." He found himself becoming a col-
lector of literary odds-and-ends. If he did not formulate this feeling
clearly, he at least knew. He found that the literary life was not as
interesting as he had expected. He sought no adventures. When he
wrote, it was graceful lyrics of polite criticisms of William Collins or
Charles Lamb. These canonized saints of culture still held the field for
Miro, however. There was nothing between them and that popular
literature of the day that all good men bemoaned. Classic or popular,
"highbrow" or "lowbrow," this was the choice, and Miro unquestion-
ingly took the orthodox heaven. In 1912 the most popular of Miro's
English professors had never heard of Galsworthy, and another was
creating a flurry of scandal in the department by recommending Chesterton to his classes. It would scarcely have been in college that Miro
would have learned of an escape from the closed dichotomy of culture.
Bored with the "classic," and frozen with horror at the "popular," his
career as a man of culture must have come to a dragging end if he had
not been suddenly liberated by a chance lecture which he happened to
hear while he was at home for the holidays.

The literary radical who appeared before the Lyceum Club of Miro's
village was none other than Professor William Lyon Phelps, and it is
to that evening of cultural audacity Miro thinks he owes all his later
emancipation. The lecturer grappled with the "modern novel," and
tossed Hardy, Tolstoi, Turgenev, Meredith, even Trollope, into the
minds of the charmed audience with such effect that the virgin shelves
of the village library were ravished for days to come by the eager minds
upon whom these great names dawned for the first time. "Jude the
Obscure" and "Resurrection" were of course kept officially away from
the vulgar, but Miro managed to find "Smoke" and "Virgin Soil" and
"Anna Karenina" and "The Warden" and "A Pair of Blue Eyes" and
"The Return of the Native." Later at college he explored the forbidden
realms. It was as if some devout and restless saint had suddenly been
introduced to the Apocrypha. A new world was opened to Miro that
was neither "classic" nor "popular," and yet which came to one under
the most unimpeachable auspices. There was, at first, it is true, an air
of illicit adventure about the enterprise. The lecturer who made himself
the missionary of such vigorous and piquant doctrine had the air of
being a heretic, or at least a boy playing out of school. But Miro himself returned to college a cultural revolutionist. His orthodoxies crum-

bled. He did not try to reconcile the new with the old. He applied pick and dynamite to the whole structure of the canon. Irony, humor, tragedy, sensuality, suddenly appeared to him as literary qualities in forms that he could understand. They were like oxygen to his soul.

If these qualities were in the books he had been reading, he had never felt them. The expurgated sample-books he had studied had passed too swiftly over the Elizabethans to give him a sense of their lustiness. Miro immersed himself voluptuously in the pessimism of Hardy. He fed on the poignant torture of Tolstoi. While he was read-ing "Resurrection," his class in literature was making an "intensive" study of Tennyson. It was too much. Miro rose in revolt. He forswore literary courses forever, dead rituals in which anaemic priests mumbled their trite critical commentary. Miro did not know that to naughtier critics even Mr. Phelps might eventually seem a pale and timid Gideon, himself stuck in moral sloughs. He was grateful enough for that blast of trumpets which made his own scholastic walls fall down.

The next stage in Miro's cultural life was one of frank revolt. He became as violent as a heretic as he had been docile as a believer. Mod-ern novels merely started the rift that widened into modern ideas. The professors were of little use. Indeed, when Miro joined a group of radi-cals who had started a new college paper, a relentless vendetta began with the teachers. Miro and his friends threw over everything that was mere literature. Social purpose must shine from any writing that was to rouse their enthusiasm. Literary flavor was to be permissible only where it made vivid high and revolutionary thought. Tolstoi became their god, Wells their high priest. Chesterton infuriated them. They wrote violent assaults upon him which began in imitation of his cool paradoxicality and ended in incoherent ravings. There were so many enemies to their new fervor that they scarcely knew where to begin. There were not only the old tables of stone to destroy, but there were new and threatening prophets of the eternal verities who had to be ex-posed. The nineteenth century which they had studied must be weeded of its nauseous moralists. The instructors consulted together how they might put down the revolt, and bring these sinners back to the faith of cultural scripture.

It was of no avail. In a short time Miro had been converted from an aspiration for the career of a cultivated "man of letters" to a fiery zeal for artistic and literary propaganda in the service of radical ideas. One of the results of this conversion was the discovery that he really had no standards of critical taste. Miro had been reverential so long that he had felt no preferences. Everything that was classic had to be good to him. But now that he had thrown away the books that were stamped with the mark of the classic mint, and was dealing with the raw ma-terials of letters, he had to become a critic and make selection. It was not enough that a book should be radical. Some of the books he read, though impeccably revolutionary as to ideas, were clearly poor as litera-ture. His muffled taste began to assert itself. He found himself impres-

sionable where before he had been only mildly acquisitive. The literature of revolt and free speculation fired him into a state of spiritual ex-
plosiveness. All that he read now stood out in brighter colors and in
sharper outlines than before. As he reached a better balance, he began
to feel the vigor of literary form, the value of sincerity and freshness
of style. He began to look for them keenly in everything he read. It
was long before Miro realized that enthusiasm not docility had made
him critical. He became a little proud of his sensitive and discriminating
reactions to the modern and the unsifted.

This pursuit had to take place without any help from the college.
After Miro graduated, it is true that it became the fashion to study literature as the record of ideas and not merely as a canon of sacred books
to be analyzed, commented upon, and absorbed. But no dent was made
upon the system in Miro's time, and, the inventory of English criticism
not going beyond Stevenson, no college course went beyond Stevenson.
The Elizabethans had been exhumed and fumigated, but the most popular attention went to the gallery of Victorians, who combined moral
soundness with literary beauty, and were therefore considered wholesome food for young men. The instructors all remained in the state of
reverence which saw all things good that had been immemorially taught.
Miro's own teacher was a fragile, earnest young man, whose robuster
parents had evidently seized upon his nature as a fortunate pledge of
what the family might produce in the way of an intellectual flower that
should surpass in culture and gentility the ambitions of his parents.
His studiousness, hopeless for his father's career as grocer, had therefore been capitalized into education.

The product now shone forth as one of the most successful and promising younger instructors in the department. He knew his subject. Card-
indexes filled his room, covering in detail the works, lives, and deaths
of the illustrious persons whom he expounded, as well as everything
that had been said about them in the way of appreciation or interpretation. An endless number of lectures and courses could be made from
this bountiful store. He never tried to write himself, but he knew all
about the different kinds of writing, and when he corrected the boys'
themes he knew infallibly what to tell them to avoid. Miro's vagaries
scandalized his teacher all the more because during his first year in
college Miro had been generally noticed as one with the proper sobriety
and scholarly patience to graduate into a similar priestly calling. Miro
found scant sympathy in the young man. To the latter, literary studies
were a science not an art, and they were to be treated with somewhat
the same cold rigor of delimitation and analysis as any other science.
Miro felt his teacher's recoil at the idea that literature was significant
only as the expression of personality or as interpretation of some social
movement. Miro saw how uneasy he became when he was confronted
with current literature. It was clear that Miro's slowly growing critical
sense had not a counterpart in the scholastic mind.

When Miro and his friends abandoned literary studies, they followed

after the teachers of history and philosophy, intellectual arenas of which
the literary professors seemed scandalously ignorant. At this ignorance
Miro boiled with contempt. Here were the profitable clues that would
give meaning to dusty literary scholarship, but the scholars had not the
wits to seize them. They lived along, playing what seemed to Miro a
rather dreary game, when they were not gaping reverently at ideas and
forms which they scarcely had the genuine personality to appreciate.
Miro felt once and for all free of these mysteries and reverences. He
was to know the world as it has been and as it is. He was to put literature into its proper place, making all "culture" serve its apprentice-
ship for him as interpretation of things larger than itself, of the course
of individual lives and the great tides of society.

Miro's later cultural life is not without interest. When he had finished
college and his architectural course, and was making headway in his
profession, his philosophy of the intellectual life began to straighten itself out. Rapid as his surrender of orthodoxy had been, it had taken
him some time to live down that early education. He found now that
he would have to live down his heresies also, and get some coherent
system of tastes that was his own and not the fruit of either docility
or the zeal of propaganda.

The old battles that were still going on helped Miro to realize his
modern position. It was a queer, musty quarrel, but it was enlisting
minds from all classes and of all intellectual fibers. The "classics" were
dying hard, as Miro recognized whenever he read, in the magazines, attacks on the "new education." He found that professors were still taken
seriously who declared in passion that without the universal study of
the Latin language in American schools all conceptions of taste, standards, criticism, the historic sense itself, would vanish from the earth.
He found that even as late as 1917 professional men were gathering
together in solemn conclave and buttressing the "value of the classics"
with testimonials from "successful men" in a variety of vocations. Miro
was amused at the fact that the mighty studies once pressed upon him
so uncritically should now require, like the patent medicines, testimonials as to their virtue. Bank presidents, lawyers, and editors had taken
the Latin language regularly for years, and had found its effects pain-
less and invigorating. He could not escape the unconscious satire that
such plump and prosperous Americans expressed when they thought it
admirable to save their cherished intellectual traditions in any such
fashion.

Other conservatives Miro saw to be abandoning the line of opposition
to science, only to fall back on the line of a defensive against "pseudo-
science," as they seemed to call whatever intellectual interests had not
yet become indubitably reputable. It was a line which would hold them
rather strongly for a time, Miro thought, because so many of the cultural
revolutionists agreed with them in hating some of these arrogant and
mechanical psychologies and sociologies that reduced life to figures or
organisms. But Miro felt also how obstructive was their fight. If the

"classics" had done little for him except to hold his mind in an uncomprehending prison, and fetter his spontaneous taste, they seemed to have done little more for even the thorough scholars. When professors had devoted scholarly lives to the "classics" only to exhibit in their own polemics none of the urbanity and intellectual command which were supposed by the believer somehow to rub off automatically on the faithful student, Miro had to conclude an absence of causal connection between the "classics" and the able modern mind. When, moreover, critical power or creative literary work became almost extinct among these defenders of the "old education," Miro felt sure that a revolution was needed in the materials and attitudes of "culture."

The case of the defenders was all the weaker because their enemies were not wanton infidels, ignorant of the holy places they profaned. They were rather cultural "Modernists," reforming the church from within. They had the classic background, these young vandals, but they had escaped from its flat and unorientated surface. Abreast of the newer objective, impersonal standards of thinking, they saw the weakness of these archaic minds which could only appeal to vested interests in culture and testimonials from successful men.

The older critics had long since disavowed the intention of discriminating among current writers. These men, who had to have an Academy to protect them, lumped the younger writers of verse and prose together as "anarchic" and "naturalistic," and had become, in these latter days, merely peevish and querulous, protesting in favor of standards that no longer represented our best values. Everyone, in Miro's time, bemoaned the lack of critics, but the older critics seemed to have lost all sense of hospitality and to have become tired and a little spitefully disconsolate, while the newer ones were too intent on their crusades against puritanism and philistinism to have time for a constructive pointing of the way.

Miro had a very real sense of standing at the end of an era. He and his friends had lived down both their old orthodoxies of the classics and their new orthodoxies of propaganda. Gone were the priggishness and self-consciousness which had marked their teachers. The new culture would be more personal than the old, but it would not be held as a personal property. It would be democratic in the sense that it would represent each person's honest spontaneous taste. The old attitude was only speciously democratic. The assumption was that if you pressed your material long enough and winningly enough upon your culturable public, they would acquire it. But the material was sometimes handed down, not grown in the garden of their own appreciations. Under these conditions the critic and appreciator became a mere impersonal register of orthodox opinion. The cultivated person, in confronting his judgments to what was authoritatively taught him, was really a member of the herd—a cultivated herd, it is true, but still a herd. It was the mass that spoke through the critic and not his own discrimination. These authoritative judgments might, of course, have come—probably had come—to the herd through discerning critics, but in Miro's time judgment in the schools had petrified. One believed not because one felt the original discernment, but because one was impressed by the weight and reputability of opinion. At least so it seemed to Miro.

Now just as the artists had become tired of conventions and were breaking through into new and personal forms, so Miro saw the younger critics breaking through these cultural conventions. To the elders the result would seem mere anarchy. But Miro's attitude did not want to destroy, it merely wanted to rearrange the materials. He wanted no more second-hand appreciations. No one's cultural store was to include anything that one could not be enthusiastic about. One's acquaintance with the best that had been said and thought should be encouraged— in Miro's ideal school—to follow the lines of one's temperament. Miro, having thrown out the old gods, found them slowly and properly coming back to him. Some would always repel him, others he hoped to understand eventually. But if it took wisdom to write the great books, did it not also take wisdom to understand them? Even the Latin writers he hoped to recover, with the aid of translations. But why bother with Greek when you could get Euripides in the marvellous verse of Gilbert Murray? Miro was willing to believe that no education was complete without at least an inoculation of the virus of the two orthodoxies that he was transcending.

As Miro looked around the American scene, he wondered where the critics were to come from. He saw, on the one hand, Mr. Mencken and Mr. Dreiser and their friends, going heavily forth to battle with the Philistines, glorying in pachydermatous vulgarisms that hurt the polite and cultivated young men of the old school. And he saw these violent critics, in their rage against puritanism, becoming themselves moralists, with the same bigotry and tastelessness as their enemies. No, these would never do. On the other hand, he saw Mr. Stuart P. Sherman, in his youthful if somewhat belated ardor, revolting so conscientiously against the "naturalism" and crude expression of current efforts that, in his defense of *belles-lettres*, of the fine tradition of literary art, he himself became a moralist of the intensest brand, and as critic plumped for Arnold Bennett, because that clever man had a feeling for the proprieties of human conduct. No, Mr. Sherman would do even less adequately. His fine sympathies were as much out of the current as was the specious classicism of Professor Shorey. He would have to look for the critics among the young men who had an abounding sense of life, as well as a feeling for literary form. They would be men who had not been content to live on their cultural inheritance, but had gone out into the modern world and amassed a fresh fortune of their own. They would be men who were not squeamish, who did not feel the delicate differences between "animal" and "human" conduct, who were enthusiastic about Mark Twain and Gorki as well as Romain Rolland, and at the same time were thrilled by Copeau's theater.

Where was a better program for culture, for any kind of literary art? Culture as a living effort, a driving attempt both at sincere expression and at the comprehension of sincere expression wherever it was found! Appreciation to be as far removed from the "I know what I like!" as from the textbook impeccability of taste! If each mind sought its own along these lines, would not many find themselves agreed? Miro insisted on liking Amy Lowell's attempt to outline the tendencies in American poetry in a form which made clear the struggles of contemporary men and women with the tradition and against "every affectation of the mind." He began to see in the new class-consciousness of poets the ending of that old division which "culture" made between the chosen people and the gentiles. We were now to form little pools of workers and appreciators of similar temperaments and tastes. The little magazines that were starting up became voices for these new communities of sentiment. Miro thought that perhaps at first it was right to adopt a tentative superciliousness towards the rest of the world, so that both Mr. Mencken with his shudders at the vulgar Demos and Mr. Sherman with his obsession with the sanely and wholesomely American might be shut out from influence. Instead of fighting the Philistine in the name of freedom, or fighting the vulgar iconoclast in the name of wholesome human notions, it might be better to write for one's own band of comprehenders, in order that one might have something genuine with which to appeal to both the mob of the "bourgeois" and the ferocious vandals who had been dividing the field among them. Far better a quarrel among these intensely self-conscious groups than the issues that had filled *The Atlantic* and *The Nation* with their dreary obsolescence. Far better for the mind that aspired towards "culture" to be told not to conform or worship, but to search out its group, its own temperamental community of sentiment, and there deepen appreciations through sympathetic contact.

It was no longer a question of being hospitable towards the work of other countries. Miro found the whole world open to him, in these days, through the enterprise of publishers. He and his friends felt more sympathetic with certain groups in France and Russia than they did with the variegated "prominent authors" of their own land. Winston Churchill as a novelist came to seem more of an alien than Artzybashev. The fact of culture being international had been followed by a sense of its being. The old cultural attitude had been hospitable enough, but it had imported its alien culture in the form of "comparative literature." It was hospitable only in trying to mould its own taste to the orthodox canons abroad. The older American critic was mostly interested in getting the proper rank and reverence for what he borrowed. The new critic will take what suits his community of sentiment. He will want to link up not with the foreign canon, but with that group which is nearest in spirit with the effort he and his friends are making. The American has to work to interpret and portray the life he knows. He cannot be international in the sense that anything but the life in which he is saturated, with its questions and its colors, can be the material for his art. But he can be international—and must be—in the sense that he works with a certain hopeful vision of a "young world," and with certain ideal values upon which the younger men, stained and revolted by war, in all countries are agreeing.

Miro wonders sometimes whether the direction in which he is tending will not bring him around the circle again to a new classicism. The last stage in the history of the man of culture will be that "classic" which he did not understand and which his mind spent its youth in overthrowing. But it will be a classicism far different from that which was so unintelligently handed down to him in the American world. It will be something worked out and lived into. Looking into the future he will have to do what Van Wyck Brooks calls "inventing a usable past." Finding little in the American tradition that is not tainted with sweetness and light and burdened with the terrible patronage of bourgeois society, the new classicist will yet rescue Thoreau and Whitman and Mark Twain and try to tap through them a certain eternal human tradition of abounding vitality and moral freedom, and so build out the future. If the classic means power with restraint, vitality with harmony, a fusion of intellect and feeling, and a keen sense of the artistic conscience, then the revolutionary world is coming out into the classic. When Miro sees behind the minds of *The Masses* group a desire for form and for expressive beauty, and sees the radicals following Jacques Copeau and reading Chekhov, he smiles at the thought of the American critics, young and old, who do not know yet that they are dead.

### H. L. MENCKEN

*from*

## Puritanism As a Literary Force

When H. L. Mencken (1880–1956) first published the following essay in 1917, he had scarcely reached mid-career; the *American Mercury,* in which he was to make his reputation, was still seven years away; most of the issues about which he was to be so precisely critical were characteristics of the postwar years. Yet "Puritanism As a Literary Force" is a classic of its kind, surely an excellent example of Mencken's rhetoric of vituperation, his abundance of documentation, his characteristic sweep through centuries of history in search of evidence. It is also almost a model of the kind of "anti-Puritan" diatribe which, from one perspective or another, was to become so prominent in the twenties. The image of the Puritan presented here, and defended by a massive accumula-

tion of "evidence," has characteristic flourishes: the distinction between the early, introspective Puritan and "militant Puritanism";
the discussion of "comstockery" (a term which from that time forward was added to the journalist's vocabulary); the phrasemaking,
which shows contempt and denunciatory vigor at one and the same
time. Much of the detail has since been proved inaccurate, and
the line of generality has a pseudo validity at best. But, as a perspective upon a certain kind of social and literary criticism, the
essay is superbly relevant, and indispensable.

1

"Calvinism," says Dr. Leon Kellner, in his excellent little history of American literature,[1] "is the natural theology of the disinherited;
it never flourished, therefore, anywhere as it did in the barren hills of
Scotland and in the wilds of North America." The learned doctor is
here speaking of theology in what may be called its narrow technical
sense—that is, as a theory of God. Under Calvinism, in the New World
as well as in the Old, it became no more than a luxuriant demonology;
even God himself was transformed into a superior sort of devil, ever
wary and wholly merciless. That primitive demonology still survives in
the barbaric doctrines of the Methodists and Baptists, particularly in the
South; but it has been ameliorated, even there, by a growing sense of
the divine grace, and so the old God of Plymouth Rock, as practically
conceived, is now scarcely worse than the average jail warden or Italian
padrone. On the ethical side, however, Calvinism is dying a much harder
death, and we are still a long way from the enlightenment. Save where
Continental influences have measurably corrupted the Puritan idea—e.g.,
in such cities as New York, St. Louis and New Orleans, the prevailing
American view of the world and its mysteries is still a purely moral one,
and no other human concern gets half the attention that is endlessly
lavished upon the problem of conduct, particularly of the other fellow.
It needed no announcement of a President of the United States to define the republic's destiny as that of an international expert in morals,
and the mentor and exemplar of the less righteous nations. Within, as
well as without, the eternal rapping of knuckles and proclaiming of
new austerities goes on. The American, save in moments of conscious
and swiftly lamented deviltry, casts up all ponderable values, including
even the values of beauty, in terms of right and wrong. He is beyond
all things else, a judge and a policeman; he believes firmly that there
is a mysterious power in law; he supports and embellishes its operation
with a fanatical vigilance.

Naturally enough, this moral obsession has given a strong colour to
American literature. In truth, it has coloured it so brilliantly that Ameri-

[1] *American Literature,* tr. by Julia Franklin; New York, Doubleday, Page
& Co., 1915.

can literature is set off sharply from all other literatures. In none other will you find so wholesale and ecstatic a sacrifice of aesthetic ideas, of all the fine gusto of passion and beauty, to notions of what is meet, proper and nice. From the books of grisly sermons that were the first American contribution to letters down to that amazing literature of "inspiration" which now flowers so prodigiously, with two literary Presidents among its chief virtuosi, one observes no relaxation of the moral pressure. In the history of every other literature there have been periods of what might be called moral innocence—periods in which a naif *joie de vivre* has broken through all concepts of duty and responsibility, and the wonder and glory of the universe have been hymned with unashamed zest. The age of Shakespeare comes to mind at once: the violence of the Puritan reaction offers a measure of the pendulum's wild swing. But in America no such general rising of the blood has ever been seen. The literature of the nation, even the literature of the enlightened minority, has been under harsh Puritan restraints from the beginning, and despite a few stealthy efforts at revolt—usually quite without artistic value or even common honesty, as in the case of the cheap fiction magazines and that of smutty plays on Broadway, and always very short-lived—it shows not the slightest sign of emancipating itself today. The American, try as he will, can never imagine any work of the imagination as wholly devoid of moral content. It must either tend toward the promotion of virtue, or be suspect and abominable.

.     .     .     .     .

2

In studying the anatomy and physiology of American Puritanism, and its effects upon the national literature, one quickly discerns two main streams of influence. On the one hand, there is the influence of the original Puritans—whether of New England or of the South—, who came to the New World with a ready-made philosophy of the utmost clarity, positiveness and inclusiveness of scope, and who attained to such a position of political and intellectual leadership that they were able to force it almost unchanged upon the whole population, and to endow it with such vitality that it successfully resisted alien opposition later on. And on the other hand, one sees a complex of social and economic conditions which worked in countless irresistible ways against the rise of that dionysian spirit, that joyful acquiescence in life, that philosophy of the *Ja-sager,* which offers to Puritanism, today as in times past, its chief and perhaps only effective antagonism. In other words, the American of the days since the Revolution has had Puritanism diligently pressed upon him from without, and at the same time he has led, in the main, a life that has engendered a chronic hospitality to it, or at all events to its salient principles, within.

Dr. Kellner accurately described the process whereby the aesthetic spirit, and its concomitant spirit of joy, were squeezed out of the original

New Englanders, so that no trace of it showed in their literature, or even in their lives, for a century and a half after the first settlements. "Absorption in God," he says, "seems incompatible with the presentation (i.e., aesthetically) of mankind. The God of the Puritans was in this respect a jealous God who brooked no sort of creative rivalry. The inspired moments of the loftiest souls were filled with the thought of God and His designs; spiritual life was wholly dominated by solicitude regarding salvation, the hereafter, grace; how could such petty concerns as personal experience of a lyric nature, the transports or the pangs of love, find utterance? What did a lyric occurrence like the first call of the cuckoo, elsewhere so welcome, or the first sight of the snowdrop, signify compared with the last Sunday's sermon and the new interpretation of the old riddle of evil in the world? And apart from the fact that everything of a personal nature must have appeared so trivial, all the sources of secular lyric poetry were offensive and impious to Puritan theology. . . . One thing is an established fact: up to the close of the eighteenth century America had no belletristic literature."

This Puritan bedevilment by the idea of personal sin, this reign of the God-crazy, gave way in later years, as we shall see, to other and somewhat milder forms of pious enthusiasm. At the time of the Revolution, indeed, the importation of French political ideas was accompanied by an importation of French theological ideas, and such men as Franklin and Jefferson dallied with what, in those days at least, was regarded as downright atheism. Even in New England this influence made itself felt; there was a gradual letting down of Calvinism to the softness of Unitarianism, and that change was presently to flower in the vague temporizing of Transcendentalism. But as Puritanism, in the strict sense, declined in virulence and took deceptive new forms, there was a compensating growth of its brother, Philistinism, and by the first quarter of the nineteenth century, the distrust of beauty, and of the joy that is its object, was as firmly established throughout the land as it had ever been in New England. The original Puritans had at least been men of a certain education, and even of a certain austere culture. They were inordinately hostile to beauty in all its forms, but one somehow suspects that much of their hostility was due to a sense of their weakness before it, a realization of its disarming psychical pull. But the American of the new republic was of a different kidney. He was not so much hostile to beauty as devoid of any consciousness of it; he stood as unmoved before its phenomena as a savage before a table of logarithms. What he had set upon on this continent, in brief, was a commonwealth of peasants and small traders, a paradise of the third-rate, and its national philosophy, almost wholly unchecked by the more sophisticated and civilized ideas of an aristocracy, was precisely the philosophy that one finds among peasants and small traders at all times and everywhere. The difference between the United States and any other nation did not lie in any essential difference between American peasants and other peasants, but simply in the fact that here, alone, the voice of the peasant was the single voice of the nation—that here, alone, the only way to eminence and public influence was the way of acquiescence in the opinions and prejudices of the stupid and Philistine mob. Jackson was the *Stammvater* of the new statesmen and philosophers; he carried the mob's distrust of good taste even into the field of conduct; he was the first to put the rewards of conformity above the dictates of common decency; he founded a whole hierarchy of Philistine messiahs, the roaring of which still belabours the ear.

Once established, this culture of the intellectually disinherited tended to defend and perpetuate itself. On the one hand, there was no appearance of a challenge from within, for the exigeant problems of existence in a country that was yet but half settled and organized left its people with no energy for questioning what at least met their grosser needs, and so met the pragmatic test. And on the other hand, there was no critical pressure from without, for the English culture which alone reached over the sea was itself entering upon its Victorian decline, and the influence of the native aristocracy—the degenerating *Junkers* of the great estates and the boorish magnates of the city *bourgeoisie*—was quite without any cultural direction at all. The chief concern of the American people, even above the bread-and-butter question, was politics. They were incessantly hag-ridden by political difficulties, both internal and external, of an inordinate complexity, and these occupied all the leisure they could steal from the sordid work of everyday. More, their new and troubled political ideas tended to absorb all the rancorous certainty of their fading religious ideas, so that devotion to a theory or a candidate became translated into devotion to a revelation, and the game of politics turned itself into a holy war. The custom of connecting purely political doctrines with pietistic concepts of an inflammable nature, then firmly set up by skilful persuaders of the mob, has never quite died out in the United States. There has not been a presidential contest since Jackson's day without its Armageddons, its marching of Christian soldiers, its crosses of gold, its crowns of thorns. The most successful American politicians, beginning with the anti-slavery agitators, have been those most adept at twisting the ancient gauds and shibboleths of Puritanism to partisan uses. Every campaign that we have seen for eighty years has been, on each side, a pursuit of bugaboos, a denunciation of heresies, a snouting up of immoralities.

.   .   .   .   .   .

.  .  . As I shall show later on, the shock of it [the Civil War] completely reorganized the American scheme of things, and even made certain important changes in the national Puritanism, or, at all events, in its machinery. Whitman, whose career straddled, so to speak, the four years of the war, was the leader—and for a long while, the only trooper —of a double revolt. On the one hand he offered a courageous challenge to the intolerable prudishness and dirty-mindedness of Puritanism, and on the other hand he boldly sought the themes and even the modes of expression of his poetry in the arduous, contentious and highly melo-dramatic life that lay all about him. Whitman, however, was clearly before his time. His countrymen could see him only as immoralist; save for a pitiful few of them, they were dead to any understanding of his stature as artist, and even unaware that such a category of men existed. He was put down as an invader of the public decencies, a disturber of the public peace; even his eloquent war poems, surely the best of all his work, were insufficient to get him a hearing; the sentimental rubbish of "The Blue and the Gray" and the ecstatic super-naturalism of "The Battle Hymn of the Republic" were far more to the public taste. Where Whitman failed, indeed, all subsequent explorers of the same field have failed with him, and the great war has left no more mark upon Ameri-can letters than if it had never been fought. Nothing remotely approach-ing the bulk and beam of Tolstoi's "War and Peace," or, to descend to a smaller scale, Zola's "The Attack on the Mill," has come out of it. Its appeal to the national imagination was undoubtedly of the most pro-found character; it coloured politics for fifty years, and is today a domi-nating influence in the thought of whole sections of the American peo-ple. But in all that stirring up there was no upheaval of artistic con-sciousness, for the plain reason that there was no artistic consciousness there to heave up, and all we have in the way of Civil War literature is a few conventional melodramas, a few half-forgotten short stories by Ambrose Bierce and Stephen Crane, and a half dozen idiotic popular songs in the manner of Randall's "Maryland, My Maryland."

In the seventies and eighties, with the appearance of such men as Henry James, William Dean Howells, Mark Twain and Bret Harte, a better day seemed to be dawning. Here, after a full century of infantile romanticizing, were four writers who at least deserved respectful con-sideration as literary artists, and what is more, three of them turned from the conventionalized themes of the past to the teeming and colour-ful life that lay under their noses. But this promise of better things was soon found to be no more than a promise. Mark Twain, after "The Gilded Age," slipped back into romanticism tempered by Philistinism, and was presently in the era before the Civil War, and finally in the Middle Ages, and even beyond. Harte, a brilliant technician, had dis-played his whole stock when he had displayed his technique: his stories were not even superficially true to the life they presumed to depict; one searched them in vain for an interpretation of it; they were simply idle tales. As for Howells and James, both quickly showed that timorous-ness and reticence which are the distinguishing marks of the Puritan, even in his most intellectual incarnations. The American scene that they depicted with such meticulous care was chiefly peopled with marionettes. They shrunk, characteristically, from those larger, harsher clashes of will and purpose which one finds in all truly first-rate literature. In particu-lar, they shrunk from any interpretation of life which grounded itself upon an acknowledgment of its inexorable and inexplicable tragedy. In the vast combat of instincts and aspirations about them they saw only

a feeble jousting of comedians, unserious and insignificant. Of the great
questions that have agitated the minds of men in Howells' time one gets
no more than a faint and far-away echo in his novels. His investigations,
one may say, are carried on *in vacuo;* his discoveries are not expressed
in terms of passion, but in terms of giggles.

· · · · · ·

. . . There have been intermittent rebellions against the prevailing
pecksniffery and sentimentality ever since the days of Irving and Hawthorne. Poe led one of them—as critic more than as creative artist. His
scathing attacks upon the Gerald Stanley Lees, the Hamilton Wright
Mabies and the George E. Woodberrys of his time keep a liveliness and
appositeness that the years have not staled; his criticism deserves to be
better remembered. Poe sensed the Philistine pull of a Puritan civilization as none had before him, and combated it with his whole artillery
of rhetoric. Another rebel, of course, was Whitman; how he came to
grief is too well known to need recalling. What is less familiar is the
fact that both the *Atlantic Monthly* and the *Century* (first called *Scrib-
ner's*) were set up by men in revolt against the reign of mush, as *Putnam's* and the *Dial* had been before them. The salutatory of the *Dial,*
dated 1840, stated the case against the national mugginess clearly. The
aim of the magazine, it said, was to oppose "that rigour of our conventions of religion and education which is turning us to stone" and to
give expression to "new views and the dreams of youth." Alas, for these
brave *révoltés! Putnam's* succumbed to the circumambient rigours and
duly turned to stone, and is now no more. The *Atlantic,* once so hereti-
cal, has become as respectable as the New York *Evening Post.* As for the
*Dial,* it was until lately the very pope of orthodoxy and jealously
guarded the college professors who read it from the pollution of ideas.
Only the *Century* has kept the faith unbrokenly. It is, indeed, the one
first-class American magazine that has always welcomed newcomers, and
that maintains an intelligent contact with the literature that is in being,
and that consistently tries to make the best terms possible with the
dominant Philistinism. It cannot go the whole way without running into
danger; let it be said to the credit of its editors that they have more
than once braved that danger.

The tale might be lengthened. Mark Twain, in his day, felt the
stirrings of revolt, and not all his Philistinism was sufficient to hold him
altogether in check. If you want to find out about the struggle that went
on within him, read the biography by Albert Bigelow Paine, or, better
still, "The Mysterious Stranger" and "What is Man?" Alive, he had his
position to consider; dead, he now speaks out. In the preface to "What
is Man?" dated 1905, there is a curious confession of his incapacity for
defying the taboos which surrounded him. The studies for the book,
he says, were begun "twenty-five or twenty-seven years ago"—the period
of "A Tramp Abroad" and "The Prince and the Pauper." It was actually
written "seven years ago"—that is, just after "Following the Equator"

and "Personal Recollections of Joan of Arc." And why did it lie so long in manuscript, and finally go out stealthily, under a private imprint? [2] Simply because, as Mark frankly confesses, he "dreaded (*and could not bear*) the disapproval of the people around" him. He knew how hard his fight for recognition had been; he knew what direful penalties outraged orthodoxy could inflict; he had in him the somewhat pathetic discretion of a respectable family man. But, dead, he is safely beyond reprisal, and so, after a prudent interval, the faithful Paine begins printing books in which, writing knowingly behind six feet of earth, he could set down his true ideas without fear. Some day, perhaps, we shall have his microbe story, and maybe even his picture of the court of Elizabeth.

·    ·    ·    ·    ·

3

All this may be called the Puritan impulse from within. It is, indeed, but a single manifestation of one of the deepest prejudices of a religious and half-cultured people—the prejudice against beauty as a form of debauchery and corruption—the distrust of all ideas that do not fit readily into certain accepted axioms—the belief in the eternal validity of moral concepts—in brief, the whole mental sluggishness of the lower orders of men. But in addition to this internal resistance, there has been laid upon American letters the heavy hand of a Puritan authority from without, and no examination of the history and present condition of our literature could be of any value which did not take it constantly into account, and work out the means of its influence and operation. That authority, as I shall show, transcends both in power and in alertness the natural reactions of the national mind, and is incomparably more potent in combating ideas. It is supported by a body of law that is unmatched in any other country of Christendom, and it is exercised with a fanatical harshness and vigilance that make escape from its operations well nigh impossible. Some of its effects, both direct and indirect, I shall describe later, but before doing so it may be well to trace its genesis and development.

At bottom, of course, it rests upon the inherent Puritanism of the people; it could not survive a year if they were opposed to the principle visible in it. That deep-seated and uncorrupted Puritanism, that conviction of the pervasiveness of sin, of the supreme importance of moral correctness, of the need of savage and inquisitorial laws, has been a dominating force in American life since the very beginning. There has never been any question before the nation, whether political or economic, religious or military, diplomatic or sociological, which did not resolve itself, soon or late, into a purely moral question. Nor has there ever been any surcease of the spiritual eagerness which lay at the

---

[2] The first edition for public sale did not appear until June, 1917, and in it the preface was suppressed.

bottom of the original Puritan's moral obsession: the American has been, from the very start, a man genuinely interested in the eternal mysteries, and fearful of missing their correct solution. The frank theocracy of the New England colonies had scarcely succumbed to the libertarianism of a godless Crown before there came the Great Awakening of 1734, with its orgies of homiletics and its restoration of talmudism to the first place among polite sciences. The Revolution, of course, brought a set-back: the colonists faced so urgent a need of unity in politics that they declared a sort of *Treuga Dei* in religion, and that truce, armed though it was, left its imprint upon the First Amendment to the Constitution. But immediately the young Republic emerged from the stresses of adolescence, a missionary army took to the field again, and before long the Asbury revival was paling that of Whitefield, Wesley and Jonathan Edwards, not only in its hortatory violence but also in the length of its lists of slain.

Thereafter, down to the outbreak of the Civil War, the country was rocked again and again by furious attacks upon the devil. On the one hand, this great campaign took a purely theological form, with a hundred new and fantastic creeds as its fruits; on the other hand, it crystallized into the hysterical temperance movement of the 30's and 40's, which penetrated to the very floor of Congress and put "dry" laws upon the statute-books of ten States; and on the third hand, as it were, it established a prudery in speech and thought from which we are yet but half delivered. Such ancient and innocent words as "bitch" and "bastard" disappeared from the American language; Bartlett tells us, indeed, in his "Dictionary of Americanisms," [3] that even "bull" was softened to "male cow." This was the Golden Age of euphemism, as it was of euphuism; the worst inventions of the English mid-Victorians were adopted and improved. The word "woman" became a term of opprobrium, verging close upon downright libel; legs became the inimitable "limbs"; the stomach began to run from the "bosom" to the pelvic arch; pantaloons faded into "unmentionables"; the newspapers spun their parts of speech into such gossamer webs as "a statutory offence," "a house of questionable repute" and "an interesting condition."

·     ·     ·     ·     ·

. . . The distinguishing mark of the elder Puritanism, at least after it had attained to the stature of a national philosophy, was its appeal to the individual conscience, its exclusive concern with the elect, its strong flavour of self-accusing. Even the rage against slavery was, in large measure, an emotion of the mourners' bench. The thing that worried the more ecstatic Abolitionists was their sneaking sense of responsibility, the fear that they themselves were flouting the fire by letting slavery go on. The thirst to punish the concrete slave-owner, as an end in itself, did not appear until opposition had added exasperation

[3] Second edition; Boston, Little, Brown & Co., 1859, xxvi.

to fervour. In most of the earlier harangues against his practice, indeed, you will find a perfect willingness to grant that slave-owner's good faith, and even to compensate him for his property. But the new Puritanism— or, perhaps more accurately, considering the shades of prefixes, the neo-Puritanism—is a frank harking back to the primitive spirit. The original Puritan of the bleak New England coast was not content to flay his own wayward carcass: full satisfaction did not sit upon him until he had jailed a Quaker. That is to say, the sinner who excited his highest zeal and passion was not so much himself as his neighbour; to borrow a term from psychopathology, he was less the masochist than the sadist. And it is that very peculiarity which sets off his descendant of today from the ameliorated Puritan of the era between the Revolution and the Civil War. The new Puritanism is not ascetic, but militant. Its aim is not to lift up saints but to knock down sinners. Its supreme manifestation is the vice crusade, an armed pursuit of helpless outcasts by the whole military and naval forces of the Republic. Its supreme hero is Comstock Himself, with his pious boast that the sinners he jailed during his astounding career, if gathered into one penitential party, would have filled a train of sixty-one coaches, allowing sixty to the coach.

•       •       •       •       •

. . . Wealth, discovering its power, has reached out its long arms to grab the distant and innumerable sinner; it has gone down into its deep pockets to pay for his costly pursuit and flaying; it has created the Puritan *entrepreneur,* the daring and imaginative organizer of Puritanism, the baron of moral endeavour, the invincible prophet of new austerities. And, by the same token, it has issued its letters of marque to the Puritan mercenary, the professional hound of heaven, the moral *Junker,* the Comstock, and out of his skill at his trade there has arisen the whole machinery, so complicated and so effective, of the new Holy Office.

•       •       •       •       •

4

This is the essential fact of the new Puritanism; its recognition of the moral expert, the professional sinhound, the virtuoso of virtue. Under the original Puritan theocracy, as in Scotland, for example, the chase and punishment of sinners was a purely ecclesiastical function, and during the slow disintegration of the theocracy the only change introduced was the extension of that function to lay helpers, and finally to the whole body of laymen. This change, however, did not materially corrupt the ecclesiastical quality of the enterprise: the leader in the so-called militant field still remained the same man who led in the spiritual field. But with the capitalization of Puritan effort there came a radical overhauling of method. The secular arm, as it were, conquered as it helped. That is to say, the special business of forcing sinners to be good was taken away from the preachers and put into the hands of laymen trained in its technique and mystery, and there it remains. The new Puritanism has created an army of gladiators who are not only distinct from the hierarchy, but who in many instances, actually command and intimidate the hierarchy. This is conspicuously evident in the case of the Anti-Saloon League, an enormously effective fighting organization, with a large staff of highly accomplished experts in its service. These experts do not wait for ecclesiastical support, nor even ask for it; they force it. The clergyman who presumes to protest against their war upon the saloon, even upon the quite virtuous ground that it is not effective enough, runs a risk of condign and merciless punishment. So plainly is this understood, indeed, that in more than one State the clergy of the Puritan denominations openly take orders from these specialists in excoriation, and court their favour without shame. Here a single moral enterprise, heavily capitalized and carefully officered, has engulfed the entire Puritan movement, and a part has become more than the whole.[4]

.　　.　　.　　.　　.

But does all this argue a total lack of justice in the American character, or even a lack of common decency? I doubt that it would be well to go so far in accusation. What it does argue is a tendency to put moral considerations above all other considerations, and to define morality in the narrow Puritan sense. The American, in other words, thinks that the sinner has no rights that any one is bound to respect, and he is prone to mistake an unsupported charge of sinning, provided it be made violently enough, for actual proof and confession. What is more, he takes an intense joy in the mere chase: he has the true Puritan taste for an *auto da fé* in him. "I am ag'inst capital punishment," said Mr. Dooley, "but we won't get rid av it so long as the people enjie it so much." But though he is thus an eager spectator, and may even be lured into taking part in the pursuit, the average American is not disposed to initiate it, nor to pay for it. The larger Puritan enterprises of today are not popular in the sense of originating in the bleachers, but only in the sense of being applauded from the bleachers. The burdens of the fray, both of toil and of expense, are always upon a relatively small number of men. In a State rocked and racked by a war upon the saloon, it was recently shown, for example, that but five per cent. of the members of the Puritan denominations contributed to the war-chest. And yet the Anti-Saloon League of that State was so sure of support from below that it presumed to stand as the spokesman of the whole Christian community, and even ventured to launch excommunications upon contumacious Christians, both lay and clerical, who object to its methods. Moreover, the great majority of the persons included in the contributing five per cent. gave no more than a few cents a year. The

---

[4] An instructive account of the organization and methods of the Anti-Saloon League, a thoroughly typical Puritan engine, is to be found in *Alcohol and Society*, by John Koren; New York, Henry Holt & Co., 1916.

whole support of the League devolved upon a dozen men, all of them
rich and all of them Puritans of purest ray serene. These men supported a costly organization for their private entertainment and stimulation. It was their means of recreation, their sporting club. They were
willing to spend a lot of money to procure good sport for themselves—
i.e., to procure the best crusading talent available—and they were so
successful in that endeavour that they enchanted the populace too, and
so shook the State.

· · · · · ·

### 5

I have gone into the anatomy and physiology of militant Puritanism
because, so far as I know, the inquiry has not been attempted before,
and because a somewhat detailed acquaintance with the forces behind
so grotesque a manifestation as comstockery, the particular business of
the present essay, is necessary to an understanding of its workings, and of
its prosperity, and of its influence upon the arts. Save one turn to
England or to the British colonies, it is impossible to find a parallel for
the astounding absolutism of Comstock and his imitators in any civilized country. No other nation has laws which oppress the arts so
ignorantly and so abominably as ours do, nor has any other nation handed
over the enforcement of the statutes which exist to agencies so openly
pledged to reduce all aesthetic expression to the service of a stupid and
unworkable scheme of rectitude. I have before me as I write a
pamphlet in explanation of his aims and principles, prepared by Comstock himself and presented to me by his successor. Its very title is a
sufficient statement of the Puritan position: "MORALS, Not Art or
Literature." [5] The capitals are in the original. And within, as a sort of
general text, the idea is amplified: "It is a question of peace, good order
and morals, and not art, literature or science." Here we have a statement
of principle that, at all events, is at least quite frank. There is not the
slightest effort to beg the question; there is no hypocritical pretension to
a desire to purify or safeguard the arts; they are dismissed at once as
trivial and degrading. And jury after jury has acquiesced in this; it was
old Anthony's boast, in his last days, that his percentage of convictions,
in 40 years, had run to 98.5.[6]

Comstockery is thus grounded firmly upon that profound national
suspicion of the arts, that truculent and almost unanimous Philistinism,
which I have described. It would be absurd to dismiss it as an ex-

[5] New York (1914).
[6] I quote from page 157 of *Anthony Comstock, Fighter,* the official biography. On page 239 the number of his prosecutions is given as 3,646, with
2,682 convictions, which works out to but 73 per cent. He is credited with
having destroyed 50 tons of books, 28,425 pounds of stereotype plates, 16,900
photographic negatives, and 3,984,063 photographs—enough to fill "sixteen
freight cars, fifteen loaded with ten tons each, and the other nearly full."

crescence, and untypical of the American mind. But it is typical, too, in the manner in which it has gone beyond that mere partiality to the accumulation of a definite power, and made that power irresponsible and almost irresistible. It was Comstock himself, in fact, who invented the process whereby his followers in other fields of moral endeavour have forced laws into the statute books upon the pretence of putting down John Doe, an acknowledged malefactor, and then turned them savagely upon Richard Roe, a peaceable, well-meaning and hitherto law-abiding man. And it was Comstock who first capitalized moral endeavour like baseball or the soap business, and made himself the first of its kept professors, and erected about himself a rampart of legal and financial immunity which rid him of all fear of mistakes and their consequences, and so enabled him to pursue his jehad with all the advantages in his favour. He was, in brief, more than the greatest Puritan gladiator of his time; he was the Copernicus of a quite new art and science, and he devised a technique and handed down a professional ethic that no rival has been able to better.

.    .    .    .    .

[The serious author] finds opposing him a flat denial of his decent purpose as an artist, and a stupid and ill-natured logic that baffles sober answer. He finds on his side only the half-hearted support of a publisher whose interest in a single book is limited to his profits from it, and who desires above all things to evade a nuisance and an expense. Not a few publishers, knowing the constant possibility of sudden and arbitrary attack, insert a clause in their contracts whereby an author must secure them against damage from any "immoral" matter in his book. They read and approve the manuscript, they print the book and sell it—but if it is unlucky enough to attract the comstockian lightning, the author has the whole burden to bear,[7] and if they seek safety and economy by yielding as often happens, he must consent to the mutilation or even the suppression of his work. The result is that a writer in such a situation is practically beaten before he can offer a defence. The professional book-

---

[7] For example, the printed contract of the John Lane Co., publisher of Dreiser's The "Genius," contains this provision: "The author hereby guarantees . . . that the work . . . contains nothing of a scandalous, an immoral or a libelous nature." The contract for the publication of the "Genius" was signed on July 30, 1914. The manuscript had been carefully read by representatives of the publisher, and presumably passed as not scandalous or immoral, inasmuch as the publication of a scandalous or immoral book would have exposed the publisher to prosecution. About 8,000 copies were sold under this contract. Two years later, in July, 1916, the Society for the Suppression of Vice threatened to begin a prosecution unless the book was withdrawn. It was withdrawn forthwith, and Dreiser was compelled to enter suit for a performance of the contract. The withdrawal, it will be noticed, was not in obedience to a court order, but followed a mere comstockian threat. Yet Dreiser was at once deprived of his royalties, and forced into expensive litigation. Had it not been that eminent counsel volunteered for his defence, his personal means would have been insufficient to have got him even a day in court.

baiters have laws to their liking, and courts pliant to their exactions; they fill the newspapers with inflammatory charges before the accused gets his day in court; they have the aid of prosecuting officers who fear the political damage of their enmity, and of the enmity of their wealthy and influential backers; above all, they have the command of far more money than any author can hope to muster. Finally, they derive an advantage from two of the most widespread of human weaknesses, the first being envy and the second being fear. When an author is attacked, a good many of his rivals see only a personal benefit in his difficulties, and not a menace to the whole order, and a good many others are afraid to go to his aid because of the danger of bringing down the moralists' rage upon themselves. Both of these weaknesses revealed themselves very amusingly in the Dreiser case, and I hope to detail their operations at some length later on, when I describe that *cause célèbre* in a separate work.

. . . . . .

## 6

So beset, it is no wonder that the typical American maker of books becomes a timorous and ineffective fellow, whose work tends inevitably toward a feeble superficiality. Sucking in the Puritan spirit with the very air he breathes, and perhaps burdened inwardly with an inheritance of the actual Puritan stupidity, he is further kept upon the straight path of chemical purity by the very real perils that I have just rehearsed. The result is a literature full of the mawkishness that the late Henry James so often roared against—a literature almost wholly detached from life as men are living it in the world—in George Moore's phrase, a literature still at nurse. It is on the side of sex that the appointed virtuosi of virtue exercise their chief repressions, for it is sex that especially fascinates the lubricious Puritan mind; but the conventual reticence that thus becomes the enforced fashion in one field extends itself to all others. Our fiction, in general, is marked by an artificiality as marked as that of Eighteenth Century poetry or the later Georgian drama. The romance in it runs to set forms and stale situations; the revelation, by such a book as "The Titan," that there may be a glamour as entrancing in the way of a conqueror of men as in the way of a youth with a maid, remains isolated and exotic. We have no first-rate political or religious novel; we have no first-rate war story; despite all our national engrossment in commercial enterprise, we have few second-rate tales of business. Romance, in American fiction, still means only a somewhat childish amorousness and sentimentality—the love affairs of Paul and Virginia, or the pale adulteries of their elders. And on the side of realism there is an almost equal vacuity and lack of veracity. The action of all the novels of the Howells school goes on within four walls of painted canvas; they begin to shock once they describe an attack of asthma or a steak burning below stairs; they never penetrate beneath the flow of social concealments and urbanities to the passions that actually move men and women to their acts, and the great forces that circumscribe and condition personality. So obvious a piece of reporting as Upton Sinclair's "The Jungle" or Robert Herrick's "Together" makes a sensation; the appearance of a "Jennie Gerhardt" or a "Hagar Revelly" brings forth a growl of astonishment and rage.

In all this dread of free inquiry, this childish skittishness in both writers and public, this dearth of courage and even of curiosity, the influence of comstockery is undoubtedly to be detected. It constitutes a sinister and ever-present menace to all men of ideas; it affrights the publisher and paralyzes the author; no one on the outside can imagine its burden as a practical concern. I am, in moments borrowed from more palatable business, the editor of an American magazine, and I thus know at first hand what the burden is. That magazine is anything but a popular one, in the current sense. It sells at a relatively high price; it contains no pictures or other baits for the childish; it is frankly addressed to a sophisticated minority. I may thus assume reasonably, I believe, that its readers are not sex-curious and itching adolescents, just as my colleague of the *Atlantic Monthly* may assume reasonably that his readers are not Italian immigrants. Nevertheless, as a practical editor, I find that the Comstocks, near and far, are oftener in my mind's eye than my actual patrons. The thing I always have to decide about a manuscript offered for publication, before ever I give any thought to its artistic merit and suitability, is the question whether its publication will be permitted—not even whether it is intrinsically good or evil, moral or immoral, but whether some roving Methodist preacher, self-commissioned to keep watch on letters, will read indecency into it. Not a week passes that I do not decline some sound and honest piece of work for no other reason. I have a long list of such things by American authors, well-devised, well-imagined, well-executed, respectable as human documents and as works of art—but never to be printed in mine or any other American magazine. It includes four or five short stories of the very first rank, and the best one-act play yet done, to my knowledge, by an American. All of these pieces would go into type at once on the Continent; no sane man would think of objecting to them; they are no more obscene, to a normal adult, than his own bare legs. But they simply cannot be printed in the United States, with the law what it is and the courts what they are.

I know many other editors. All of them are in the same boat. Some of them try to get around the difficulty by pecksniffery more or less open—for example, by fastening a moral purpose upon works of art, and hawking them as uplifting.[8] Others, facing the intolerable fact,

---

[8] For example, the magazine which printed David Graham Phillips' *Susan Lenox: Her Rise and Fall* as a serial prefaced it with a moral encomium by the Rev. Charles H. Parkhurst. Later, when the novel appeared in book form, the Comstocks began an action to have it suppressed, and forced the publisher to bowdlerize it.

yield to it with resignation. And if they didn't? Well, if one of them didn't, any professional moralist could go before a police magistrate, get a warrant upon a simple affidavit, raid the office of the offending editor, seize all the magazines in sight, and keep them impounded until after the disposition of the case. Editors cannot afford to take this risk. Magazines are perishable goods. Even if, after a trial has been had, they are returned, they are worthless save as waste paper. And what may be done with copies found in the actual office of publication may be done too with copies found on news-stands, and not only in one city, but in two, six, a dozen, a hundred. All the costs and burdens of the contest are on the defendant. Let him be acquitted with honour, and invited to dinner by the judge, he has yet lost his property, and the Comstock hiding behind the warrant cannot be made to pay. In this concealment, indeed, lurk many sinister things—not forgetting personal enmity and business rivalry. The actual complainant is seldom uncovered; Comstockery, taking on a semi-judicial character, throws its chartered immunity around the whole process. A hypothetical outrage? By no means. It has been perpetrated, in one American city or another, upon fully half of the magazines of general circulation published today. Its possibility sticks in the consciousness of every editor and publisher like a recurrent glycosuria.

But though the effects of comstockery are thus abominably insane and irritating, the fact is not to be forgotten that, after all, the thing is no more than an effect itself. The fundamental causes of all the grotesque (and often half-fabulous) phenomena flowing out of it are to be sought in the habits of mind of the American people. They are, as I have shown, besotted by moral concepts, a moral engrossment, a delusion of moral infallibility. In their view of the arts they are still unable to shake off the naïve suspicion of the Fathers. A work of the imagination can justify itself, in their sight, only if it show a moral purpose, and that purpose must be obvious and unmistakable. Even in their slow progress toward a revolt against the ancestral Philistinism, they cling to this ethical bemusement: a new gallery of pictures is welcomed as "improving," to hear Beethoven "makes one better." Any questioning of the moral ideas that prevail—the principal business, it must be plain, of the novelist, the serious dramatist, the professed inquirer into human motives and acts—is received with the utmost hostility. To attempt such an enterprise is to disturb the peace—and the disturber of the peace, in the national view, quickly passes over into the downright criminal.

· · · · ·

The new generation, urged to curiosity and rebellion by its mounting sap, is rigourously restrained, regimented, policed. The ideal is vacuity, guilelessness, imbecility. "We are looking at this particular book," said Comstock's successor of "The 'Genius,' " "from the standpoint of its harmful effect on female readers of immature mind." [9] To be curious is

---

[9] In a letter to Felix Shay, Nov. 24, 1916.

to be lewd; to know is to yield to fornication. Here we have the mediaeval doctrine still on its legs: a chance word may arouse "a libidinous passion" in the mind of a "modest" woman. Not only youth must be safeguarded, but also the "female," the untrustworthy one, the temptress. "Modest," is a euphemism; it takes laws to keep her "pure." The "locks of chastity" rust in the Cluny Museum; in place of them we have comstockery. . . .

But, as I have said in hymning Huneker, there is yet the munyonic consolation. Time is a great legalizer, even in the field of morals. We have yet no delivery, but we have at least the beginnings of a revolt, or, at all events, of a protest. We have already reached, in Howells, our Hannah More; in Clemens, our Swift; in Henry James, our Horace Walpole; in Woodberry, Robinson *et al.*, our Cowpers, Southeys and Crabbes; perhaps we might even make a composite and call it our Johnson. We are sweating through our Eighteenth Century, our era of sentiment, our spiritual measles. Maybe a new day is not quite so far off as it seems to be, and with it we may get our Hardy, our Conrad, our Swinburne, our Thoma, our Moore, our Meredith and our Synge.

## D. H. LAWRENCE

# Nathaniel Hawthorne and "The Scarlet Letter"

When Lawrence (1885–1930) wrote the first version of the following essay (published in the *English Review* for May, 1919), he had not visited the United States, but was engaged in a series of essays, which were eventually to be published as *Studies in Classic American Literature* (1923). In order to appreciate his curious perspective upon American literature, it is wise to know also that before the book appeared, he had published two long essays on psychoanalysis and related matters: *Psychoanalysis and the Unconscious* (1921) and *Fantasia of the Unconscious* (1922). He was preoccupied with the conflict of the unconscious and the mind, and invented a variety of metaphors to account for it. Lawrence's view of the American past allowed him to make it an especially appropriate illustration of his theories. The discussions of the predatory American will, its "Puritan" imbalance, combine with the more theoretical analyses of the general relationship of the sexes to remind one of the two essays mentioned above. Throughout, there is an extremely personal rhetoric and style, which make his American book more a series of brilliant impressions than the "Studies" the title claimed them to be. But this approach makes for flashes of insight, typical of the general revision of view of the American past, as well as of Lawrence's own struggle for definitions. As such, the *Studies* belong to a forward-looking critical revaluation of modern American and traditional cultures.

*N*athaniel Hawthorne writes romance.

And what's romance? Usually, a nice little tale where you have everything As You Like It, where rain never wets your jacket and gnats never bite your nose and it's always daisy-time. *As You Like It* and *Forest Lovers,* etc. *Morte D'Arthur.*

Hawthorne obviously isn't this kind of romanticist: though nobody has muddy boots in *The Scarlet Letter,* either.

But there is more to it. *The Scarlet Letter* isn't a pleasant, pretty romance. It is a sort of parable, an earthly story with a hellish meaning.

All the time there is this split in the American art and art-consciousness. On the top it is as nice as pie, goody-goody and lovey-dovey. Like Hawthorne being such a blue-eyed darling, in life, and Longfellow and the rest such sucking doves. Hawthorne's wife said she "never saw him in time," which doesn't mean she saw him too late. But always in the "frail effulgence of eternity."

Serpents they were. Look at the inner meaning of their art and see what demons they were.

You *must* look through the surface of American art, and see the inner diabolism of the symbolic meaning. Otherwise it is all mere childishness.

That blue-eyed darling Nathaniel knew disagreeable things in his inner soul. He was careful to send them out in disguise.

Always the same. The deliberate consciousness of Americans so fair and smooth-spoken, and the under-consciousness so devilish. *Destroy! destroy! destroy!* hums the under-consciousness. *Love and produce! Love and produce!* cackles the upper consciousness. And the world hears only the Love-and-produce cackle. Refuses to hear the hum of destruction underneath. Until such time as it will *have* to hear.

The American has got to destroy. It is his destiny. It is his destiny to destroy the whole corpus of the white psyche, the white consciousness. And he's got to do it secretly. As the growing of a dragon-fly inside a chrysalis or cocoon destroys the larva grub, secretly.

Though many a dragon-fly never gets out of the chrysalis case: dies inside. As America might.

So the secret chrysalis of *The Scarlet Letter,* diabolically destroying the old psyche inside.

*Be good! Be good!* warbles Nathaniel. *Be good, and never sin! Be sure your sins will find you out.*

So convincingly that his wife never saw him "as in time."

Then listen to the diabolic undertone of *The Scarlet Letter.*

Man ate of the tree of knowledge, and became ashamed of himself.

Do you imagine Adam had never lived with Eve before that apple episode? Yes, he had. As a wild animal with his mate.

It didn't become "sin" till the knowledge-poison entered. That apple of Sodom.

We are divided in ourselves, against ourselves. And that is the meaning of the cross symbol.

In the first place, Adam knew Eve as a wild animal knows its mate, momentaneously, but vitally, in blood-knowledge. Blood-knowledge, not mind-knowledge. Blood-knowledge, that seems utterly to forget, but doesn't. Blood-knowledge, instinct, intuition, all the vast vital flux of knowing that goes on in the dark, antecedent to the mind.

Then came that beastly apple, and the other sort of knowledge started.

Adam began to look at himself. "My hat!" he said. "What's this? My Lord! What the deuce!—And Eve! I wonder about Eve."

Thus starts KNOWING. Which shortly runs to UNDERSTANDING, when the devil gets his own.

When Adam went and took Eve, *after* the apple, he didn't do any more than he had done many a time before, in act. But in consciousness he did something very different. So did Eve. Each of them kept an eye on what they were doing, they watched what was happening to them. They wanted to KNOW. And that was the birth of sin. Not *doing* it, but KNOWING about it. Before the apple, they had shut their eyes and their minds had gone dark. Now, they peeped and pried and imagined. They watched themselves. And they felt uncomfortable after. They felt self-conscious. So they said, "The *act* is sin. Let's hide. We've sinned."

No wonder the Lord kicked them out of the Garden. Dirty hypocrites. The sin was the self-watching, self-consciousness. The sin, and the doom. Dirty understanding.

Nowadays men do hate the idea of dualism. It's no good, dual we are. The Cross. If we accept the symbol, then, virtually, we accept the fact. We are divided against ourselves.

For instance, the blood *hates* being KNOWN by the mind. It feels itself destroyed when it is KNOWN. Hence the profound instinct of privacy.

And on the other hand, the mind and the spiritual consciousness of man simply *hates* the dark potency of blood-acts: hates the genuine dark sensual orgasms, which do, for the time being, actually obliterate the mind and the spiritual consciousness, plunge them in a suffocating flood of darkness.

You can't get away from this.

Blood-consciousness overwhelms, obliterates, and annuls mind-consciousness.

Mind-consciousness extinguishes blood-consciousness, and consumes the blood.

We are all of us conscious in both ways. And the two ways are antagonistic in us.

They will always remain so.

That is our cross. /

The antagonism is so obvious, and so far-reaching, that it extends to the smallest thing. The cultured, highly-conscious person of to-day *loathes* any form of physical, "menial" work: such as washing dishes or sweeping a floor or chopping wood. This menial work is an insult to the spirit. "When I see men carrying heavy loads, doing brutal work, it always makes me want to cry," said a beautiful, cultured woman to me.

"When you say that, it makes me want to beat you," said I, in reply. "When I see you with your beautiful head pondering heavy thoughts, I just want to hit you. It outrages me."

My father hated books, hated the sight of anyone reading or writing.

My mother hated the thought that any of her sons should be condemned to manual labour. Her sons must have something higher than that.

She won. But she died first.

He laughs longest who laughs last.

There is a basic hostility in all of us between the physical and the mental, the blood and the spirit. The mind is "ashamed" of the blood. And the blood is destroyed by the mind, actually. Hence pale-faces.

At present the mind-consciousness and the so-called spirit triumphs. In America supremely. In America, nobody does anything from the blood. Always from the nerves, if not from the mind. The blood is chemically reduced by the nerves, in American activity.

When an Italian labourer labours, his mind and nerves sleep, his blood acts ponderously.

Americans, when they are *doing* things, never seem really to be doing them. They are "busy about" it. They are always busy "about" something. But truly *immersed* in *doing* something, with the deep blood-consciousness active, that they never are.

They *admire* the blood-conscious spontaneity. And they want to get it in their heads. "Live from the body," they shriek. It is their last mental shriek. *Co-ordinate.*

It is a further attempt still to rationalize the body and blood. "Think about such and such a muscle," they say, "and relax there."

And every time you "conquer" the body with the mind (you can say "heal" it, if you like) you cause a deeper, more dangerous complex or tension somewhere else.

Ghastly Americans, with their blood no longer blood. A yellow spiritual fluid.

The Fall.

There have been lots of Falls.

We *fell* into *knowledge* when Eve bit the apple. Self-conscious knowledge. For the first time the mind put up a fight against the blood. Wanting to UNDERSTAND. That is to intellectualize the blood.

The blood must be *shed*, says Jesus.

Shed on the cross of our own divided psyche.

Shed the blood, and you become mind-conscious. Eat the body and drink the blood, self-cannibalizing, and you become extremely conscious, like Americans and some Hindus. Devour yourself, and God knows what a lot you'll know, what a lot you'll be conscious of.

Mind you don't choke yourself.

For a long time men *believed* that they could be perfected through the mind, through the spirit. They believed, passionately. They had their ecstasy in pure consciousness. They *believed* in purity, chastity, and the wings of the spirit.

America soon plucked the bird of the spirit. America soon killed the *belief* in the spirit. But not the practice. The practice continued with a sarcastic vehemence. America, with a perfect inner contempt for the spirit and the consciousness of man, practises the same spirituality and universal love and KNOWING all the time, incessantly, like a drug habit. And inwardly gives not a fig for it. Only for the *sensation*. The pretty-pretty *sensation* of love, loving all the world. And the nice fluttering aeroplane *sensation* of knowing, knowing, knowing. Then the prettiest of all sensations, the sensation of UNDERSTANDING. Oh, what a lot they understand, the darlings! So good at the trick, they are. Just a trick of self-conceit.

*The Scarlet Letter* gives the show away.

You have your pure-pure young parson Dimmesdale.

You have the beautiful Puritan Hester at his feet.

And the first thing she does is to seduce him.

And the first thing he does is to be seduced.

And the second thing they do is to hug their sin in secret, and gloat over it, and try to understand.

Which is the myth of New England.

Deerslayer refused to be seduced by Judith Hutter. At least the Sodom apple of sin didn't fetch him.

But Dimmesdale was seduced gloatingly. Oh, luscious Sin!

He was such a pure young man.

That he had to make a fool of purity.

The American psyche.

Of course the best part of the game lay in keeping up pure appearances.

The greatest triumph a woman can have, especially an American woman, is the triumph of seducing a man: especially if he is pure.

And he gets the greatest thrill of all, in falling.—"Seduce me, Mrs. Hercules."

And the pair of them share the subtlest delight in keeping up pure appearances, when everybody knows all the while. But the power of pure appearances is something to exult in. All America gives in to it. *Look* pure!

To seduce a man. To have everybody know. To keep up appearances of purity. Pure!

This is the great triumph of woman.

*A.* The Scarlet Letter. Adulteress! The great Alpha. Alpha! Adulteress! The new Adam and Adama! American!

*A.* Adulteress! Stitched with gold thread, glittering upon the bosom. The proudest insignia.

Put her upon the scaffold and worship her there. Worship her there. The Woman, the Magna Mater. *A.* Adulteress! Abel!

Abel! Abel! Abel! Admirable!

It becomes a farce.

The fiery heart. *A.* Mary of the Bleeding Heart. Mater Adolerata! *A.* Capital *A.* Adulteress. Glittering with gold thread. Abel! Adultery. Admirable!

It is, perhaps, the most colossal satire ever penned. *The Scarlet Letter.* And by a blue-eyed darling of a Nathaniel.

Not Bumppo, however.

The human spirit, fixed in a lie, adhering to a lie, giving itself perpetually the lie.

All begins with *A.*

Adulteress. Alpha. Abel, Adam. *A.* America.

*The Scarlet Letter.*

"Had there been a Papist among the crowd of Puritans, he might have seen in this beautiful woman, so picturesque in her attire and mien, and with the infant at her bosom, an object to remind him of the image of Divine Maternity, which so many illustrious painters have vied with one another to represent; something which should remind him, indeed, but only by contrast, of that sacred image of sinless Motherhood, whose infant was to redeem the world."

Whose infant was to redeem the world indeed! It will be a startling redemption the world will get from the American infant.

"Here was a taint of deepest sin in the most sacred quality of human life, working such effect that the world was only the darker for this woman's beauty, and more lost for the infant she had borne."

Just listen to the darling. Isn't he a master of apology?

Of symbols, too.

His pious blame is a chuckle of praise all the while.

Oh, Hester, you are a demon. A man *must* be pure, just that you can seduce him to a fall. Because the greatest thrill in life is to bring down the Sacred Saint with a flop into the mud. Then when you've brought him down, humbly wipe off the mud with your hair, another Magdalen. And then go home and dance a witch's jig of triumph, and stitch yourself a Scarlet Letter with gold thread, as duchesses used to stitch themselves coronets. And then stand meek on the scaffold and fool the world. Who will all be envying you your sin, and beating you because you've stolen an advantage over them.

Hester Prynne is the great nemesis of woman. She is the KNOWING Ligeia risen diabolic from the grave. Having her own back. UNDERSTANDING.

This time it is Mr. Dimmesdale who dies. She lives on and is Abel.

His spiritual love was a lie. And prostituting the woman to his spiritual love, as popular clergymen do, in his preachings and loftiness, was a tall white lie. Which came flop.

We are so pure in spirit. Hi-tiddly-i-ty!

Till she tickled him in the right place, and he fell.

Flop.

Flop goes spiritual love.

But keep up the game. Keep up appearances. Pure are the pure. To the pure all things, etc.

Look out, Mister, for the Female Devotee. Whatever you do, don't let her start tickling you. She knows your weak spot. Mind your Purity.

When Hester Prynne seduced Arthur Dimmesdale it was the beginning of the end. But from the beginning of the end to the end of the end is a hundred years or two.

Mr. Dimmesdale also wasn't at the end of his resources. Previously, he had lived by governing his body, ruling it, in the interests of his spirit. Now he has a good time all by himself torturing his body, whipping it, piercing it with thorns, macerating himself. It's a form of masturbation. He wants to get a mental grip on his body. And since he can't quite manage it with the mind, witness his fall—he will give it what for, with whips. His will shall *lash* his body. And he enjoys his pains. Wallows in them. To the pure all things are pure.

It is the old self-mutilation process, gone rotten. The mind wanting to get its teeth in the blood and flesh. The ego exulting in the tortures of the mutinous flesh. I, the ego, I *will* triumph over my own flesh. Lash! Lash! I am a grand free spirit. *Lash!* I am the master of my soul! *Lash! Lash!* I am the captain of my soul. *Lash!* Hurray! "In the fell clutch of circumstance," etc., etc.

Good-bye Arthur. He depended on women for his Spiritual Devotees, spiritual brides. So, the woman just touched him in his weak spot, his Achilles Heel of the flesh. Look out for the spiritual bride. She's after the weak spot.

It is the battle of wills.

"For the will therein lieth, which dieth not——"

The Scarlet Woman becomes a Sister of Mercy. Didn't she just, in the late war. Oh, Prophet Nathaniel!

Hester urges Dimmesdale to go away with her, to a new country, to a new life. He isn't having any.

He knows there is no new country, no new life on the globe to-day. It is the same old thing, in different degrees, everywhere. *Plus ça change, plus c'est la même chose.*

Hester thinks, with Dimmesdale for her husband, and Pearl for her child, in Australia, maybe, she'd have been perfect.

But she wouldn't. Dimmesdale had already fallen from his integrity as a minister of the Gospel of the Spirit. He had lost his manliness. He didn't see the point of just leaving himself between the hands of a woman, and going away to a "new country," to be her thing entirely. She'd only have despised him more, as every woman despises a man who has "fallen" to her: despises him with her tenderest lust.

He stood for nothing any more. So let him stay where he was and dree out his weird.

She had dished him and his spirituality, so he hated her. As Angel Clare was dished, and hated Tess. As Jude in the end hated Sue: or should have done. The women make fools of them, the spiritual men. And when, as men, they've gone flop in their spirituality, they can't pick themselves up whole any more. So they just crawl, and die detesting the female, or the females, who made them fall.

The saintly minister gets a bit of his own back, at the last minute, by making public confession from the very scaffold where she was exposed. Then he dodges into death. But he's had a bit of his own back, on everybody.

" 'Shall we not meet again?' whispered she, bending her face down close to him. 'Shall we not spend our immortal life together? Surely, surely we have ransomed one another with all this woe! Thou lookest far into eternity with those bright dying eyes. Tell me what thou seest!' "

" 'Hush, Hester—hush,' said he, with tremulous solemnity. 'The law we broke!—the sin here so awfully revealed! Let these alone be in thy thoughts. I fear! I fear!' "

So he dies, throwing the "sin" in her teeth, and escaping into death.

The law we broke, indeed. You bet!

Whose law?

But it is truly a law, that man must either stick to the belief he has grounded himself on, and obey the laws of that belief. Or he must admit the belief itself to be inadequate, and prepare himself for a new thing.

There was no change in belief, either in Hester or in Dimmesdale or in Hawthorne or in America. The same old treacherous belief, which was really cunning disbelief, in the Spirit, in Purity, in Selfless Love, and in Pure Consciousness. They would go on following this belief, for the sake of the sensationalism of it. But they would make a fool of it all the time. Like Woodrow Wilson, and the rest of modern Believers. The rest of modern Saviours.

If you meet a Saviour, to-day, be sure he is trying to make an innermost fool of you. Especially if the saviour be an UNDERSTANDING WOMAN, offering her love.

Hester lives on, pious as pie, being a public nurse. She becomes at last an acknowledged saint, Abel of the Scarlet Letter.

She would, being a woman. She has had her triumph over the individual man, so she quite loves subscribing to the whole spiritual life of society. She will make herself as false as hell, for society's sake, once she's had her real triumph over Saint Arthur.

Blossoms out into a Sister-of-Mercy Saint.

But it's a long time before she really takes anybody in. People kept on thinking her a witch, which she was.

As a matter of fact, unless a woman is held, by man, safe within the bounds of belief, she becomes inevitably a destructive force. She can't help herself. A woman is almost always vulnerable to pity. She can't bear to see anything *physically* hurt. But let a woman loose from the bounds and restraints of man's fierce belief, in his gods and in himself, and she becomes a gentle devil. She becomes subtly diabolic. The colossal evil of the united spirit of Woman. WOMAN, German woman or American woman, or every other sort of woman, in the last war, was something frightening. As every *man* knows.

Woman becomes a helpless, would-be-loving demon. She is helpless. Her very love is a subtle poison.

Unless a man believes in himself and his gods, *genuinely*: unless he fiercely obeys his own Holy Ghost; his woman will destroy him. Woman is the nemesis of doubting man. She can't help it.

And with Hester, after Ligeia, woman becomes a nemesis to man. She bolsters him up from the outside, she destroys him from the inside. And he dies hating her, as Dimmesdale did.

Dimmesdale's spirituality had gone on too long, too far. It had become a false thing. He found his nemesis in woman. And he was done for.

Woman is a strange and rather terrible phenomenon, to man. When the subconscious soul of woman recoils from its creative union with man, it becomes a destructive force. It exerts, willy-nilly, an invisible destructive influence. The woman herself may be as nice as milk, to all appearance, like Ligeia. But she is sending out waves of silent destruction of the faltering spirit in men, all the same. She doesn't know it. She can't even help it. But she does it. The devil is in her.

The very women who are most busy saving the bodies of men, and saving the children: these women-doctors, these nurses, these educationalists, these public-spirited women, these female saviours: they are all, from the inside, sending out waves of destructive malevolence which eat out the inner life of a man, like a cancer. It is so, it will be so, till men realize it and react to save themselves.

God won't save us. The women are so devilish godly. Men must save themselves in this strait, and by no sugary means either.

A woman can use her sex in sheer malevolence and poison, while she is *behaving* as meek and good as gold. Dear darling, she is really snow-white in her blamelessness. And all the while she is using her sex as a she-devil, for the endless hurt of her man. She doesn't know it. She will never believe it if you tell her. And if you give her a slap in the face for her fiendishness, she will rush to the first magistrate, in indignation. She is so *absolutely* blameless, the she-devil, the dear, dutiful creature.

Give her the great slap, just the same, just when she is being most angelic. Just when she is bearing her cross most meekly.

Oh, woman out of bounds is a devil. But it is man's fault. Woman never *asked*, in the first place, to be cast out of her bit of an Eden of belief and trust. It is man's business to bear the responsibility of belief. If he becomes a spiritual fornicator and liar, like Ligeia's husband and Arthur Dimmesdale, how *can* a woman believe in him? Belief doesn't go by choice. And if a woman doesn't believe in a *man*, she believes, essentially, in nothing. She becomes, willy-nilly, a devil.

A devil she is, and a devil she will be. And most men will succumb to her devilishness.

Hester Prynne was a devil. Even when she was so meekly going round as a sick-nurse. Poor Hester. Part of her wanted to be saved from her own devilishness. And another part wanted to go on and on in devilishness, for revenge. Revenge! REVENGE! It is this that fills the unconscious spirit of woman to-day. Revenge against man, and against the spirit of man, which has betrayed her into unbelief. Even when she is most sweet and a salvationist, she is her most devilish, is woman. She gives her man the sugar-plum of her own submissive sweetness. And when he's taken this sugar-plum in his mouth, a scorpion comes out of it. After he's taken this Eve to his bosom, oh, so loving, she destroys him inch by inch. Woman and her revenge! She will have it, and go on having it, for decades and decades, unless she's stopped. And to stop her you've got to believe in yourself and your gods, your own Holy Ghost, Sir Man; and then you've got to fight her, and never give in. She's a devil. But in the long run she is conquerable. And just a tiny bit of her wants to be conquered. You've got to fight three-quarters of her, in absolute hell, to get at the final quarter of her that wants a release, at last, from the hell of her own revenge. But it's a long last. And not yet.

"She had in her nature a rich, voluptuous, oriental characteristic—a taste for the gorgeously beautiful." This is Hester. This is American. But she repressed her nature in the above direction. She would not even allow herself the luxury of labouring at fine, delicate stitching. Only she dressed her little sin-child Pearl vividly, and the scarlet letter was gorgeously embroidered. Her Hecate and Astarte insignia.

"A voluptuous, oriental characteristic—" That lies waiting in American women. It is probable that the Mormons are the forerunners of the coming real America. It is probable that men will have more than one wife, in the coming America. That you will have again a half-oriental womanhood, and a polygamy.

The grey nurse, Hester. The Hecate, the hellcat. The slowly-evolving voluptuous female of the new era, with a whole new submissiveness to the dark, phallic principle.

But it takes time. Generation after generation of nurses and political women and salvationists. And in the end, the dark erection of the images of sex-worship once more, and the newly submissive woman. That kind of depth. Deep women in that respect. When we have at last broken this insanity of mental-spiritual consciousness. And the women *choose* to experience again the great submission.

"The poor, whom she sought out to be the objects of her bounty, often reviled the hand that was stretched to succour them."

Naturally. The poor hate a salvationist. They smell the devil underneath.

"She was patient—a martyr indeed—but she forbore to pray for her enemies, lest, in spite of her forgiving aspirations, the words of the blessing should stubbornly twist themselves into a curse."

So much honesty, at least. No wonder the old witch-lady Mistress Hibbins claimed her for another witch.

"She grew to have a dread of children; for they had imbibed from their parents a vague idea of something horrible in this dreary woman gliding silently through the town, with never any companion but only one child."

"A vague idea!" Can't you see her "gliding silently"? It's not a question of a vague idea imbibed, but a definite feeling directly received.

"But sometimes, once in many days, or perchance in many months, she felt an eye—a human eye—upon the ignominious brand, that seemed to give a momentary relief, as if half her agony were shared. The next instant, back it all rushed again, with a still deeper throb of pain; for in that brief interval she had sinned again. Had Hester sinned alone?"

Of course not. As for sinning again, she would go on all her life silently, changelessly "sinning." She never repented. Not she. Why should she? She had brought down Arthur Dimmesdale, that too-too snow-white bird, and that was her life-work.

As for sinning again when she met two dark eyes in a crowd, why of course. Somebody who understood as she understood.

I always remember meeting the eyes of a gypsy woman, for one moment, in a crowd, in England. She knew, and I knew. What did we know? I was not able to make out. But we knew.

Probably the same fathomless hate of this spiritual-conscious society in which the outcast woman and I both roamed like meek-looking wolves. Tame wolves waiting to shake off their tameness. Never able to.

And again, that "voluptuous, oriental" characteristic that knows the mystery of the ithyphallic gods. She would not betray the ithyphallic gods to this white, leprous-white society of "lovers." Neither will I, if I can help it. These leprous-white, seducing, spiritual women, who "understand" so much. One has been too often seduced, and "understood." "I can read him like a book," said my first lover of me. The book is in several volumes, dear. And more and more comes back to me the gulf of dark hate and *other* understanding, in the eyes of the gypsy woman. So different from the hateful white light of understanding which floats like scum on the eyes of white, oh, so white English and American women, with their understanding voices and their deep, sad words, and their profound, *good* spirits. Pfui!

Hester was scared only of one result of her sin: Pearl. Pearl, the scarlet letter incarnate. The little girl. When women bear children, they produce either devils or sons with gods in them. And it is an evolutionary process. The devil in Hester produced a purer devil in Pearl. And the devil in Pearl will produce—she married an Italian Count—a piece of purer devilishness still.

And so from hour to hour we ripe and ripe.

And then from hour to hour we rot and rot.

There was that in the child "which often impelled Hester to ask in bitterness of heart, whether it were for good or ill that the poor little creature had been born at all."

For ill, Hester. But don't worry. Ill is as necessary as good. Malevolence is as necessary as benevolence. If you have brought forth, spawned, a young malevolence, be sure there is a rampant falseness in the world against which this malevolence must be turned. Falseness has to be bitten and bitten, till it is bitten to death. Hence Pearl.

Pearl. Her own mother compares her to the demon of plague, or scarlet fever, in her red dress. But then plague is necessary to destroy a rotten, false humanity.

Pearl, the devilish girl-child, who can be so tender and loving and *understanding*, and then, when she has understood, will give you a hit across the mouth, and turn on you with a grin of sheer diabolic jeering.

Serves you right, you shouldn't be *understood*. That is your vice. You shouldn't want to be loved, and then you'd not get hit across the mouth. Pearl will love you: marvellously. And she'll hit you across the mouth: oh, so neatly. And serves you right.

Pearl is perhaps the most modern child in all literature.

Old-fashioned Nathaniel, with his little-boy charm, he'll tell you what's what. But he'll cover it with smarm.

Hester simply *hates* her child, from one part of herself. And from another, she cherishes her child as her one precious treasure. For Pearl is the continuing of her female revenge on life. But female revenge hits both ways. Hits back at its own mother. The female revenge in Pearl hits back at Hester, the mother, and Hester is simply livid with fury and "sadness," which is rather amusing.

"The child could not be made amenable to rules. In giving her existence a great law had been broken; and the result was a being whose elements were perhaps beautiful and brilliant, but all in disorder, or with an order peculiar to themselves, amidst which the point of variety and arrangement was difficult or impossible to discover."

Of course the order is peculiar to themselves. But the point of variety is this: "Draw out the loving, sweet soul, draw it out with marvellous understanding; and then spit in its eye."

Hester, of course, didn't at all like it when her sweet child drew out her motherly soul, with yearning and deep understanding: and then spit in the motherly eye, with a grin. But it was a process the mother had started.

Pearl had a peculiar look in her eyes: "a look so intelligent, yet so inexplicable, so perverse, sometimes so malicious, but generally accompanied by a wild flow of spirits, that Hester could not help questioning at such moments whether Pearl was a human child."

A little demon! But her mother, and the saintly Dimmesdale, had borne her. And Pearl, by the very openness of her perversity, was more straightforward than her parents. She flatly refuses any Heavenly Father, seeing the earthly one such a fraud. And she has the pietistic Dimmesdale on toast, spits right in his eye: in both his eyes.

Poor, brave, tormented little soul, always in a state of recoil, she'll be a devil to men when she grows up. But the men deserve it. If they'll let themselves be "drawn," by her loving understanding, they deserve that she shall slap them across the mouth the moment they *are* drawn. The chickens! Drawn and trussed.

Poor little phenomenon of a modern child, she'll grow up into the devil of a modern woman. The nemesis of weak-kneed modern men, craving to be love-drawn.

The third person in the diabolic trinity, or triangle, of the Scarlet Letter, is Hester's first husband, Roger Chillingworth. He is an old Elizabethan physician with a grey beard and a long-furred coat and a twisted shoulder. Another healer. But something of an alchemist, a magician. He is a magician on the verge of modern science, like Francis Bacon.

Roger Chillingworth is of the old order of intellect, in direct line from the mediæval Roger Bacon alchemists. He has an old, intellectual belief in the dark sciences, the Hermetic philosophies. He is no Christian, no selfless aspirer. He is not an aspirer. He is the old authoritarian in man. The old male authority. But without passional belief. Only intellectual belief in himself and his male authority.

Shakespeare's whole tragic wail is because of the downfall of the true male authority, the ithyphallic authority and masterhood. It fell with Elizabeth. It was trodden underfoot with Victoria.

But Chillingworth keeps on the *intellectual* tradition. He hates the new spiritual aspirers, like Dimmesdale, with a black, crippled hate. He is the old male authority, in intellectual tradition.

You can't keep a wife by force of an intellectual tradition. So Hester took to seducing Dimmesdale.

Yet her only marriage, and her last oath, is with the old Roger. He and she are accomplices in pulling down the spiritual saint.

"Why dost thou smile so at me—" she says to her old, vengeful husband. "Art thou not like the Black Man that haunts the forest around us? Hast thou not enticed me into a bond which will prove the ruin of my soul?"

"Not thy soul!" he answered with another smile. "No, not thy soul!"

It is the soul of the pure preacher, that false thing, which they are after. And the crippled physician—this other healer—blackly vengeful in his old, distorted male authority, and the "loving" woman, they bring down the saint between them.

A black and complementary hatred, akin to love, is what Chillingworth feels for the young, saintly parson. And Dimmesdale responds, in a hideous kind of love. Slowly the saint's life is poisoned. But the black old physician smiles, and tries to keep him alive. Dimmesdale goes in for self-torture, self-lashing, lashing his own white, thin, spiritual saviour's body. The dark old Chillingworth listens outside the door and laughs, and prepares another medicine, so that the game can go on longer. And the saint's very soul goes rotten. Which is the supreme triumph. Yet he keeps up appearances still.

The black, vengeful soul of the crippled, masterful male, still dark in his authority: and the white ghastliness of the fallen saint! The two halves of manhood mutually destroying one another.

Dimmesdale has a "coup" in the very end. He gives the whole show away by confessing publicly on the scaffold, and dodging into death, leaving Hester dished, and Roger as it were, doubly cuckolded. It is a neat last revenge.

Down comes the curtain, as in Ligeia's poem.

But the child Pearl will be on in the next act, with her Italian Count and a new brood of vipers. And Hester greyly Abelling, in the shadows, after her rebelling.

It is a marvellous allegory. It is to me one of the greatest allegories in all literature, *The Scarlet Letter*. Its marvellous under-meaning! And its perfect duplicity.

The absolute duplicity of that blue-eyed *Wunderkind* of a Nathaniel. The American wonder-child, with his magical allegorical insight.

But even wonder-children have to grow up in a generation or two.

And even SIN becomes stale.

# THE DIGNITY AND RESPONSIBILITY
# OF ART

*T. E. HULME*

## Romanticism and Classicism

T. E. Hulme (1883–1917) was, for a brief time, one of the most stimulating of English critics. In London, in the years before and during World War I, he set about educating his contemporaries in the reform of attitudes toward poetry and criticism. He was also a translator of works by Henri Bergson and Georges Sorel. His own philosophy existed only in a few essays, suggestive but not yet given final definition at the time of his death on the Western front, in 1917. Modern criticism is indebted to him chiefly for two contributions: his elaborate critique of Humanism (or, Humanitarianism), and the contrast of it with what he called the "religious attitude"; and his attempts to convert contemporaries to a "new classicism" in criticism and poetry. In both cases, he was allied informally with Ezra Pound and T. S. Eliot. "Romanticism and Classicism" is a germinal essay. It defines, in Hulme's own eccentric ways, the two terms of its title, and tries to prove, through an amateurish historical "survey," the need for a new classicism in poetics. Many of the ideas of this essay were repeated, with their own variants, by Pound and Eliot in the years from 1913 to 1930. The Anglo-American debates over Imagism in these years derive partly from Hulme's pioneering work.

*I* want to maintain that after a hundred years of romanticism, we are in for a classical revival, and that the particular weapon of this new

57

classical spirit, when it works in verse, will be fancy. And in this I imply the superiority of fancy—not superior generally or absolutely, for that would be obvious nonsense, but superior in the sense that we use the word good in empirical ethics—good for something, superior for something. I shall have to prove then two things, first that a classical revival is coming, and, secondly, for its particular purposes, fancy will be superior to imagination.

So banal have the terms Imagination and Fancy become that we imagine they must have always been in the language. Their history as two differing terms in the vocabulary of criticism is comparatively short. Originally, of course, they both mean the same thing; they first began to be differentiated by the German writers on æsthetics in the eighteenth century.

I know that in using the words "classic" and "romantic" I am doing a dangerous thing. They represent five or six different kinds of antitheses, and while I may be using them in one sense you may be interpreting them in another. In this present connection I am using them in a perfectly precise and limited sense. I ought really to have coined a couple of new words, but I prefer to use the ones I have used, as I then conform to the practice of the group of polemical writers who make most use of them at the present day, and have almost succeeded in making them political catchwords. I mean Maurras, Lasserre and all the group connected with L'Action Française.

At the present time this is the particular group with which the distinction is most vital. Because it has become a party symbol. If you asked a man of a certain set whether he preferred the classics or the romantics, you could deduce from that what his politics were.

The best way of gliding into a proper definition of my terms would be to start with a set of people who are prepared to fight about it—for in them you will have no vagueness. (Other people take the infamous attitude of the person with catholic tastes who says he likes both.)

About a year ago, a man whose name I think was Fauchois gave a lecture at the Odéon on Racine, in the course of which he made some disparaging remarks about his dullness, lack of invention and the rest of it. This caused an immediate riot: fights took place all over the house; several people were arrested and imprisoned, and the rest of the series of lectures took place with hundreds of gendarmes and detectives scattered all over the place. These people interrupted because the classical ideal is a living thing to them and Racine is the great classic. That is what I call a real vital interest in literature. They regard romanticism as an awful disease from which France had just recovered.

The thing is complicated in their case by the fact that it was romanticism that made the revolution. They hate the revolution, so they hate romanticism.

I make no apology for dragging in politics here; romanticism both in England and France is associated with certain political views, and it is in taking a concrete example of the working out of a principle in action that you can get its best definition.

What was the positive principle behind all the other principles of '89? I am talking here of the revolution in as far as it was an idea; I leave out material causes—they only produce the forces. The barriers which could easily have resisted or guided these forces had been previously rotted away by ideas. This always seems to be the case in successful changes; the privileged class is beaten only when it has lost faith in itself, when it has itself been penetrated with the ideas which are working against it.

It was not the rights of man—that was a good solid practical war-cry. The thing which created enthusiasm, which made the revolution practically a new religion, was something more positive than that. People of all classes, people who stood to lose by it, were in a positive ferment about the idea of liberty. There must have been some idea which enabled them to think that something positive could come out of so essentially negative a thing. There was, and here I get my definition of romanticism. They had been taught by Rousseau that man was by nature good, that it was only bad laws and customs that had suppressed him. Remove all these and the infinite possibilities of man would have a chance. This is what made them think that something positive could come out of disorder, this is what created the religious enthusiasm. Here is the root of all romanticism: that man, the individual, is an infinite reservoir of possibilities; and if you can so rearrange society by the destruction of oppressive order then these possibilities will have a chance and you will get Progress.

One can define the classical quite clearly as the exact opposite to this. Man is an extraordinarily fixed and limited animal whose nature is absolutely constant. It is only by tradition and organisation that anything decent can be got out of him.

This view was a little shaken at the time of Darwin. You remember his particular hypothesis, that new species came into existence by the cumulative effect of small variations—this seems to admit the possibility of future progress. But at the present day the contrary hypothesis makes headway in the shape of De Vries's mutation theory, that each new species comes into existence, not gradually by the accumulation of small steps, but suddenly in a jump, a kind of sport, and that once in existence it remains absolutely fixed. This enables me to keep the classical view with an appearance of scientific backing.

Put shortly, these are the two views, then. One, that man is intrinsically good, spoilt by circumstance; and the other that he is intrinsically limited, but disciplined by order and tradition to something fairly decent. To the one party man's nature is like a well, to the other like a bucket. The view which regards man as a well, a reservoir full of possibilities, I call the romantic; the one which regards him as a very finite and fixed creature, I call the classical.

One may note here that the Church has always taken the classical view since the defeat of the Pelagian heresy and the adoption of the sane classical dogma of original sin.

It would be a mistake to identify the classical view with that of materialism. On the contrary it is absolutely identical with the normal religious attitude. I should put it in this way: That part of the fixed nature of man is the belief in the Deity. This should be as fixed and true for every man as belief in the existence of matter and in the objective world. It is parallel to appetite, the instinct of sex, and all the other fixed qualities. Now at certain times, by the use of either force or rhetoric, these instincts have been suppressed—in Florence under Savonarola, in Geneva under Calvin, and here under the Roundheads. The inevitable result of such a process is that the repressed instinct bursts out in some abnormal direction. So with religion. By the perverted rhetoric of Rationalism, your natural instincts are suppressed and you are converted into an agnostic. Just as in the case of the other instincts, Nature has her revenge. The instincts that find their right and proper outlet in religion must come out in some other way. You don't believe in a God, so you begin to believe that man is a god. You don't believe in Heaven, so you begin to believe in a heaven on earth. In other words, you get romanticism. The concepts that are right and proper in their own sphere are spread over, and so mess up, falsify and blur the clear outlines of human experience. It is like pouring a pot of treacle over the dinner table. Romanticism then, and this is the best definition I can give of it, is spilt religion.

I must now shirk the difficulty of saying exactly what I mean by romantic and classical in verse. I can only say that it means the result of these two attitudes towards the cosmos, towards man, in so far as it gets reflected in verse. The romantic, because he thinks man infinite, must always be talking about the infinite; and as there is always the bitter contrast between what you think you ought to be able to do and what man actually can, it always tends, in its later stages at any rate, to be gloomy. I really can't go any further than to say it is the reflection of these two temperaments, and point out examples of the different spirits. On the one hand I would take such diverse people as Horace, most of the Elizabethans and the writers of the Augustan age, and on the other side Lamartine, Hugo, parts of Keats, Coleridge, Byron, Shelley and Swinburne.

I know quite well that when people think of classical and romantic in verse, the contrast at once comes into their mind between, say, Racine and Shakespeare. I don't mean this; the dividing line that I intend is here misplaced a little from the true middle. That Racine is on the extreme classical side I agree, but if you call Shakespeare romantic, you are using a different definition to the one I give. You are thinking of the difference between classic and romantic as being merely one between restraint and exuberance. I should say with Nietzsche that there are two kinds of classicism, the static and the dynamic. Shakespeare is the classic of motion.

What I mean by classical in verse, then, is this. That even in the most imaginative flights there is always a holding back, a reservation. The classical poet never forgets this finiteness, this limit of man. He remembers always that he is mixed up with earth. He may jump, but he always returns back; he never flies away into the circumambient gas.

You might say if you wished that the whole of the romantic attitude seems to crystallise in verse round metaphors of flight. Hugo is always flying, flying over abysses, flying up into the eternal gases. The word infinite in every other line.

In the classical attitude you never seem to swing right along to the infinite nothing. If you say an extravagant thing which does exceed the limits inside which you know man to be fastened, yet there is always conveyed in some way at the end an impression of yourself standing outside it, and not quite believing it, or consciously putting it forward as a flourish. You never go blindly into an atmosphere more than the truth, an atmosphere too rarefied for man to breathe for long. You are always faithful to the conception of a limit. It is a question of pitch; in romantic verse you move at a certain pitch of rhetoric which you know, man being what he is, to be a little high falutin. The kind of thing you get in Hugo or Swinburne. In the coming classical reaction that will feel just wrong. For an example of the opposite thing, a verse written in the proper classical spirit, I can take the song from Cymbeline beginning with "Fear no more the heat of the sun." I am just using this as a parable. I don't quite mean what I say here. Take the last two lines:

> "Golden lads and girls all must,
> Like chimney sweepers come to dust."

Now, no romantic would have ever written that. Indeed, so ingrained is romanticism, so objectionable is this to it, that people have asserted that these were not part of the original song.

Apart from the pun, the thing that I think quite classical is the word lad. Your modern romantic could never write that. He would have to write golden youth, and take up the thing at least a couple of notes in pitch.

I want now to give the reasons which make me think that we are nearing the end of the romantic movement.

The first lies in the nature of any convention or tradition in art. A particular convention or attitude in art has a strict analogy to the phenomena of organic life. It grows old and decays. It has a definite period of life and must die. All the possible tunes get played on it and then it is exhausted; moreover its best period is its youngest. Take the case of the extraordinary efflorescence of verse in the Elizabethan period. All kinds of reasons have been given for this—the discovery of the new world and all the rest of it. There is a much simpler one. A new medium had been given them to play with—namely, blank verse. It was new and so it was easy to play new tunes on it.

The same law holds in other arts. All the masters of painting are born into the world at a time when the particular tradition from which they start is imperfect. The Florentine tradition was just short of full ripeness when Raphael came to Florence, the Bellinesque was still young when Titian was born in Venice. Landscape was still a toy or an appanage of figure-painting when Turner and Constable arose to reveal its independent power. When Turner and Constable had done with landscape they left little or nothing for their successors to do on the same lines. Each field of artistic activity is exhausted by the first great artist who gathers a full harvest from it.

This period of exhaustion seems to me to have been reached in romanticism. We shall not get any new efflorescence of verse until we get a new technique, a new convention, to turn ourselves loose in.

Objection might be taken to this. It might be said that a century as an organic unity doesn't exist, that I am being deluded by a wrong metaphor, that I am treating a collection of literary people as if they were an organism or state department. Whatever we may be in other things, an objector might urge, in literature in as far as we are anything at all—in as far as we are worth considering—we are individuals, we are persons, and as distinct persons we cannot be subordinated to any general treatment. At any period at any time, an individual poet may be a classic or a romantic just as he feels like it. You at any particular moment may think that you can stand outside a movement. You may think that as an individual you observe both the classic and the romantic spirit and decide from a purely detached point of view that one is superior to the other.

The answer to this is that no one, in a matter of judgment of beauty, can take a detached standpoint in this way. Just as physically you are not born that abstract entity, man, but the child of particular parents, so you are in matters of literary judgment. Your opinion is almost entirely of the literary history that came just before you, and you are governed by that whatever you may think. Take Spinoza's example of a stone falling to the ground. If it had a conscious mind it would, he said, think it was going to the ground because it wanted to. So you with your pretended free judgment about what is and what is not beautiful. The amount of freedom in man is much exaggerated. That we are free on certain rare occasions, both my religion and the views I get from metaphysics convince me. But many acts which we habitually label free are in reality automatic. It is quite possible for a man to write a book almost automatically. I have read several such products. Some observations were recorded more than twenty years ago by Robertson on reflex speech, and he found that in certain cases of dementia, where the people were quite unconscious so far as the exercise of reasoning went, that very intelligent answers were given to a succession of questions on politics and such matters. The meaning of these questions could not possibly have been understood. Language here acted after the manner of a reflex. So that certain extremely complex mechanisms, subtle enough to imitate beauty, can work by themselves—I certainly think that this is the case with judgments about beauty.

I can put the same thing in slightly different form. Here is a question of a conflict of two attitudes, as it might be of two techniques. The critic, while he has to admit that changes from one to the other occur, persists in regarding them as mere variations to a certain fixed normal, just as a pendulum might swing. I admit the analogy of the pendulum as far as movement, but I deny the further consequence of the analogy, the existence of the point of rest, the normal point.

When I say that I dislike the romantics, I dissociate two things: the part of them in which they resemble all the great poets, and the part in which they differ and which gives them their character as romantics. It is this minor element which constitutes the particular note of a century, and which, while it excites contemporaries, annoys the next generation. It was precisely that quality in Pope which pleased his friends, which we detest. Now, anyone just before the romantics who felt that, could have predicted that a change was coming. It seems to me that we stand just in the same position now. I think that there is an increasing proportion of people who simply can't stand Swinburne.

When I say that there will be another classical revival I don't necessarily anticipate a return to Pope. I say merely that now is the time for such a revival. Given people of the necessary capacity, it may be a vital thing; without them we may get a formalism something like Pope. When it does come we may not even recognise it as classical. Although it will be classical it will be different because it has passed through a romantic period. To take a parallel example: I remember being very surprised, after seeing the Post Impressionists, to find in Maurice Denis's account of the matter that they consider themselves classical in the sense that they were trying to impose the same order on the mere flux of new material provided by the impressionist movement, that existed in the more limited materials of the painting before.

There is something now to be cleared away before I get on with my argument, which is that while romanticism is dead in reality, yet the critical attitude appropriate to it still continues to exist. To make this a little clearer: For every kind of verse, there is a corresponding receptive attitude. In a romantic period we demand from verse certain qualities. In a classical period we demand others. At the present time I should say that this receptive attitude has outlasted the thing from which it was formed. But while the romantic tradition has run dry, yet the critical attitude of mind, which demands romantic qualities from verse, still survives. So that if good classical verse were to be written to-morrow very few people would be able to stand it.

I object even to the best of the romantics. I object still more to the receptive attitude. I object to the sloppiness which doesn't consider that a poem is a poem unless it is moaning or whining about something or

other. I always think in this connection of the last line of a poem of
John Webster's which ends with a request I cordially endorse:

> "End your moan and come away."

The thing has got so bad now that a poem which is all dry and hard,
a properly classical poem, would not be considered poetry at all. How
many people now can lay their hands on their hearts and say they like
either Horace or Pope? They feel a kind of chill when they read them.

The dry hardness which you get in the classics is absolutely repugnant
to them. Poetry that isn't damp isn't poetry at all. They cannot see that
accurate description is a legitimate object of verse. Verse to them always
means a bringing in of some of the emotions that are grouped round the
word infinite.

The essence of poetry to most people is that it must lead them to a
beyond of some kind. Verse strictly confined to the earthly and the
definite (Keats is full of it) might seem to them to be excellent writing,
excellent craftsmanship, but not poetry. So much has romanticism de-
bauched us, that, without some form of vagueness, we deny the highest.

In the classic it is always the light of ordinary day, never the light
that never was on land or sea. It is always perfectly human and never
exaggerated: man is always man and never a god.

But the awful result of romanticism is that, accustomed to this strange
light, you can never live without it. Its effect on you is that of a drug.

There is a general tendency to think that verse means little else than
the expression of unsatisfied emotion. People say: "But how can you
have verse without sentiment?" You see what it is: the prospect alarms
them. A classical revival to them would mean the prospect of an arid
desert and the death of poetry as they understand it, and could only
come to fill the gap caused by that death. Exactly why this dry classical
spirit should have a positive and legitimate necessity to express itself in
poetry is utterly inconceivable to them. What this positive need is, I
shall show later. It follows from the fact that there is another quality,
not the emotion produced, which is at the root of excellence in verse.
Before I get to this I am concerned with a negative thing, a theoretical
point, a prejudice that stands in the way and is really at the bottom of
this reluctance to understand classical verse.

It is an objection which ultimately I believe comes from a bad metaphysic of art. You are unable to admit the existence of beauty without
the infinite being in some way or another dragged in.

I may quote for purposes of argument, as a typical example of this
kind of attitude made vocal, the famous chapters in Ruskin's *Modern
Painters*, Vol. II, on the imagination. I must say here, parenthetically,
that I use this word without prejudice to the other discussion with
which I shall end the paper. I only use the word here because it is Ruskin's word. All that I am concerned with just now is the attitude behind
it, which I take to be the romantic.

"Imagination cannot but be serious; she sees too far, too darkly, too solemnly, too earnestly, ever to smile. There is something in the heart of everything, if we can reach it, that we shall not be inclined to laugh at. . . . Those who have so pierced and seen the melancholy deeps of things, are filled with intense passion and gentleness of sympathy." (Part III, Chap. III, § 9.)

"There is in every word set down by the imaginative mind an awful undercurrent of meaning, and evidence and shadow upon it of the deep places out of which it has come. It is often obscure, often half-told; for he who wrote it, in his clear seeing of the things beneath, may have been impatient of detailed interpretation; for if we choose to dwell upon it and trace it, it will lead us always securely back to that metropolis of the soul's dominion from which we may follow out all the ways and tracks to its farthest coasts." (Part III, Chap. III, § 5.)

Really in all these matters the act of judgment is an instinct, an absolutely unstateable thing akin to the art of the tea taster. But you must talk, and the only language you can use in this matter is that of analogy. I have no material clay to mould to the given shape; the only thing which one has for the purpose, and which acts as a substitute for it, a kind of mental clay, are certain metaphors modified into theories of æsthetic and rhetoric. A combination of these, while it cannot state the essentially unstateable intuition, can yet give you a sufficient analogy to enable you to see what it was and to recognise it on condition that you yourself have been in a similar state. Now these phrases of Ruskin's convey quite clearly to me his taste in the matter.

I see quite clearly that he thinks the best verse must be serious. That is a natural attitude for a man in the romantic period. But he is not content with saying that he prefers this kind of verse. He wants to deduce his opinion like his master, Coleridge, from some fixed principle which can be found by metaphysic.

Here is the last refuge of this romantic attitude. It proves itself to be not an attitude but a deduction from a fixed principle of the cosmos.

One of the main reasons for the existence of philosophy is not that it enables you to find truth (it can never do that) but that it does provide you a refuge for definitions. The usual idea of the thing is that it provides you with a fixed basis from which you can deduce the things you want in æsthetics. The process is the exact contrary. You start in the confusion of the fighting line, you retire from that just a little to the rear to recover, to get your weapons right. Quite plainly, without metaphor this—it provides you with an elaborate and precise language in which you really can explain definitely what you mean, but what you want to say is decided by other things. The ultimate reality is the hurly-burly, the struggle; the metaphysic is an adjunct to clear-headedness in it.

To get back to Ruskin and his objection to all that is not serious. It seems to me that involved in this is a bad metaphysical æsthetic. You have the metaphysic which in defining beauty or the nature of art always drags in the infinite. Particularly in Germany, the land where theories of æsthetics were first created, the romantic æsthetes collated all beauty to an impression of the infinite involved in the identification of our being in absolute spirit. In the least element of beauty we have a total intuition of the whole world. Every artist is a kind of pantheist.

Now it is quite obvious to anyone who holds this kind of theory that any poetry which confines itself to the finite can never be of the highest kind. It seems a contradiction in terms to them. And as in metaphysics you get the last refuge of a prejudice, so it is now necessary for me to refute this.

Here follows a tedious piece of dialectic, but it is necessary for my purpose. I must avoid two pitfalls in discussing the idea of beauty. On the one hand there is the old classical view which is supposed to define it as lying in conformity to certain standard fixed forms; and on the other hand there is the romantic view which drags in the infinite. I have got to find a metaphysic between these two which will enable me to hold consistently that a neo-classic verse of the type I have indicated involves no contradiction in terms. It is essential to prove that beauty may be in small, dry things.

The great aim is accurate, precise and definite description. The first thing is to recognise how extraordinarily difficult this is. It is no mere matter of carefulness; you have to use language, and language is by its very nature a communal thing; that is, it expresses never the exact thing but a compromise—that which is common to you, me and everybody. But each man sees a little differently, and to get out clearly and exactly what he does see, he must have a terrific struggle with language, whether it be with words or the technique of other arts. Language has its own special nature, its own conventions and communal ideas. It is only by a concentrated effort of the mind that you can hold it fixed to your own purpose. I always think that the fundamental process at the back of all the arts might be represented by the following metaphor.* You know what I call architect's curves—flat pieces of wood with all different kinds of curvature. By a suitable selection from these you can draw approximately any curve you like. The artist I take to be the man who simply can't bear the idea of that 'approximately.' He will get the exact curve of what he sees whether it be an object or an idea in the mind. I shall here have to change my metaphor a little to get the process in his mind. Suppose that instead of your curved pieces of wood you have a springy piece of steel of the same types of curvature as the wood. Now the state of tension or concentration of mind, if he is doing anything really good in this struggle against the ingrained habit of the tech-

---

* [This metaphor is used elsewhere by Hulme—in dealing with Bergson's Theory of Art (p. 160 *infra*)—but I have refrained from deleting it here because of its particular relevancy. (Note by Herbert Read, editor of *Speculations*)]

nique, may be represented by a man employing all his fingers to bend the steel out of its own curve and into the exact curve which you want. Something different to what it would assume naturally.

There are then two things to distinguish, first the particular faculty of mind to see things as they really are, and apart from the conventional ways in which you have been trained to see them. This is itself rare enough in all consciousness. Second, the concentrated state of mind, the grip over oneself which is necessary in the actual expression of what one sees. To prevent one falling into the conventional curves of ingrained technique, to hold on through infinite detail and trouble to the exact curve you want. Wherever you get this sincerity, you get the fundamental quality of good art without dragging in infinite or serious.

I can now get at that positive fundamental quality of verse which constitutes excellence, which has nothing to do with infinity, with mystery or with emotions.

This is the point I aim at, then, in my argument. I prophesy that a period of dry, hard, classical verse is coming. I have met the preliminary objection founded on the bad romantic æsthetic that in such verse, from which the infinite is excluded, you cannot have the essence of poetry at all.

After attempting to sketch out what this positive quality is, I can get on to the end of my paper in this way: That where you get this quality exhibited in the realm of the emotions you get imagination, and that where you get this quality exhibited in the contemplation of finite things you get fancy.

In prose as in algebra concrete things are embodied in signs or counters which are moved about according to rules, without being visualised at all in the process. There are in prose certain type situations and arrangements of words, which move as automatically into certain other arrangements as do functions in algebra. One only changes the X's and the Y's back into physical things at the end of the process. Poetry, in one aspect at any rate, may be considered as an effort to avoid this characteristic of prose. It is not a counter language, but a visual concrete one. It is a compromise for a language of intuition which would hand over sensations bodily. It always endeavours to arrest you, and to make you continuously see a physical thing, to prevent you gliding through an abstract process. It chooses fresh epithets and fresh metaphors, not so much because they are new, and we are tired of the old, but because the old cease to convey a physical thing and become abstract counters. A poet says a ship 'coursed the seas' to get a physical image, instead of the counter word 'sailed.' Visual meanings can only be transferred by the new bowl of metaphor; prose is an old pot that lets them leak out. Images in verse are not mere decoration, but the very essence of an intuitive language. Verse is a pedestrian taking you over the ground, prose—a train which delivers you at a destination.

I can now get on to a discussion of two words often used in this connection, "fresh" and "unexpected." You praise a thing for being "fresh." I understand what you mean, but the word besides conveying the truth conveys a secondary something which is certainly false. When you say a poem or drawing is fresh, and so good, the impression is somehow conveyed that the essential element of goodness is freshness, that it is good because it is fresh. Now this is certainly wrong, there is nothing particularly desirable about freshness *per se*. Works of art aren't eggs. Rather the contrary. It is simply an unfortunate necessity due to the nature of language and technique that the only way the element which does constitute goodness, the only way in which its presence can be detected externally, is by freshness. Freshness convinces you, you feel at once that the artist was in an actual physical state. You feel that for a minute. Real communication is so very rare, for plain speech is unconvincing. It is in this rare fact of communication that you get the root of æsthetic pleasure.

I shall maintain that wherever you get an extraordinary interest in a thing, a great zest in its contemplation which carries on the contemplator to accurate description in the sense of the word accurate I have just analysed, there you have sufficient justification for poetry. It must be an intense zest which heightens a thing out of the level of prose. I am using contemplation here just in the same way that Plato used it, only applied to a different subject; it is a detached interest. "The object of æsthetic contemplation is something framed apart by itself and regarded without memory or expectation, simply as being itself, as end not means, as individual not universal."

To take a concrete example. I am taking an extreme case. If you are walking behind a woman in the street, you notice the curious way in which the skirt rebounds from her heels. If that peculiar kind of motion becomes of such interest to you that you will search about until you can get the exact epithet which hits it off, there you have a properly æsthetic emotion. But it is the zest with which you look at the thing which decides you to make the effort. In this sense the feeling that was in Herrick's mind when he wrote "the tempestuous petticoat" was exactly the same as that which in bigger and vaguer matters makes the best romantic verse. It doesn't matter an atom that the emotion produced is not of dignified vagueness, but on the contrary amusing; the point is that exactly the same activity is at work as in the highest verse. That is the avoidance of conventional language in order to get the exact curve of the thing.

I have still to show that in the verse which is to come, fancy will be the necessary weapon of the classical school. The positive quality I have talked about can be manifested in ballad verse by extreme directness and simplicity, such as you get in "On Fair Kirkconnel Lea." But the particular verse we are going to get will be cheerful, dry and sophisticated, and here the necessary weapon of the positive quality must be fancy.

Subject doesn't matter; the quality in it is the same as you get in the more romantic people.

It isn't the scale or kind of emotion produced that decides, but this one fact: Is there any real zest in it? Did the poet have an actually realised visual object before him in which he delighted? It doesn't matter if it were a lady's shoe or the starry heavens.

Fancy is not mere decoration added on to plain speech. Plain speech is essentially inaccurate. It is only by new metaphors, that is, by fancy, that it can be made precise.

When the analogy has not enough connection with the thing described to be quite parallel with it, where it overlays the thing it described and there is a certain excess, there you have the play of fancy— that I grant is inferior to imagination.

But where the analogy is every bit of it necessary for accurate description in the sense of the word accurate I have previously described, and your only objection to this kind of fancy is that it is not serious in the effect it produces, then I think the objection to be entirely invalid. If it is sincere in the accurate sense, when the whole of the analogy is necessary to get out the exact curve of the feeling or thing you want to express—there you seem to me to have the highest verse, even though the subject be trivial and the emotions of the infinite far away.

It is very difficult to use any terminology at all for this kind of thing. For whatever word you use is at once sentimentalised. Take Coleridge's word "vital." It is used loosely by all kinds of people who talk about art, to mean something vaguely and mysteriously significant. In fact, vital and mechanical is to them exactly the same antithesis as between good and bad.

Nothing of the kind; Coleridge uses it in a perfectly definite and what I call dry sense. It is just this: A mechanical complexity is the sum of its parts. Put them side by side and you get the whole. Now vital or organic is merely a convenient metaphor for a complexity of a different kind, that in which the parts cannot be said to be elements as each one is modified by the other's presence, and each one to a certain extent is the whole. The leg of a chair by itself is still a leg. My leg by itself wouldn't be.

Now the characteristic of the intellect is that it can only represent complexities of the mechanical kind. It can only make diagrams, and diagrams are essentially things whose parts are separate one from another. The intellect always analyses—when there is a synthesis it is baffled. That is why the artist's work seems mysterious. The intellect can't represent it. This is a necessary consequence of the particular nature of the intellect and the purposes for which it is formed. It doesn't mean that your synthesis is ineffable, simply that it can't be definitely stated.

Now this is all worked out in Bergson, the central feature of his whole philosophy. It is all based on the clear conception of these vital complexities which he calls "intensive" as opposed to the other kind which he calls "extensive," and the recognition of the fact that the intellect can only deal with the extensive multiplicity. To deal with the intensive you must use intuition.

Now, as I said before, Ruskin was perfectly aware of all this, but he had no such metaphysical background which would enable him to state definitely what he meant. The result is that he has to flounder about in a series of metaphors. A powerfully imaginative mind seizes and combines at the same instant all the important ideas of its poem or picture, and while it works with one of them, it is at the same instant working with and modifying all in their relation to it and never losing sight of their bearings on each other—as the motion of a snake's body goes through all parts at once and its volition acts at the same instant in coils which go contrary ways.

A romantic movement must have an end of the very nature of the thing. It may be deplored, but it can't be helped—wonder must cease to be wonder.

I guard myself here from all the consequences of the analogy, but it expresses at any rate the inevitableness of the process. A literature of wonder must have an end as inevitably as a strange land loses its strangeness when one lives in it. Think of the lost ecstasy of the Elizabethans. "Oh my America, my new found land," think of what it meant to them and of what it means to us. Wonder can only be the attitude of a man passing from one stage to another, it can never be a permanently fixed thing.

## EZRA POUND

# A Retrospect[1]

The role of Ezra Pound (1885–    ) is so well known that it does not need summarizing, beyond the fact that in the years 1910–20 he was extremely and effectively active in the reform of poetic theory and practice. The two selections from him reprinted here state as well as anything else he has written the terms of his critical point of view. The great ideals were economy and precision of representation, elimination of all superfluities, and the definition of the poetic act within carefully circumscribed and

---

[1] A group of early essays and notes which appeared under this title in *Pavannes and Divisions* (1918). "A Few Don'ts" was first printed in *Poetry*, I, 6 (March, 1913).

rigidly held limits. Despite their differences of tone, the following may be considered companion pieces of Hulme's "Romanticism and Classicism," reprinted above. The letter to Harriet Monroe is characteristic of Pound's epistolary style. He is obviously speaking as a self-avowed leader or "preacher," who insists upon his doctrine and is concerned to make a complete break from the errors of the recent past.

*T*here has been so much scribbling about a new fashion in poetry, that I may perhaps be pardoned this brief recapitulation and retrospect.

In the spring or early summer of 1912, "H. D.," Richard Aldington and myself decided that we were agreed upon the three principles following:

1. Direct treatment of the "thing" whether subjective or objective.
2. To use absolutely no word that does not contribute to the presentation.
3. As regarding rhythm: to compose in the sequence of the musical phrase, not in sequence of a metronome.

Upon many points of taste and of predilection we differed, but agreeing upon these three positions we thought we had as much right to a group name, at least as much right, as a number of French "schools" proclaimed by Mr. Flint in the August number of Harold Monro's magazine for 1911.

This school has since been "joined" or "followed" by numerous people who, whatever their merits, do not show any signs of agreeing with the second specification. Indeed *vers libre* has become as prolix and as verbose as any of the flaccid varieties that preceded it. It has brought faults of its own. The actual language and phrasing is often as bad as that of our elders without even the excuse that the words are shovelled in to fill a metric pattern or to complete the noise of a rhyme-sound. Whether or no the phrases followed by the followers are musical must be left to the reader's decision. At times I can find a marked metre in "vers libres," as stale and hackneyed as any pseudo-Swinburnian, at times the writers seem to follow no musical structure whatever. But it is, on the whole, good that the field should be ploughed. Perhaps a few good poems have come from the new method, and if so it is justified.

Criticism is not a circumscription or a set of prohibitions. It provides fixed points of departure. It may startle a dull reader into alertness. That little of it which is good is mostly in stray phrases; or if it be an older artist helping a younger it is in great measure but rules of thumb, cautions gained by experience.

I set together a few phrases on practical working about the time the first remarks on imagisme were published. The first use of the word "Imagiste" was in my note to T. E. Hulme's five poems, printed at the end of my "Ripostes" in the autumn of 1912. I reprint my cautions from *Poetry* for March, 1913.

## A Few Don'ts

An "Image" is that which presents an intellectual and emotional complex in an instant of time. I use the term "complex" rather in the technical sense employed by the newer psychologists, such as Hart, though we might not agree absolutely in our application.

It is the presentation of such a "complex" instantaneously which gives that sense of sudden liberation; that sense of freedom from time limits and space limits; that sense of sudden growth, which we experience in the presence of the greatest works of art.

It is better to present one Image in a lifetime than to produce voluminous works.

All this, however, some may consider open to debate. The immediate necessity is to tabulate A LIST OF DON'TS for those beginning to write verses. I can not put all of them into Mosaic negative.

To begin with, consider the three propositions (demanding direct treatment, economy of words, and the sequence of the musical phrase), not as dogma—never consider anything as dogma—but as the result of long contemplation, which, even if it is some one else's contemplation, may be worth consideration.

Pay no attention to the criticism of men who have never themselves written a notable work. Consider the discrepancies between the actual writing of the Greek poets and dramatists, and the theories of the Graeco-Roman grammarians, concocted to explain their metres.

## Language

Use no superfluous word, no adjective which does not reveal something.

Don't use such an expression as "dim lands *of peace.*" It dulls the image. It mixes an abstraction with the concrete. It comes from the writer's not realizing that the natural object is always the *adequate* symbol.

Go in fear of abstractions. Do not retell in mediocre verse what has already been done in good prose. Don't think any intelligent person is going to be deceived when you try to shirk all the difficulties of the unspeakably difficult art of good prose by chopping your composition into line lengths.

What the expert is tired of today the public will be tired of tomorrow.

Don't imagine that the art of poetry is any simpler than the art of music, or that you can please the expert before you have spent at least as much effort on the art of verse as the average piano teacher spends on the art of music.

Be influenced by as many great artists as you can, but have the decency either to acknowledge the debt outright, or to try to conceal it.

Don't allow "influence" to mean merely that you mop up the particular decorative vocabulary of some one or two poets whom you happen to admire. A Turkish war correspondent was recently caught red-handed babbling in his despatches of "dove-grey" hills, or else it was "pearl-pale," I can not remember.

Use either no ornament or good ornament.

## Rhythm and Rhyme

Let the candidate fill his mind with the finest cadences he can discover, preferably in a foreign language,[2] so that the meaning of the words may be less likely to divert his attention from the movement; e.g. Saxon charms, Hebridean Folk Songs, the verse of Dante, and the lyrics of Shakespeare—if he can dissociate the vocabulary from the cadence. Let him dissect the lyrics of Goethe coldly into their component sound values, syllables long and short, stressed and unstressed, into vowels and consonants.

It is not necessary that a poem should rely on its music, but if it does rely on its music that music must be such as will delight the expert.

Let the neophyte know assonance and alliteration, rhyme immediate and delayed, simple and polyphonic, as a musician would expect to know harmony and counterpoint and all the minutiae of his craft. No time is too great to give to these matters or to any one of them, even if the artist seldom have need of them.

Don't imagine that a thing will "go" in verse just because it's too dull to go in prose.

Don't be "viewy"—leave that to the writers of pretty little philosophic essays. Don't be descriptive; remember that the painter can describe a landscape much better than you can, and that he has to know a deal more about it.

When Shakespeare talks of the "Dawn in russet mantle clad" he presents something which the painter does not present. There is in this line of his nothing that one can call description; he presents.

Consider the way of the scientists rather than the way of an advertising agent for a new soap.

The scientist does not expect to be acclaimed as a great scientist until he has *discovered* something. He begins by learning what has been discovered already. He goes from that point onward. He does not bank on being a charming fellow personally. He does not expect his friends to applaud the results of his freshman class work. Freshmen in poetry are unfortunately not confined to a definite and recognizable class room. They are "all over the shop." Is it any wonder "the public is indifferent to poetry?"

---

[2] This is for rhythm, his vocabulary must of course be found in his native tongue.

Don't chop your stuff into separate *iambs*. Don't make each line stop dead at the end, and then begin every next line with a heave. Let the beginning of the next line catch the rise of the rhythm wave, unless you want a definite longish pause.

In short, behave as a musician, a good musician, when dealing with that phase of your art which has exact parallels in music. The same laws govern, and you are bound by no others.

Naturally, your rhythmic structure should not destroy the shape of your words, or their natural sound, or their meaning. It is improbable that, at the start, you will be able to get a rhythm-structure strong enough to affect them very much, though you may fall a victim to all sorts of false stopping due to line ends and cæsurae.

The Musician can rely on pitch and the volume of the orchestra. You can not. The term harmony is misapplied in poetry; it refers to simultaneous sounds of different pitch. There is, however, in the best verse a sort of residue of sound which remains in the ear of the hearer and acts more or less as an organ-base.

A rhyme must have in it some slight element of surprise if it is to give pleasure; it need not be bizarre or curious, but it must be well used if used at all.

*Vide* further Vildrac and Duhamel's notes on rhyme in *"Technique Poétique."*

That part of your poetry which strikes upon the imaginative *eye* of the reader will lose nothing by translation into a foreign tongue; that which appeals to the ear can reach only those who take it in the original.

Consider the definiteness of Dante's presentation, as compared with Milton's rhetoric. Read as much of Wordsworth as does not seem too unutterably dull.[3]

If you want the gist of the matter go to Sappho, Catullus, Villon, Heine when he is in the vein, Gautier when he is not too frigid; or, if you have not the tongues, seek out the leisurely Chaucer. Good prose will do you no harm, and there is good discipline to be had by trying to write it.

Translation is likewise good training, if you find that your original matter "wobbles" when you try to rewrite it. The meaning of the poem to be translated can not "wobble."

If you are using a symmetrical form, don't put in what you want to say and then fill up the remaining vacuums with slush.

Don't mess up the perception of one sense by trying to define it in terms of another. This is usually only the result of being too lazy to find the exact word. To this clause there are possibly exceptions.

The first three simple prescriptions will throw out nine-tenths of all the bad poetry now accepted as standard and classic; and will prevent you from many a crime of production.

"... *Mais d'abord il faut être un poète,*" as MM. Duhamel and

---

[3] Vide infra.

Vildrac have said at the end of their little book, *"Notes sur la Technique Poétique."*

Since March 1913, Ford Madox Hueffer has pointed out that Wordsworth was so intent on the ordinary or plain word that he never thought of hunting for *le mot juste.*

John Butler Yeats has handled or man-handled Wordsworth and the Victorians, and his criticism, contained in letters to his son, is now printed and available.

I do not like writing *about* art, my first, at least I think it was my first essay on the subject, was a protest against it.

## Prolegomena[4]

Time was when the poet lay in a green field with his head against a tree and played his diversion on a ha'penny whistle, and Caesar's predecessors conquered the earth, and the predecessors of golden Crassus embezzled, and fashions had their say, and let him alone. And presumably he was fairly content in this circumstance, for I have small doubt that the occasional passerby, being attracted by curiosity to know why any one should lie under a tree and blow diversion on a ha'penny whistle, came and conversed with him, and that among these passers-by there was on occasion a person of charm or a young lady who had not read *Man and Superman*; and looking back upon this naïve state of affairs we call it the age of gold.

Metastasio, and he should know if any one, assures us that this age endures—even though the modern poet is expected to holloa his verses down a speaking tube to the editors of cheap magazines—S. S. McClure, or some one of that sort—even though hordes of authors meet in dreariness and drink healths to the "Copyright Bill"; even though these things be, the age of gold pertains. Imperceivably, if you like, but pertains. You meet unkempt Amyclas in a Soho restaurant and chant together of dead and forgotten things—it is a manner of speech among poets to chant of dead, half-forgotten things, there seems no special harm in it; it has always been done—and it's rather better to be a clerk in the Post Office than to look after a lot of stinking, verminous sheep—and at another hour of the day one substitutes the drawing-room for the restaurant and tea is probably more palatable than mead and mare's milk, and little cakes than honey. And in this fashion one survives the resignation of Mr. Balfour, and the iniquities of the American customs-house, *e quel bufera infernal*, the periodical press. And then in the middle of it, there being apparently no other person at once capable and available one is stopped and asked to explain oneself.

I begin on the chord thus querulous, for I would much rather lie on what is left of Catullus' parlour floor and speculate the azure beneath

---

[4] *Poetry and Drama* (then the *Poetry Review*, edited by Harold Monro), Feb. 1912.

it and the hills off to Salo and Riva with their forgotten gods moving unhindered amongst them, than discuss any processes and theories of art whatsoever. I would rather play tennis. I shall not argue.

## Credo

*Rhythm.*—I believe in an "absolute rhythm," a rhythm, that is, in poetry which corresponds exactly to the emotion or shade of emotion to be expressed. A man's rhythm must be interpretative, it will be, therefore, in the end, his own, uncounterfeiting, uncounterfeitable.

*Symbols.*—I believe that the proper and perfect symbol is the natural object, that if a man use "symbols" he must so use them that their symbolic function does not obtrude; so that *a* sense, and the poetic quality of the passage, is not lost to those who do not understand the symbol as such, to whom, for instance, a hawk is a hawk.

*Technique.*—I believe in technique as the test of a man's sincerity; in law when it is ascertainable; in the trampling down of every convention that impedes or obscures the determination of the law, or the precise rendering of the impulse.

*Form.*—I think there is a "fluid" as well as a "solid" content, that some poems may have form as a tree has form, some as water poured into a vase. That most symmetrical forms have certain uses. That a vast number of subjects cannot be precisely, and therefore not properly rendered in symmetrical forms.

"Thinking that alone worthy wherein the whole art is employed." [5] I think the artist should master all known forms and systems of metric, and I have with some persistence set about doing this, searching particularly into those periods wherein the systems came to birth or attained their maturity. It has been complained, with some justice, that I dump my note-books on the public. I think that only after a long struggle will poetry attain such a degree of development, or if you will, modernity, that it will vitally concern people who are accustomed, in prose, to Henry James and Anatole France, in music to Debussy. I am constantly contending that it took two centuries of Provence and one of Tuscany to develop the media of Dante's masterwork, that it took the latinists of the Renaissance, and the Pleiade, and his own age of painted speech to prepare Shakespeare his tools. It is tremendously important that great poetry be written, it makes no jot of difference who writes it. The experimental demonstrations of one man may save the time of many— hence my furore over Arnaut Daniel—if a man's experiments try out one new rime, or dispense conclusively with one iota of currently accepted nonsense, he is merely playing fair with his colleagues when he chalks up his result.

No man ever writes very much poetry that "matters." In bulk, that is, no one produces much that is final, and when a man is not doing

---

[5] Dante, *De Volgari Eloquio.*

this highest thing, this saying the thing once for all and perfectly; when he is not matching Ποικιλόθρον', ἀθάνατ' 'Αφρόδιτα, or "Hist—said Kate the Queen," he had much better be making the sorts of experiment which may be of use to him in his later work, or to his successors.

"The lyf so short, the craft so long to lerne." It is a foolish thing for a man to begin his work on a too narrow foundation, it is a disgraceful thing for a man's work not to show steady growth and increasing fineness from first to last.

As for "adaptations"; one finds that all the old masters of painting recommend to their pupils that they begin by copying masterwork, and proceed to their own composition.

As for "Every man his own poet," the more every man knows about poetry the better. I believe in every one writing poetry who wants to; most do. I believe in every man knowing enough of music to play "God bless our home" on the harmonium, but I do not believe in every man giving concerts and printing his sin.

The mastery of any art is the work of a lifetime. I should not discriminate between the "amateur" and the "professional." Or rather I should discriminate quite often in favour of the amateur, but I should discriminate between the amateur and the expert. It is certain that the present chaos will endure until the Art of poetry has been preached down the amateur gullet, until there is such a general understanding of the fact that poetry is an art and not a pastime; such a knowledge of technique; of technique of surface and technique of content, that the amateurs will cease to try to drown out the masters.

If a certain thing was said once for all in Atlantis or Arcadia, in 450 Before Christ or in 1290 after, it is not for us moderns to go saying it over, or to go obscuring the memory of the dead by saying the same thing with less skill and less conviction.

My pawing over the ancients and semi-ancients has been one struggle to find out what has been done, once for all, better than it can ever be done again, and to find out what remains for us to do, and plenty does remain, for if we still feel the same emotions as those which launched the thousand ships, it is quite certain that we come on these feelings differently, through different nuances, by different intellectual gradations. Each age has its own abounding gifts yet only some ages transmute them into matter of duration. No good poetry is ever written in a manner twenty years old, for to write in such a manner shows conclusively that the writer thinks from books, convention and *cliché,* and not from life, yet a man feeling the divorce of life and his art may naturally try to resurrect a forgotten mode if he finds in that mode some leaven, or if he thinks he sees in it some element lacking in contemporary art which might unite that art again to its sustenance, life.

In the art of Daniel and Cavalcanti, I have seen that precision which I miss in the Victorians, that explicit rendering, be it of external nature, or of emotion. Their testimony is of the eyewitness, their symptoms are first hand.

As for the nineteenth century, with all respect to its achievements, I think we shall look back upon it as a rather blurry, messy sort of a period, a rather sentimentalistic, mannerish sort of a period. I say this without any self-righteousness, with no self-satisfaction.

As for there being a "movement" or my being of it, the conception of poetry as a "pure art" in the sense in which I use the term, revived with Swinburne. From the puritanical revolt to Swinburne, poetry had been merely the vehicle—yes, definitely, Arthur Symon's scruples and feelings about the word not withholding—the ox-cart and post-chaise for transmitting thoughts poetic or otherwise. And perhaps the "great Victorians," though it is doubtful, and assuredly the "nineties" continued the development of the art, confining their improvements, however, chiefly to sound and to refinements of manner.

Mr. Yeats has once and for all stripped English poetry of its perdamnable rhetoric. He has boiled away all that is not poetic—and a good deal that is. He has become a classic in his own lifetime and *nel mezzo del cammin*. He has made our poetic idiom a thing pliable, a speech without inversions.

Robert Bridges, Maurice Hewlett and Frederic Manning are[6] in their different ways seriously concerned with overhauling the metric, in testing the language and its adaptability to certain modes. Ford Hueffer is making some sort of experiments in modernity. The Provost of Oriel continues his translation of the *Divina Commedia*.

As to Twentieth century poetry, and the poetry which I expect to see written during the next decade or so, it will, I think, move against poppy-cock, it will be harder and saner, it will be what Mr. Hewlett calls "nearer the bone." It will be as much like granite as it can be, its force will lie in its truth, its interpretative power (of course, poetic force does always rest there); I mean it will not try to seem forcible by rhetorical din, and luxurious riot. We will have fewer painted adjectives impeding the shock and stroke of it. At least for myself, I want it so, austere, direct, free from emotional slither.

What is there now, in 1917, to be added?

## Re Vers Libre

I think the desire for vers libre is due to the sense of quantity reasserting itself after years of starvation. But I doubt if we can take over, for English, the rules of quantity laid down for Greek and Latin, mostly by Latin grammarians.

I think one should write vers libre only when one "must," that is to say, only when the "thing" builds up a rhythm more beautiful than that of set metres, or more real, more a part of the emotion of the "thing," more germane, intimate, interpretative than the measure of

---

[6] (Dec. 1911).

regular accentual verse; a rhythm which discontents one with set iambic or set anapaestic.

Eliot has said the thing very well when he said, "No *vers* is *libre* for the man who wants to do a good job."

As a matter of detail, there is vers libre with accent heavily marked as a drum-beat (as par example my "Dance Figure"), and on the other hand I think I have gone as far as can profitably be gone in the other direction (and perhaps too far). I mean I do not think one can use to any advantage rhythms much more tenuous and imperceptible than some I have used. I think progress lies rather in an attempt to approximate classical quantitative metres (NOT to copy them) than in a carelessness regarding such things.[7]

I agree with John Yeats on the relation of beauty to certitude. I prefer satire, which is due to emotion, to any sham of emotion.

I have had to write, or at least I have written a good deal about art, sculpture, painting and poetry. I have seen what seemed to me the best of contemporary work reviled and obstructed. Can any one write prose of permanent or durable interest when he is merely saying for one year what nearly every one will say at the end of three or four years? I have been battistrada for a sculptor, a painter, a novelist, several poets. I wrote also of certain French writers in *The New Age* in nineteen twelve or eleven.

I would much rather that people would look at Brzeska's sculpture and Lewis's drawings, and that they would read Joyce, Jules Romains, Eliot, than that they should read what I have said of these men, or that I should be asked to republish argumentative essays and reviews.

All that the critic can do for the reader or audience or spectator is to focus his gaze or audition. Rightly or wrongly I think my blasts and essays have done their work, and that more people are now likely to go to the sources than are likely to read this book.

Jammes's "Existences" in *"La Triomphe de la Vie"* is available. So are his early poems. I think we need a convenient anthology rather than descriptive criticism. Carl Sandburg wrote me from Chicago, "It's hell when poets can't afford to buy each other's books." Half the people who care, only borrow. In America so few people know each other that the difficulty lies more than half in distribution. Perhaps one should make an anthology: Romains's "Un Etre en Marche" and "Prières," Vildrac's "Visite." Retrospectively the fine wrought work of Laforgue, the flashes of Rimbaud, the hard-bit lines of Tristan Corbière, Tailhade's sketches in "Poèmes Aristophanesques," the "Litanies" of De Gourmont.

It is difficult at all times to write of the fine arts, it is almost impossible unless one can accompany one's prose with many reproductions. Still I would seize this chance or any chance to reaffirm my belief in

---

[7] Let me date this statement 20 Aug. 1917.

Wyndham Lewis's genius, both in his drawings and his writings. And I would name an out of the way prose book, the *"Scenes and Portraits"* of Frederic Manning, as well as James Joyce's short stories and novel, "Dubliners" and the now well known "Portrait of the Artist" as well as Lewis's "Tarr," if, that is, I may treat my strange reader as if he were a new friend come into the room, intent on ransacking my bookshelf.

## Only Emotion Endures

"Only emotion endures." Surely it is better for me to name over the few beautiful poems that still ring in my head than for me to search my flat for back numbers of periodicals and rearrange all that I have said about friendly and hostile writers.

The first twelve lines of Padraic Colum's "Drover"; his "O Woman shapely as a swan, on your account I shall not die"; Joyce's "I hear an army"; the lines of Yeats that ring in my head and in the heads of all young men of my time who care for poetry: Braseal and the Fisherman, "The fire that stirs about her when she stirs"; the later lines of "The Scholars," the faces of the Magi; William Carlos Williams's "Postlude," Aldington's version of "Atthis," and "H. D.'s" waves like pine tops, and her verse in "Des Imagistes" the first anthology; Hueffer's "How red your lips are" in his translation from Von der Vogelweide, his "Three Ten," the general effect of his "On Heaven"; his sense of the prose values or prose qualities in poetry; his ability to write poems that half-chant and are spoiled by a musician's additions; beyond these a poem by Alice Corbin, "One City Only," and another ending "But sliding water over a stone." These things have worn smooth in my head and I am not through with them, nor with Aldington's "In Via Sestina" nor his other poems in "Des Imagistes," though people have told me their flaws. It may be that their content is too much embedded in me for me to look back at the words.

I am almost a different person when I come to take up the argument for Eliot's poems.

*EZRA POUND*

# Letter to Harriet Monroe

*Coleman's Hatch, January*

𝒟ear H. M.: ———— Poetry must be *as well written as prose.* Its language must be a fine language, departing in no way from speech save by a heightened intensity (i.e. simplicity). There must be no book words, no periphrases, no inversions. It must be as simple as De Maupassant's best prose, and as hard as Stendhal's.

There must be no interjections. No words flying off to nothing. Granted one can't get perfection every shot, this must be one's INTENTION.

Rhythm MUST have meaning. It can't be merely a careless dash off, with no grip and no real hold to the words and sense, a tumty tum tumty tum tum ta.

There must be no clichés, set phrases, stereotyped journalese. The only escape from such is by precision, a result of concentrated attention to what is writing. The test of a writer is his ability for such concentration AND for his power to stay concentrated till he gets to the end of his poem, whether it is two lines or two hundred.

Objectivity and again objectivity, and expression: no hindside-beforeness, no straddled adjectives (as "addled mosses dank"), no Tennysonianness of speech; nothing—nothing that you couldn't, in some circumstance, in the stress of some emotion, actually say. Every literaryism, every book word, fritters away a scrap of the reader's patience, a scrap of his sense of your sincerity. When one really feels and thinks, one stammers with simple speech; it is only in the flurry, the shallow frothy excitement of writing, or the inebriety of a metre, that one falls into the easy—oh, how easy!—speech of books and poems that one has read.*

Language is made out of concrete things. General expressions in non-concrete terms are a laziness; they are talk, not art, not creation. They are the reaction of things on the writer, not a creative act *by* the writer.

"Epithets" are usually abstractions—I mean what they call "epithets" in the books about poetry. The only adjective that is worth using is the adjective that is essential to the sense of the passage, not the decorative frill adjective.

Aldington has his occasional concentrations, and for that reason it is always possible that he will do a fine thing. There is a superficial clever-

---

* 1937. It should be realized that Ford Madox Ford had been hammering this point of view into me from the time I first met him (1908 or 1909) and that I owe him anything that I don't owe myself for having saved me from the academic influences then raging in London.—E.P. *January* 1937. Footnote from Harriet Monroe's *A Poet's Life.*

ness in him, then a great and lamentable gap, then the hard point, the true centre, out of which a fine thing may come at any time.

Fletcher is sputter, bright flash, sputter. Impressionist temperament, made intense at half-seconds.

H. D. and William C. Williams both better emotional equipment than Aldington, but lacking the superficial cleverness. Ought to produce really fine things at great intervals.

Eliot is intelligent, very, but I don't know him well enough to make predictions.

Masters hits rock bottom now and again. He should comb the journalese out of his poems. I wish Lindsay all possible luck but we're not really pulling the same way, though we both pull against entrenched senility. ———

Sandburg may come out all right, but he needs to learn a *lot* about *How to Write*. I believe his intention is right.

Would to God I could see a bit more Sophoclean severity in the ambitions of mes amis et confrères. The general weakness of the writers of the new school is looseness, lack of rhythmical construction and intensity; secondly, an attempt to "apply decoration," to use what ought to be a vortex as a sort of bill-poster, or fence-wash. Hinc illae lachrymae. Too bad about Amy—why can't she conceive of herself as a Renaissance figure instead of a spiritual chief, which she ain't.

Ebbene—enough of this.

*3*

# POETRY AND BELIEF

*JOSEPH WOOD KRUTCH*

## The Genesis of a Mood

The following essay is the first chapter of *The Modern Temper* (1929), by Joseph Wood Krutch (1893–    ), a book that culminated a decade of soul-searching about the meaning of naturalism for modern man. It is also different from the two essays that follow: Eliot considers Christianity a permanent archetypal design, from which we have strayed, to which (with the aid of poets and divines) we will return; Richards is concerned with the splitting off of one discourse from another, or with the apparent triumph of the scientific over the poetic discourse. Krutch, in this excerpt and throughout *The Modern Temper,* may be called a "sentimental naturalist." He makes of pessimism a rich and insistent emotion, and his distinctions between past and present invariably give an impression of helplessness in the face of overwhelmingly defeatist evidence. The book, and its first chapter, should be considered primarily in the context of its time—as a good, illustrative formulation of its kind. Its relevance is not to facts or conclusions as such but to an emotional state or disposition which was induced by partial and eccentric interpretations of them.

*I*t is one of Freud's quaint conceits that the child in its mother's womb is the happiest of living creatures. Into his consciousness no conflict has yet entered, for he knows no limitations to his desires and the universe is exactly as he wishes it to be. All his needs are satisfied before even he becomes aware of them, and if his awareness is dim that is but the natural result of a complete harmony between the self and the environment, since, as Spencer pointed out in a remote age, to be omniscient and omnipotent would be to be without any consciousness whatsoever. The discomfort of being born is the first warning which he receives that any event can be thrust upon him; it is the first limitation of his omnipotence which he perceives, and he is cast upon the shores of the world wailing his protest against the indignity to which he has been subjected. Years pass before he learns to control the expression of enraged surprise which arises within him at every unpleasant fact with which he is confronted, and his parents conspire so to protect him that he will learn only by very slow stages how far is the world from his heart's desire.

The cradle is made to imitate as closely as may be the conditions, both physical and spiritual, of the womb. Of its occupant no effort is demanded, and every precaution is taken to anticipate each need before it can arise. If, as the result of any unforeseen circumstance, any unsatisfied desire is born, he need only raise his voice in protest to cause the entire world in so far as he knows it—his nurse or his parents—to rush to his aid. The whole of his physical universe is obedient to his will and he is justified by his experience in believing that his mere volition controls his destiny. Only as he grows older does he become aware that there are wills other than his own or that there are physical circumstances rebellious to any human will. And only after the passage of many years does he become aware of the full extent of his predicament in the midst of a world which is in very few respects what he would wish it to be.

As a child he is treated as a child, and such treatment implies much more than the physical coddling of which Freud speaks. Not only do those who surround him co-operate more completely than they ever will again to satisfy his wishes in material things, but they encourage him to live in a spiritual world far more satisfactory than their own. He is carefully protected from any knowledge of the cruelties and complexities of life; he is led to suppose that the moral order is simple and clear, that virtue triumphs, and that the world is, as the desires of whole generations of mankind have led them to try to pretend that it is, arranged according to a pattern which would seem reasonable and satisfactory to human sensibilities. He is prevented from realizing how inextricably what men call good and evil are intertwined, how careless is Nature of those values called mercy and justice and righteousness which men have come, in her despite, to value; and he is, besides, encouraged to believe in a vast mythology peopled with figments which range all the way from the Saints to Santa Claus and which represent projections of human wishes which the adult has come to recognize as no more than projections but which he is willing that the child, for the sake of his own happiness, should believe real. Aware how different is the world which experience reveals from the world which the spirit desires, the mature, as though afraid that reality could not be endured unless the mind had been gradually inured to it, allow the child to become aware of it only by slow stages, and little by little he learns, not only the limitations of his will, but the moral discord of the world. Thus it is, in a very important sense, true that the infant does come trailing clouds of glory from that heaven which his imagination creates, and that as his experience accumulates he sees it fade away into the light of common day.

Now races as well as individuals have their infancy, their adolescence, and their maturity. Experience accumulates not only from year to year but from generation to generation, and in the life of each person it plays a little larger part than it did in the life of his father. As civilization grows older it too has more and more facts thrust upon its consciousness and is compelled to abandon one after another, quite as the child does, certain illusions which have been dear to it. Like the child, it has instinctively assumed that what it would like to be true is true, and it never gives up any such belief until experience in some form compels it to do so. Being, for example, extremely important to itself, it assumes that it is extremely important to the universe also. The earth is the center of all existing things, man is the child and the protégé of those gods who transcend and who will ultimately enable him to transcend all the evils which he has been compelled to recognize. The world and all that it contains were designed for him, and even those things which seem noxious have their usefulness only temporarily hid. Since he knows but little he is free to imagine, and imagination is always the creature of desire.

## II

The world which any consciousness inhabits is a world made up in part of experience and in part of fancy. No experience, and hence no knowledge, is complete, but the gaps which lie between the solid fragments are filled in with shadows. Connections, explanations, and reasons are supplied by the imagination, and thus the world gets its patterned completeness from material which is spun out of the desires. But as time goes on and experience accumulates there remains less and less scope for the fancy. The universe becomes more and more what experience has revealed, less and less what imagination has created, and hence, since it was not designed to suit man's needs, less and less what he would have it be. With increasing knowledge his power to manipulate his physical environment increases, but in gaining the knowledge which enables him to do so he surrenders insensibly the power which in his ignorance he had to mold the universe. The forces of nature obey him, but in learning to master them he has in another sense allowed them to master him. He has exchanged the universe which his desires created, the universe made for man, for the universe of nature of which he is only a part. Like the child growing into manhood, he passes from a world which is fitted to him into a world for which he must fit himself.

If, then, the world of poetry, mythology, and religion represents the world as a man would like to have it, while science represents the world as he gradually comes to discover it, we need only compare the two to realize how irreconcilable they appear. For the cozy bowl of the sky arched in a protecting curve above him he must exchange the cold immensities of space and, for the spiritual order which he has designed, the chaos of nature. God he had loved *because* God was anthropomorphic, because He was made in man's own image, with purposes and desires which were human and hence understandable. But Nature's purpose, if purpose she can be said to have, is no purpose of his and is not understandable in his terms. Her desire merely to live and to propagate in innumerable forms, her ruthless indifference to his values, and the blindness of her irresistible will strike terror to his soul, and he comes in the fullness of his experience to realize that the ends which he proposes to himself—happiness and order and reason—are ends which he must achieve, if he achieve them at all, in her despite. Formerly he had believed in even his darkest moments that the universe was rational if he could only grasp its rationality, but gradually he comes to suspect that rationality is an attribute of himself alone and that there is no reason to suppose that his own life has any more meaning than the life of the humblest insect that crawls from one annihilation to another. Nature, in her blind thirst for life, has filled every possible cranny of the rotting earth with some sort of fantastic creature, and among them man is but one—perhaps the most miserable of all, because he is the only one in whom the instinct of life falters long enough to enable it to ask the question "Why?" As long as life is regarded as having been created, creating may be held to imply a purpose, but merely to have come into being is, in all likelihood, merely to go out of it also.

Fortunately, perhaps, man, like the individual child, was spared in his cradle the knowledge which he could not bear. Illusions have been lost one by one. God, instead of disappearing in an instant, has retreated step by step and surrendered gradually his control of the universe. Once he decreed the fall of every sparrow and counted the hairs upon every head; a little later he became merely the original source of the laws of nature, and even today there are thousands who, unable to bear the thought of losing him completely, still fancy that they can distinguish the uncertain outlines of a misty figure. But the rôle which he plays grows less and less, and man is left more and more alone in a universe to which he is completely alien. His world was once, like the child's world, three-quarters myth and poetry. His teleological concepts molded it into a form which he could appreciate and he gave to it moral laws which would make it meaningful, but step by step the outlines of nature have thrust themselves upon him, and for the dream which he made is substituted a reality devoid of any pattern which he can understand.

In the course of this process innumerable readjustments have been made, and always with the effort to disturb as little as possible the myth which is so much more full of human values than the fact which comes in some measure to replace it. Thus, for example, the Copernican theory of astronomy, removing the earth from the center of the universe and assigning it a very insignificant place among an infinitude of whirling motes, was not merely resisted as a fact but was, when finally accepted, accepted as far as possible without its implications. Even if taken entirely by itself and without the whole system of facts of which it is a part, it renders extremely improbable the assumption, fundamental in most human thought, that the universe has man as its center and is hence understandable in his terms, but this implication was disregarded just as, a little later, the implications of the theory of evolution were similarly disregarded. It is not likely that if man had been aware from the very beginning that his world was a mere detail in the universe, and himself merely one of the innumerable species of living things, he would ever have come to think of himself, as he even now tends to do, as a being whose desires must be somehow satisfiable and whose reason must be matched by some similar reason in nature. But the myth, having been once established, persists long after the assumptions upon which it was made have been destroyed, because, being born of desire, it is far more satisfactory than any fact.

Unfortunately, perhaps, experience does not grow at a constant, but at an accelerated, rate. The Greeks who sought knowledge, not through the study of nature but through the examination of their own minds, developed a philosophy which was really analogous to myth, because the laws which determined its growth were dictated by human desires and they discovered few facts capable of disturbing the pattern which they devised. The Middle Ages retreated still further into themselves, but with the Renaissance man began to surrender himself to nature, and the sciences, each nourishing the other, began their iconoclastic march. Three centuries lay between the promulgation of the Copernican theory and the publication of the *Origin of Species,* but in sixty-odd years which have elapsed since that latter event the blows have fallen with a rapidity which left no interval for recovery. The structures which are variously known as mythology, religion, and philosophy, and which are alike in that each has as its function the interpretation of experience in terms which have human values, have collapsed under the force of successive attacks and shown themselves utterly incapable of assimilating the new stores of experience which have been dumped upon the world. With increasing completeness science maps out the pattern of nature, but the latter has no relation to the pattern of human needs and feelings.

Consider, for example, the plight of ethics. Historical criticism having destroyed what used to be called by people of learning and intelligence "Christian Evidences," and biology having shown how unlikely it is that man is the recipient of any transcendental knowledge, there remains no foundation in authority for ideas of right and wrong; and if, on the other hand, we turn to the traditions of the human race anthropology is ready to prove that no consistent human tradition has ever existed. Custom has furnished the only basis which ethics have ever had, and there is no conceivable human action which custom has not at one time justified and at another condemned. Standards are imaginary things, and yet it is extremely doubtful if man can live well, either spiritually or physically, without the belief that they are somehow real. Without them society lapses into anarchy and the individual becomes aware of an intolerable disharmony between himself and the universe. Instinctively and emotionally he is an ethical animal. No known race is so low in the scale of civilization that it has not attributed a moral order to the world, because no known race is so little human as not to suppose a moral order so innately desirable as to have an inevitable existence. It is man's most fundamental myth, and life seems meaningless to him without it. Yet, as that systematized and cumulative experience which is called science displaces one after another the myths which have been generated by need, it grows more and more likely that he must remain an ethical animal in a universe which contains no ethical element.

### III

Mystical philosophers have sometimes said that they "accepted the universe." They have, that is to say, formed of it some conception which answered the emotional needs of their spirit and which brought them a sense of being in harmony with its aims and processes. They have been aware of no needs which Nature did not seem to supply and of no ideals which she too did not seem to recognize. They have felt themselves one with her because they have had the strength of imagination to make her over in their own image, and it is doubtful if any man can live at peace who does not thus feel himself at home. But as the world assumes the shape which science gives it, it becomes more and more difficult to find such emotional correspondences. Whole realms of human feeling, like the realm of ethics, find no place for themselves in the pattern of nature and generate needs for which no satisfaction is supplied. What man knows is everywhere at war with what he wants.

In the course of a few centuries his knowledge, and hence the universe of which he finds himself an inhabitant, has been completely revolutionized, but his instincts and his emotions have remained, relatively at least, unchanged. He is still, as he always was, adjusted to the orderly, purposeful, humanized world which all peoples unburdened by experience have figured to themselves, but that world no longer exists. He has the same sense of dignity to which the myth of his descent from the gods was designed to minister, and the same innate purposefulness which led him to attribute a purpose to nature, but he can no longer think in terms appropriate to either. The world which his reason and his investigation reveal is a world which his emotions cannot comprehend.

Casually he accepts the spiritual iconoclasm of science, and in the detachment of everyday life he learns to play with the cynical wisdom of biology and psychology, which explain away the awe of emotional experience just as earlier science explained away the awe of conventional piety. Yet, under the stress of emotional crises, knowledge is quite incapable of controlling his emotions or of justifying them to himself. In love, he calls upon the illusions of man's grandeur and dignity to help him accept his emotions, and faced with tragedy he calls upon illusion to dignify his suffering; but lyric flight is checked by the rationality which he has cultivated, and in the world of metabolism and hormones, repressions and complexes, he finds no answer for his needs. He is feeling about love, for example, much as the troubadour felt, but he thinks about it in a very different way. Try as he may, the two halves of his soul can hardly be made to coalesce, and he cannot either feel as his intelligence tells him that he should feel or think as his emotions would have him think, and thus he is reduced to mocking his torn and divided soul. In the grip of passion he cannot, as some romanticist might have done, accept it with a religious trust in the mystery of love, nor yet can he regard it as a psychiatrist, himself quite free from emotion, might suggest—merely as an interesting specimen of psychical botany. Man *qua* thinker may delight in the intricacies of psychology, but man *qua* lover has not learned to feel in its terms; so that, though complexes and ductless glands may serve to explain the feelings of another, one's own still demand all those symbols of the ineffable in which one has long ceased to believe.

Time was when the scientist, the poet, and the philosopher walked hand in hand. In the universe which the one perceived the other found himself comfortably at home. But the world of modern science is one in which the intellect alone can rejoice. The mind leaps, and leaps perhaps with a sort of elation, through the immensities of space, but the spirit, frightened and cold, longs to have once more above its head the inverted bowl beyond which may lie whatever paradise its desires may create. The lover who surrendered himself to the Implacable Aphrodite or who fancied his foot upon the lowest rung of the Platonic ladder of love might retain his self-respect, but one can neither resist nor yield gracefully to a carefully catalogued psychosis. A happy life is a sort of poem, with a poem's elevation and dignity, but emotions cannot be dignified unless they are first respected. They must seem to correspond with, to be justified by, something in the structure of the universe itself; but though it was the function of religion and philosophy to hypostatize some such correspondence, to project a humanity upon nature, or at least to conceive of a humane force above and beyond her, science finds no justification for such a process and is content instead to show how illusions were born.

The most ardent love of truth, the most resolute determination to follow nature no matter to what black abyss she may lead, need not blind one to the fact that many of the lost illusions had, to speak the language of science, a survival value. Either individuals or societies whose life is imbued with a cheerful certitude, whose aims are clear, and whose sense of the essential rightness of life is strong, live and struggle with an energy unknown to the skeptical and the pessimistic. Whatever the limitations of their intellects as instruments of criticism, they possess the physical and emotional vigor which is, unlike critical intelligence, analogous to the processes of nature. They found empires and conquer wildernesses, and they pour the excess of their energy into works of art which the intelligence of more sophisticated peoples continues to admire even though it has lost the faith in life which is requisite for the building of a Chartres or the carving of a Venus de Milo. The one was not erected to a law of nature or the other designed to celebrate the libido, for each presupposed a sense of human dignity which science nowhere supports.

Thus man seems caught in a dilemma which his intellect has devised. Any deliberately managed return to a state of relative ignorance, however desirable it might be argued to be, is obviously out of the question. We cannot, as the naïve proponents of the various religions, new and old, seem to assume, believe one thing and forget another merely because we happen to be convinced that it would be desirable to do so; and it is worth observing that the new psychology, with its penetrating analysis of the influence of desire upon belief, has so adequately warned the reason of the tricks which the will can play upon it that it has greatly decreased the possibility of beneficent delusion and serves to hold the mind in a steady contemplation of that from which it would fain escape. Weak and uninstructed intelligences take refuge in the monotonous repetition of once living creeds, or are even reduced to the desperate expedient of going to sleep amid the formulae of the flabby pseudo-religions in which the modern world is so prolific. But neither of these classes affords any aid to the robust but serious mind which is searching for some terms upon which it may live.

And if we are, as by this time we should be, free from any teleological delusion, if we no longer make the unwarranted assumption that every human problem is somehow of necessity solvable, we must confess it may be that for the sort of being whom we have described no survival is possible in any form like that which his soul has now taken. He is a fantastic thing that has developed sensibilities and established values beyond the nature which gave him birth. He is of all living creatures the one to whom the earth is the least satisfactory. He has arrived at a point where he can no longer delude himself as to the extent of his predicament, and should he either become modified or disappear the earth would continue to spin and the grass to grow as it has always done. Of the thousands of living species the vast majority would be as unaware of his passing as they are unaware now of his presence, and he would go as a shadow goes. His arts, his religions, and his civilizations— these are fair and wonderful things, but they are fair and wonderful to him alone. With the extinction of his poetry would come also the extinction of the only sensibility for which it has any meaning, and there would remain nothing capable of feeling a loss. Nothing would be left to label the memory of his discontent "divine," and those creatures who find in nature no lack would resume their undisputed possession of the earth.

Anthropoid in form some of them might continue to be, and possessed as well of all of the human brain that makes possible a cunning adaptation to the conditions of physical life. To them nature might yield up subtler secrets than any yet penetrated; their machines might be more wonderful and their bodies more healthy than any yet known—even though there had passed away, not merely all myth and poetry, but the need for them as well. Cured of his transcendental cravings, content with things as they are, accepting the universe as experience had shown it to be, man would be freed of his soul and, like the other animals, either content or at least desirous of nothing which he might not hope ultimately to obtain.

Nor can it be denied that certain adumbrations of this type have before now come into being. Among those of keener intellect there are scientists to whom the test tube and its contents are all-sufficient, and among those of coarser grain, captains of finance and builders of mills, there are those to whom the acquirement of wealth and power seems to constitute a life in which no lack can be perceived. Doubtless they are not new types; doubtless they have always existed; but may they not be the strain from which Nature will select the coming race? Is not their creed the creed of Nature, and are they not bound to triumph over those whose illusions are no longer potent because they are no longer really believed? Certain philosophers, clinging desperately to the ideal of a humanized world, have proposed a retreat into the imagination. Bertrand Russell in his popular essay, *A Free Man's Worship,* Unamuno and Santayana *passim* throughout their works, have argued that the way of salvation lay in a sort of ironic belief, in a determination to act as though one still believed the things which once were really held true. But is not this a desperate expedient, a last refuge likely to appeal only to the leaders of a lost cause? Does it not represent the last, least substantial, phase of fading faith, something which borrows what little substance it seems to have from a reality of the past? If it seems half real to the sons of those who lived in the spiritual world of which it is a shadow, will it not seem, a little further removed, only a faint futility? Surely it has but little to oppose to those who come armed with the certitudes of science and united with, not fleeing from, the nature amid which they live.

And if the dilemma here described is itself a delusion it is at least as vividly present and as terribly potent as those other delusions which have shaped or deformed the human spirit. There is no significant contemporary writer upon philosophy, ethics, or aesthetics whose speculations do not lead him to it in one form or another, and even the less reflective are aware of it in their own way. Both our practical morality and our emotional lives are adjusted to a world which no longer exists. In so far as we adhere to a code of conduct, we do so largely because certain habits still persist, not because we can give any logical reason for preferring them, and in so far as we indulge ourselves in the primitive emotional satisfactions—romantic love, patriotism, zeal for justice, and so forth—our satisfaction is the result merely of the temporary suspension of our disbelief in the mythology upon which they are founded. Traditionalists in religion are fond of asserting that our moral codes are flimsy because they are rootless; but, true as this is, it is perhaps not so important as the fact that our emotional lives are rootless too.

If the gloomy vision of a dehumanized world which has just been evoked is not to become a reality, some complete readjustment must be made, and at least two generations have found themselves unequal to the task. The generation of Thomas Henry Huxley, so busy with destruction as never adequately to realize how much it was destroying, fought with such zeal against frightened conservatives that it never took time to do more than assert with some vehemence that all would be well, and the generation that followed either danced amid the ruins or sought by various compromises to save the remains of a few tottering structures. But neither patches nor evasions will serve. It is not a changed world but a new one in which man must henceforth live if he lives at all, for all his premises have been destroyed and he must proceed to new conclusions. The values which he thought established have been swept away along with the rules by which he thought they might be attained.

To this fact many are not yet awake, but our novels, our poems, and our pictures are enough to reveal that a generation aware of its predicament is at hand. It has awakened to the fact that both the ends which its fathers proposed to themselves and the emotions from which they drew their strength seem irrelevant and remote. With a smile, sad or mocking, according to individual temperament, it regards those works of the past in which were summed up the values of life. The romantic ideal of a world well lost for love and the classic ideal of austere dignity seem equally ridiculous, equally meaningless when referred, not to the temper of the past, but to the temper of the present. The passions which swept through the once major poets no longer awaken any profound response, and only in the bleak, tortuous complexities of a T. S. Eliot does it find its moods given adequate expression. Here disgust speaks with a robust voice and denunciation is confident, but ecstasy, flickering and uncertain, leaps fitfully up only to sink back among the cinders. And if the poet, with his gift of keen perceptions and his power of organization, can achieve only the most momentary and unstable adjustments, what hope can there be for those whose spirit is a less powerful instrument?

And yet it is with such as he, baffled, but content with nothing which plays only upon the surface, that the hope for a still humanized future must rest. No one can tell how many of the old values must go or how new the new will be. Thus, while under the influence of the old mythology the sexual instinct was transformed into romantic love and tribal solidarity into the religion of patriotism, there is nothing in the modern consciousness capable of effecting these transmutations. Neither the one nor the other is capable of being, as it once was, the *raison d'être* of a life or the motif of a poem which is not, strictly speaking, derivative and anachronistic. Each is fading, each becoming as much a shadow as devotion to the cult of purification through self-torture. Either the instincts upon which they are founded will achieve new transformations or they will remain merely instincts, regarded as having no particular emotional significance in a spiritual world which, if it exists at all, will be as different from the spiritual world of, let us say, Robert Browning as that world is different from the world of Cato the Censor.

As for this present unhappy time, haunted by ghosts from a dead world and not yet at home in its own, its predicament is not, to return to the comparison with which we began, unlike the predicament of the adolescent who has not yet learned to orient himself without reference to the mythology amid which his childhood was passed. He still seeks in the world of his experience for the values which he had found there, and he is aware only of a vast disharmony. But boys—most of them, at least —grow up, and the world of adult consciousness has always held a relation to myth intimate enough to make readjustment possible. The finest spirits have bridged the gulf, have carried over with them something of a child's faith, and only the coarsest have grown into something which was no more than finished animality. Today the gulf is broader, the adjustment more difficult, than ever it was before, and even the possibility of an actual human maturity is problematic. There impends for the human spirit either extinction or a readjustment more stupendous than any made before.

## T. S. ELIOT

# Baudelaire

The criticism of Eliot (1888–    ) is noteworthy on many counts. He might have been cited for his notorious analogy of the catalyst ("Tradition and the Individual Talent"), or for his role in attracting critical attention to seventeenth-century English poetry ("The Metaphysical Poets"), or for his discussions of religion and tradition (*After Strange Gods, Notes Towards the Definition of Culture,* and other essays). The "Baudelaire" here reprinted is the best of several he wrote on the French poet, and it is especially important for what it says about the problems of evil and belief in modern society. Published in 1930, it indirectly suggests the tendency of Eliot's poetry from *The Waste Land* through *Ash-*

*Wednesday* (the latter was published in the same year as the essay). It is important for at least two reasons: it is a review of the psychological problem of belief which Eliot felt so acutely in the twenties; and it is a testimony of his regard for Baudelaire and of his special indebtedness to him.

*A*nything like a just appreciation of Baudelaire has been slow to arrive in England, and still is defective or partial even in France. There are, I think, special reasons for the difficulty in estimating his worth and finding his place. For one thing, Baudelaire was in some ways far in advance of the point of view of his own time, and yet was very much of it, very largely partook of its limited merits, faults, and fashions. For one thing, he had a great part in forming a generation of poets after him; and in England he had what is in a way the misfortune to be first and extravagantly advertised by Swinburne, and taken up by the followers of Swinburne. He was universal, and at the same time confined by a fashion which he himself did most to create. To dissociate the permanent from the temporary, to distinguish the man from his influence, and finally to detach him from the associations of those English poets who first admired him, is no small task. His comprehensiveness itself makes difficulty, for it tempts the partisan critic, even now, to adopt Baudelaire as the patron of his own beliefs.

It is the purpose of this essay to affirm the importance of Baudelaire's prose works, a purpose justified by the translation of one of those works which is indispensable for any student of his poetry.[1] This is to see Baudelaire as something more than the author of the *Fleurs du Mal,* and consequently to revise somewhat our estimate of that book. Baudelaire came into vogue at a time when "Art for Art's sake" was a dogma. The care which he took over his poems, and the fact that contrary to the fluency of his time, both in France and England he restricted himself to this one volume, encouraged the opinion that Baudelaire was an artist exclusively for art's sake. The doctrine does not, of course, really apply to anybody; no one applied it less than Pater, who spent many years, not so much in illustrating it, as in expounding it as a *theory of life,* which is not the same thing at all. But it was a doctrine which did affect criticism and appreciation, and which did obstruct a proper judgment of Baudelaire. He is in fact a greater man than was imagined, though perhaps not such a perfect poet.

Baudelaire has, I believe, been called a fragmentary Dante, for what that description is worth. It is true that many people who enjoy Dante enjoy Baudelaire; but the differences are as important as the similarities. Baudelaire's inferno is very different in quality and significance from that of Dante. Truer, I think, would be the description of Baudelaire as a later and more limited Goethe. As we begin to see him now, he rep-

---

[1] *Intimes,* translated by Christopher Isherwood, and published by the Blackamore Press.

resents his own age in somewhat the same way as that in which Goethe represents an earlier age. As a critic of the present generation, Mr. Peter Quennell has recently said in his book, *Baudelaire and the Symbolists*:

He had enjoyed a *sense of his own age,* had recognized its pattern while the pattern was yet incomplete, and—because it is only our misapprehension of the present which prevents our looking into the immediate future, our ignorance of today and of its real as apart from its spurious tendencies and requirements—had anticipated many problems, both on the aesthetic and on the moral plane, in which the fate of modern poetry is still concerned.

Now the man who has this sense of his age is hard to analyse. He is exposed to its follies as well as sensitive to its inventions; and in Baudelaire, as well as in Goethe, is some of the outmoded nonsense of his time. The parallel between the German poet who has always been the symbol of perfect "health" in every sense, as well as of universal curiosity, and the French poet who has been the symbol of morbidity in mind and concentrated interests in work, may seem paradoxical. But after this lapse of time the difference between "health" and "morbidity" in the two men becomes more negligible; there is something artificial and even priggish about Goethe's healthiness, as there is about Baudelaire's unhealthiness; we have passed beyond both fashions, of health or malady, and they are both merely men with restless, critical, curious minds and the "sense of the age"; both men who understood and foresaw a great deal. Goethe, it is true, was interested in many subjects which Baudelaire left alone; but by Baudelaire's time it was no longer necessary for a man to embrace such varied interests in order to have the sense of the age; and in retrospect some of Goethe's studies seem to us (not altogether justly) to have been merely dilettante hobbies. The most of Baudelaire's prose writings (with the exception of the translations from Poe, which are of less interest to an English reader) are as important as the most of Goethe. They throw light on the *Fleurs du Mal* certainly, but they also expand immensely our appreciation of their author.

It was once the mode to take Baudelaire's Satanism seriously, as it is now the tendency to present Baudelaire as a serious and Catholic Christian. Especially as a prelude to the *Journaux Intimes* this diversity of opinion needs some discussion. I think that the latter view—that Baudelaire is essentially Christian—is nearer the truth than the former, but it needs considerable reservation. When Baudelaire's Satanism is dissociated from its less creditable paraphernalia, it amounts to a dim intuition of a part, but a very important part, of Christianity. Satanism itself, so far as not merely an affectation, was an attempt to get into Christianity by the back door. Genuine blasphemy, genuine in spirit and not purely verbal, is the product of partial belief, and is as impossible to the complete atheist as to the perfect Christian. It is a way of affirming belief. This state of partial belief is manifest throughout the *Journaux Intimes.*

What is significant about Baudelaire is his theological innocence. He is discovering Christianity for himself; he is not assuming it as a fashion or weighing social or political reasons, or any other accidents. He is beginning, in a way, at the beginning; and being a discoverer, is not altogether certain what he is exploring and to what it leads; he might almost be said to be making again, as one man, the effort of scores of generations. His Christianity is rudimentary or embryonic; at best, he has the excesses of a Tertullian (and even Tertullian is not considered wholly orthodox and well balanced). His business was not to practise Christianity, but—what was much more important for his time—to assert its *necessity*.

Baudelaire's morbidity of temperament cannot, of course, be ignored: and no one who has looked at the work of Crépet or the recent small biographical study of François Porché can forget it. We should be misguided if we treated it as an unfortunate ailment which can be discounted or to attempt to detach the sound from the unsound in his work. Without the morbidity none of his work would be possible or significant; his weaknesses can be composed into a larger whole of strength, and this is implied in my assertion that neither the health of Goethe nor the malady of Baudelaire matters in itself: it is what both men made of their endowments that matters. To the eye of the world, and quite properly for all questions of private life, Baudelaire was thoroughly perverse and insufferable: a man with a talent for ingratitude and unsociability, intolerably irritable, and with a mulish determination to make the worst of everything; if he had money, to squander it; if he had friends, to alienate them; if he had any good fortune, to disdain it. He had the pride of the man who feels in himself great weakness and great strength. Having great genius, he had neither the patience nor the inclination, had he had the power, to overcome his weakness; on the contrary, he exploited it for theoretical purposes. The morality of such a course may be a matter for endless dispute; for Baudelaire, it was the way to liberate his mind and give us the legacy and lesson that he has left.

He was one of those who have great strength, but strength merely to *suffer*. He could not escape suffering and could not transcend it, so he *attracted* pain to himself. But what he could do, with that immense passive strength and sensibilities which no pain could impair, was to study his suffering. And in this limitation he is wholly unlike Dante, not even like any character in Dante's Hell. But, on the other hand, such suffering as Baudelaire's implies the possibility of a positive state of beatitude. Indeed, in his way of suffering is already a kind of presence of the supernatural and of the superhuman. He rejects always the purely natural and the purely human; in other words, he is neither "naturalist" nor "humanist." Either because he cannot adjust himself to the actual world he has to reject it in favour of Heaven and Hell, or because he has the perception of Heaven and Hell he rejects the present world: both ways of putting it are tenable. There is in his statements a good deal of romantic detritus; *ses ailes de géant l'empêchent de marcher,* he says of the Poet and of the Albatross, but not convincingly; but there is also truth about himself and about the world. His *ennui* may of course be explained, as everything can be explained in psychological or pathological terms; but it is also, from the opposite point of view, a true form of *acedia,* arising from the unsuccessful struggle towards the spiritual life.

## II

From the poems alone, I venture to think, we are not likely to grasp what seems to me the true sense and significance of Baudelaire's mind. Their excellence of form, their perfection of phrasing, and their superficial coherence, may give them the appearance of presenting a definite and final state of mind. In reality, they seem to me to have the external but not the internal form of classic art. One might even hazard the conjecture that the care for perfection of form, among some of the romantic poets of the nineteenth century, was an effort to support, or to conceal from view, an inner disorder. Now the true claim of Baudelaire as an artist is not that he found a superficial form, but that he was searching for a form of life. In minor form he never indeed equalled Théophile Gautier, to whom he significantly dedicated his poems: in the best of the slight verse of Gautier there is a satisfaction, a balance of inwards and form, which we do not find in Baudelaire. He had a greater technical ability than Gautier, and yet the content of feeling is constantly bursting the receptacle. His apparatus, by which I do not mean his command of words and rhythms, but his stock of imagery (and every poet's stock of imagery is circumscribed somewhere), is not wholly perdurable or adequate. His prostitutes, mulattoes, Jewesses, serpents, cats, corpses, form a machinery which has not worn very well; his Poet, or his Don Juan, has a romantic ancestry which is too clearly traceable. Compare with the costumery of Baudelaire the stock of imagery of the *Vita Nuova,* or of Cavalcanti, and you find Baudelaire's does not everywhere wear as well as that of several centuries earlier; compare him with Dante or Shakespeare, for what such a comparison is worth, and he is found not only a much smaller poet, but one in whose work much more that is perishable has entered.

To say this is only to say that Baudelaire belongs to a definite place in time. Inevitably the offspring of romanticism, and by his nature the first counter-romantic in poetry, he could, like any one else, only work with the materials which were there. It must not be forgotten that a poet in a romantic age cannot be a "classical" poet except in tendency. If he is sincere, he must express with individual differences the general state of mind—not as a *duty,* but simply because he cannot help participating in it. For such poets, we may expect often to get much help from reading their prose works and even notes and diaries; help in deciphering the discrepancies between head and heart, means and end, material and ideals.

What preserves Baudelaire's poetry from the fate of most French poetry of the nineteenth century up to his time, and has made him, as M. Valéry has said in a recent introduction to the *Fleurs du Mal,* the one modern French poet to be widely read abroad, is not quite easy to conclude. It is partly that technical mastery which can hardly be overpraised, and which has made his verse an inexhaustible study for later poets, not only in his own language. When we read

> Maint joyau dort enseveli
> Dans les ténèbres et l'oubli,
> Bien loin des pioches et des sondes;
> Mainte fleur épanche à regret
> Son parfum doux comme un secret
> Dans les solitudes profondes,*

we might for a moment think it a more lucid bit of Mallarmé; and so original is the arrangement of words that we might easily overlook its borrowing from Gray's *Elegy.* When we read

> Valse mélancolique et langoureux vertige! †

we are already in the Paris of Laforgue. Baudelaire gave to French poets as generously as he borrowed from English and American poets. The renovation of the versification of Racine has been mentioned often enough; quite genuine, but might be overemphasized, as it sometimes comes near to being a trick. But even without this, Baudelaire's variety and resourcefulness would still be immense.

Furthermore, besides the stock of images which he used that seems already second-hand, he gave new possibilities to poetry in a new stock of imagery of contemporary life.

> . . . Au cœur d'un vieux faubourg, labyrinthe fangeux
> Où l'humanité grouille en ferments orageux,
>
> On voit un vieux chiffonnier qui vient, hochant le tête
> Buttant, et se cognant aux murs comme un poëte.‡

---

* [Stanzas 3 and 4 of "Le Guignon." Eliot does not mark the stanza break. The following translation is by Roy Campbell, and is included in Marthiel and Jackson Mathews' collection of the best translations of Baudelaire (New York: New Directions, 1955), pp. 19–20:—Ed.]

> —Yet many a gem lies hidden still
> Of whom no pick-axe, spade, or drill
> The lonely secrecy invades
>
> And many a flower, to heal regret,
> Pours forth its fragrant secret yet
> Amidst the solitary shades.

† [Stanza 1, line 4, of "Harmonie du Soir": "A mournful waltz, a languorous whirling flight!" is an approximation of the meaning, which really cannot be translated.—Ed.]

‡ [Lines 3–4 of stanza 1, lines 1–2 of stanza 2, of "Le Vin des Chiffonniers" (roughly: "The Ragpickers' Wine"). The translation is by C. F. Mac-

This introduces something new, and something universal in modern life. (The last line quoted, which in ironic terseness anticipates Corbière, might be contrasted with the whole poem *Bénédiction* which begins the volume.) It is not merely in the use of imagery of common life, not merely in the use of imagery of the sordid life of a great metropolis, but in the elevation of such imagery to the *first intensity*—presenting it as it is, and yet making it represent something much more than itself— that Baudelaire has created a mode of release and expression for other men.

This invention of language, at a moment when French poetry in particular was famishing for such invention, is enough to make of Baudelaire a great poet, a great landmark in poetry. Baudelaire is indeed the greatest exemplar in *modern* poetry in any language, for his verse and language is the nearest thing to a complete renovation that we have experienced. But his renovation of an attitude towards life is no less radical and no less important. In his verse, he is now less a model to be imitated or a source to be drained than a reminder of the duty, the consecrated task, of sincerity. From a fundamental sincerity he could not deviate. The superficies of sincerity (as I think has not always been remarked) is not always there. As I have suggested, many of his poems are insufficiently removed from their romantic origins, from Byronic paternity and Satanic fraternity. The "satanism" of the Black Mass was very much in the air; in exhibiting it Baudelaire is the voice of his time; but I would observe that in Baudelaire, as in no one else, it is redeemed by *meaning something else*. He uses the same paraphernalia, but cannot limit its symbolism even to all that of which he is conscious. Compare him with Huysmans in *A rebours, En route,* and *Là-Bas.* Huysmans, who is a first-rate realist of his time, only succeeds in making his diabolism interesting when he treats it externally, when he is merely describing a manifestation of his period (if such it was). His own interest in such matters is, like his interest in Christianity, a petty affair. Huysmans merely provides a document. Baudelaire would not even provide that, if he had been really absorbed in that ridiculous hocus-pocus. But actually Baudelaire is concerned, not with demons, black masses, and romantic blasphemy, but with the real problem of good and evil. It is hardly more than an accident of time that he uses the current imagery and vocabulary of blasphemy. In the middle nineteenth cen-

---

Intyre (in Mathews, *ibid.,* p 136; I include all of stanzas 1 and 2, because the translator has, quite rightly, rearranged the syntax):—Ed.]

> In the muddy maze of some old neighborhood,
> Often, where the street lamp gleams like blood,
> As the wind whips the flame, rattles the glass
> Where human beings ferment in a stormy mass,
>
> One sees a ragpicker knocking against the walls,
> Paying no heed to the spies of the cops, his thralls,
> But stumbling like a poet lost in dreams;
> He pours his heart out in stupendous schemes.

tury, the age which (at its best) Goethe had prefigured, an age of bustle, programmes, platforms, scientific progress, humanitarianism and revolutions which improved nothing, an age of progressive degradation, Baudelaire perceived that what really matters is Sin and Redemption. It is a proof of his honesty that he went as far as he could honestly go and no further. To a mind observant of the post-Voltaire France (*Voltaire . . . le prédicateur des concierges*), a mind which saw the world of *Napoléon le petit* more lucidly than did that of Victor Hugo, a mind which at the same time had no affinity for the *Saint-Sulpicerie* of the day, the recognition of the reality of Sin is a New Life; and the possibility of damnation is so immense a relief in a world of electoral reform, plebiscites, sex reform and dress reform, that damnation itself is an immediate form of salvation—of salvation from the ennui of modern life, because it at last gives some significance to living. It is this, I believe, that Baudelaire is trying to express; and it is this which separates him from the modernist Protestantism of Byron and Shelley. It is apparently Sin in the Swinburnian sense, but really Sin in the permanent Christian sense, that occupies the mind of Baudelaire.

Yet, as I said, the sense of Evil implies the sense of good. Here too, as Baudelaire apparently confuses, and perhaps did confuse, Evil with its theatrical representations, Baudelaire is not always certain in his notion of the Good. The romantic idea of Love is never quite exorcised, but never quite surrendered to. In *Le Balcon,* which M. Valéry considers, and I think rightly, one of Baudelaire's most beautiful poems, there is all the romantic idea, but something more: the reaching out towards something which cannot be had *in,* but which may be had partly *through,* personal relations. Indeed, in much romantic poetry the sadness is due to the exploitation of the fact that no human relations are adequate to human desires, but also to the disbelief in any further object for human desires than that which, being human, fails to satisfy them. One of the unhappy necessities of human existence is that we have to "find things out for ourselves." If it were not so, the statement of Dante would have, at least for poets, have done once for all. Baudelaire has all the romantic sorrow, but invents a new kind of romantic nostalgia, a derivative of his nostalgia being the *poésie des départs,* the *poésie des salles d'attente.** In a beautiful paragraph of the volume in question, *Mon cœur mis à nu,* he imagines the vessels lying in harbour as saying: *Quand partons-nous vers le bonheur?* and his minor successor Laforgue exclaims: *Comme ils sont beaux, les trains manqués.*† The poetry of flight—which, in contemporary France, owes a great debt to the poems of the A. O. Barnabooth of Valery Larbaud—is, in its origin in this paragraph of Baudelaire, a dim recognition of the direction of beatitude.

---

\* ["Poetry of flight"; "poetry of waiting-rooms"—Ed.]
† ["When do we leave (on our journey) to happiness?" "How beautiful they are, the trains that we do not have."—Ed.]

But in the adjustment of the natural to the spiritual, of the bestial to the human and the human to the supernatural, Baudelaire is a bungler compared with Dante; the best that can be said, and that is a very great deal, is that what he knew he found out for himself. In his book, the *Journaux Intimes,* and especially in *Mon cœur mis à nu,* he has a great deal to say of the love of man and woman. One aphorism which has been especially noticed is the following: *La volupté unique et suprême de l'amour gît dans la certitude de faire le mal.*\* This means, I think, that Baudelaire has perceived that what distinguishes the relations of man and woman from the copulation of beasts is the knowledge of Good and Evil (of *moral* Good and Evil which are not natural Good and Bad or puritan Right and Wrong). Having an imperfect, vague romantic conception of Good, he was at least able to understand that the sexual act as evil is more dignified, less boring, than as the natural, "life-giving," cheery automatism of the modern world. For Baudelaire, sexual operation is at least something not analogous to Kruschen Salts.

So far as we are human, what we do must be either evil or good;[2] so far as we do evil or good, we are human; and it is better, in a paradoxical way, to do evil than to do nothing: at least, we exist. It is true to say that the glory of man is his capacity for salvation; it is also true to say that his glory is his capacity for damnation. The worst that can be said of most of our malefactors, from statesmen to thieves, is that they are not men enough to be damned. Baudelaire was man enough for damnation: whether he *is* damned is, of course, another question, and we are not prevented from praying for his repose. In all his humiliating traffic with other beings, he walked secure in this high vocation, that he was capable of a damnation denied to the politicians and the newspaper editors of Paris.

### III

Baudelaire's notion of beatitude certainly tended to the wishy-washy; and even in one of the most beautiful of his poems, *L'Invitation au voyage,* he hardly exceeds the *poésie des départs.* And because his vision is here so restricted, there is for him a gap between human love and divine love. His human love is definite and positive, his divine love vague and uncertain: hence his insistence upon the evil of love, hence his constant vituperations of the female. In this there is no need to pry for psychopathological causes, which would be irrelevant at best; for his attitude towards women is consistent with the point of view which he had reached. Had he been a woman he would, no doubt, have held

---

\* ["The unique and supreme voluptuousness of love lies in the certainty that it does (literally: makes for) evil."—Ed.]

[2] "Know ye not, that to whom ye yield yourselves servants to obey, his servants ye are to whom ye obey: whether of sin unto death, or of obedience unto righteousness?"—Romans vi. 16.

the same views about men. He has arrived at the perception that a woman must be to some extent a symbol; he did not arrive at the point of harmonising his experience with his ideal needs. The complement, and the correction to the *Journaux Intimes*, so far as they deal with the relations of man and woman, is the *Vita Nuova*, and the *Divine Comedy*. But—I cannot assert it too strongly—Baudelaire's view of life, such as it is, is objectively apprehensible, that is to say, his idiosyncrasies can partly explain his view of life, but they cannot explain it away. And this view of life is one which has grandeur and which exhibits heroism; it was an evangel to his time and to ours. *La vraie civilisation,* he wrote, *n'est pas dans le gaz, ni dans la vapeur, ni dans les tables tournantes. Elle est dans la diminution des traces du péché originel.** It is not quite clear exactly what *diminution* here implies, but the tendency of his thought is clear, and the message is still accepted by but few. More than half a century later T. E. Hulme left behind him a paragraph which Baudelaire would have approved:

In the light of these absolute values, man himself is judged to be essentially limited and imperfect. He is endowed with Original Sin. While he can occasionally accomplish acts which partake of perfection, he can never himself *be* perfect. Certain secondary results in regard to ordinary human action in society follow from this. A man is essentially bad, he can only accomplish anything of value by discipline—ethical and political. Order is thus not merely negative, but creative and liberating. Institutions are necessary.

## I. A. RICHARDS

### SCIENCE AND POETRY †

*Science and Poetry* by I. A. Richards (1893–    ) makes a number of useful contributions. It provides a substantial summary of Richards' analysis, in *Principles of Literary Criticism* (1924), of the experiencing of poetry; it offers a number of curious observations on Richards' contemporaries; and its major discussion concentrates on the relation of the two kinds of discourse suggested in the title. While this discussion may be considered unnecessarily alarmist and arbitrary, it is also typical of the kind of "emergency" debate that took place in the twenties, over the grow-

* [From the *Journaux Intimes*. A rather literal translation: "True civilization does not exist in gas, nor in steam, nor in turn-tables (round-houses, where trains change tracks). It exists in the lessening of the traces of original sin."—Ed.]

† The spelling in this selection has been Americanized by the editor.

ing prestige (and the human limitations) of science. Implicitly, and explicitly at times, Richards is concerned with the problem of preserving belief in a time of serious doubt. But he is also involved with poetry as a humanistic exercise, and with its psychological influence upon the development of the sensitive personality who submits to it.

*The future of poetry is immense, because in poetry, where it is worthy of its high destinies, our race, as time goes on, will find an ever surer and surer stay. There is not a creed which is not shaken, not an accredited dogma which is not shown to be questionable, not a received tradition which does not threaten to dissolve. Our religion has materialised itself in the fact, in the supposed fact; it has attached its emotion to the fact, and now the fact is failing it. But for poetry the idea is everything.—* MATTHEW ARNOLD

## 1. The General Situation

*M*an's prospects are not at present so rosy that he can neglect any means of improving them. He has recently made a number of changes in his customs and ways of life, partly with intention, partly by accident. These changes are involving such widespread further changes that the fairly near future is likely to see an almost complete reorganization of our lives, in their intimate aspects as much as in their public. Man himself is changing, together with his circumstances; he has changed in the past, it is true, but never perhaps so swiftly. His circumstances are not known ever to have changed so much or so suddenly before, with psychological as well as with economic, social and political dangers. This suddenness threatens us. Some parts of human nature resist change more than others. We risk disaster if some of our customs change while others which should change with them stay as they are.

Habits that have endured for many thousands of years are not easy to throw off—least of all when they are habits of thought and when they do not come into open conflict with changing circumstances, or do not clearly involve us in loss or inconvenience. Yet the loss may be great without our knowing anything about it. Before 1590 no one knew how inconvenient were our natural habits of thought about the ways in which a stone may fall; yet the modern world began when Galileo discovered what really happens. Before 1800 only persons thought to be crazy knew that ordinary traditional ideas as to cleanliness are dangerously inadequate. The infant's average "expectation of life" has increased by about 30 years since Lister upset them. Nobody before Sir Ronald Ross knew what were the consequences of thinking about malaria in terms of influences and miasmas instead of in terms of mosquitoes. The Roman Empire might perhaps have still been flourishing if some one had found this out before A.D. 100.

With such examples all about us we can no longer, in any department of life, so easily accept what was good enough for our fathers as good enough for ourselves or for our children. We are forced to wonder whether our ideas, even upon subjects apparently of little practical importance, such as poetry, may not be dangerously inadequate. It becomes indeed somewhat alarming to recognize, as we must, that our habits of thought remain, as regards most of our affairs, much as they were 5,000 years ago. The Sciences are, of course, simply the exceptions to this rule. Outside the Sciences—and the greater part of our thinking still goes on outside the Sciences—we think very much as our ancestors thought a hundred or two hundred generations ago. Certainly this is so as regards official views about poetry. Is it not possible that these are wrong, as wrong as most ideas of an equally hoary antiquity? Is it not possible that to the men of the future our life today will seem a continual, ceaseless disaster due only to our own stupidity, to the nervelessness with which we accept and transmit ideas which do not apply and never have applied to anything?

*The average educated man is growing more conscious,* an extraordinarily significant change. It is probably due to the fact that his life is becoming more complex, more intricate, his desires and needs more varied and more apt to conflict. And as he becomes more conscious he can no longer be content to drift in unreflecting obedience to custom. He is forced to reflect. And if reflection often takes the form of inconclusive worrying, that is no more than might be expected in view of the unparalleled difficulty of the task. To live reasonably is much more difficult today than it was in Dr. Johnson's time, and even then, as Boswell shows, it was difficult enough.

To live reasonably is not to live by reason alone—the mistake is easy, and, if carried far, disastrous—but to live in a way of which reason, a clear full sense of the whole situation, would approve. And the most important part of the whole situation, as always, is ourselves, our own psychological make-up. The more we learn about the physical world, about our bodies, for example, the more points we find at which our ordinary behavior is out of accord with the facts, inapplicable, wasteful, disadvantageous, dangerous or absurd. Witness our habit of boiling our vegetables. We have still to learn how to feed ourselves satisfactorily. Similarly, the little that is yet known about the mind already shows that our ways of thinking and feeling about very many of the things with which we concern ourselves are out of accord with the facts. This is pre-eminently true of our ways of thinking and feeling about poetry. We think and talk in terms of states of affairs which have never existed. We attribute to ourselves and to things, powers which neither we nor they possess. And equally we overlook or misuse powers which are all-important to us.

Day by day, in recent years, man is getting more out of place in Nature. Where he is going to he does not yet know, he has not yet decided. As a consequence he finds life more and more bewildering, more and more difficult to live coherently. Thus he turns to consider himself, his own nature. For the first step towards a reasonable way of life is a better understanding of human nature.

It has long been recognized that if only something could be done in psychology remotely comparable to what has been achieved in physics, practical consequences might be expected even more remarkable than any that the engineer can contrive. The first positive steps in the science of the mind have been slow in coming, but already they are beginning to change man's whole outlook.

## 2. The Poetic Experience

Extraordinary claims have often been made for poetry—Matthew Arnold's words quoted at the head of this essay are an example—claims which very many people are inclined to view with astonishment or with the smile which tolerance gives to the enthusiast. Indeed a more representative modern view would be that the future of poetry is *nil*. Peacock's conclusion in his *The Four Ages of Poetry* finds a more general acceptance. "A poet in our times is a semi-barbarian in a civilized community. He lives in the days that are past. . . . In whatever degree poetry is cultivated, it must necessarily be to the neglect of some branch of useful study: and it is a lamentable thing to see minds, capable of better things, running to seed in the specious indolence of these empty aimless mockeries of intellectual exertion. Poetry was the mental rattle that awakened the attention of intellect in the infancy of civil society: but for the maturity of mind to make a serious business of the playthings of its childhood, is as absurd as for a grown man to rub his gums with coral, and cry to be charmed asleep by the jingle of silver bells." And with more regret many others—Keats was among them— have thought that the inevitable effect of the advance of science would be to destroy the possibility of poetry.

What is the truth in this matter? How is our estimate of poetry going to be affected by science? And how will poetry itself be influenced? The extreme importance which has in the past been assigned to poetry is a fact which must be accounted for whether we conclude that it was rightly assigned or not, and whether we consider that poetry will continue to be held in such esteem or not. It indicates that the case for poetry, whether right or wrong, is one which turns on momentous issues. We shall not have dealt adequately with it unless we have raised questions of great significance.

Very much toil has gone to the endeavor to explain the high place of poetry in human affairs, with, on the whole, few satisfactory or convincing results. This is not surprising. For in order to show how poetry is important it is first necessary to discover to some extent what it is. Until recently this preliminary task could only be very incompletely carried out; the psychology of instinct and emotion was too little advanced; and, moreover, the wild speculations natural in pre-scientific enquiry definitely stood in the way. Neither the professional psychologist, whose interest in poetry is frequently not intense, nor the man of letters, who as a rule has no adequate ideas of the mind as a whole, has been equipped for the investigation. Both a passionate knowledge of poetry and a capacity for dispassionate psychological analysis are required if it is to be satisfactorily prosecuted.

It will be best to begin by asking "What *kind of a thing,* in the widest sense is poetry?" When we have answered this we shall be ready to ask "How can we use and misuse it?" and "What reasons are there for thinking it valuable?"

Let us take an experience, ten minutes of a person's life, and describe it in broad outline. It is now possible to indicate its general structure, to point out what is important in it, what trivial and accessory, which features depend upon which, how it has arisen, and how it is probably going to influence his future experience. There are, of course, wide gaps in this description, none the less it *is* at last possible to understand in general how the mind works in an experience, and what sort of stream of events the experience is.

A poem, let us say Wordsworth's *Westminster Bridge* sonnet, is such an experience, it is the experience the right kind of reader has when he peruses the verses. And the first step to an understanding of the place and future of poetry in human affairs is to see what the general structure of such an experience is. Let us begin by reading it very slowly, preferably aloud, giving every syllable time to make its full effect upon us. And let us read it experimentally, repeating it, varying our tone of voice until we are satisfied that we have caught its rhythm as well as we are able, and—whether our reading is such as to please other people or not—we ourselves at least are certain how it should "go."

> Earth has not anything to show more fair:
> Dull would he be of soul who could pass by
> A sight so touching in its majesty:
> This City now doth like a garment wear
> The beauty of the morning: silent, bare,
> Ships, towers, domes, theatres and temples lie
> Open to the fields, and to the sky;
> All bright and glittering in the smokeless air.
> Never did sun more beautifully steep
> In his first splendour valley, rock or hill;
> Ne'er saw I, never felt, a calm so deep!
> The river glideth at its own sweet will:
> Dear God! the very houses seem asleep
> And all that mighty heart is lying still!

We may best make our analysis of the experience that arises through reading these lines from the surface inwards, to speak metaphorically. The surface is the impression of the printed words on the retina. This sets up an agitation which we must follow as it goes deeper and deeper.

The first things to occur (if they do not, the rest of the experience will be gravely inadequate) are the sound of the words "in the mind's

ear" and the feel of the words imaginarily spoken.[1] These together give
the *full body,* as it were, to the words, and it is with the full bodies
of words that the poet works, not with their printed signs. But many
people lose nearly everything in poetry through these indispensable parts
escaping them.

Next arise various pictures "in the mind's eye"; not of words but of
things for which the words stand; perhaps of ships, perhaps of hills;
and together with them, it may be, other images of various sorts. Images
of what it feels like to stand leaning on the parapet of Westminster
Bridge. Perhaps that odd thing an image of "silence." But, unlike the
image-bodies of the words themselves, those other images of things are
not vitally important. Those who have them may very well think them
indispensable, and *for them* they may be necessary; but other people
may not require them at all. This is a point at which differences between individual minds are very marked.

Thence onwards the agitation which is the experience divides into a
major and a minor branch, though the two streams have innumerable
interconnections and influence one another intimately. Indeed it is only
as an expositor's artifice that we may speak of them as two streams.

The minor branch we may call the intellectual stream; the other,
which we may call the active, or emotional, stream, is made up of the
play of our interests.

The intellectual stream is fairly easy to follow; it follows itself, so to
speak; but it is the less important of the two. In poetry it matters only
*as a means;* it directs and excites the active stream. It is made up of
thoughts, which are not static little entities that bob up into consciousness and down again out of it, but fluent happenings, events, which
reflect or point to the things the thoughts are of. Exactly how they do
this is a matter which is still much disputed.

This pointing to or reflecting things is all that thoughts do. They
appear to do much more; which is our chief illusion. The realm of
thought is never a sovereign state. Our thoughts are the servants of our
interests, and even when they seem to rebel it is usually our interests
that are in disorder. Our thoughts are pointers and it is the other, the
active, stream which deals with the things which thoughts reflect or
point to.

Some people who read verse (they do not often read much of it) are
so constituted that very little more happens than this intellectual stream
of thoughts. It is perhaps superfluous to point out that they miss the real
poem. To exaggerate this part of the experience, and give it too much
importance on its own account, is a notable current tendency, and for
many people explains why they do not read poetry.

The active branch is what really matters; for from it all the energy

---

[1] The view of the mind-body problem assumed here is defended and main-
tained with references to the contemporary authorities who hold it, in *The
Meaning of Psychology* by C. K. Ogden, Chapter II. (London, Kegan Paul;
New York, Harpers; 1926).

of the whole agitation comes. The thinking which goes on is somewhat like the play of an ingenious and invaluable "governor" run by, but controlling, the main machine. Every experience is essentially some interest or group of interests swinging back to rest.

To understand what an interest is we should picture the mind as a system of very delicately poised balances, a system which so long as we are in health is constantly growing. Every situation we come into disturbs some of these balances to some degree. The ways in which they swing back to a new equipoise are the impulses with which we respond to the situation. And the chief balances in the system are our chief interests.

Suppose that we carry a magnetic compass about in the neighborhood of powerful magnets. The needle waggles as we move and comes to rest pointing in a new direction whenever we stand still in a new position. Suppose that instead of a single compass we carry an arrangement of many magnetic needles, large and small, swung so that they influence one another, some able only to swing horizontally, others vertically, others hung freely. As we move, the perturbations in this system will be very complicated. But for every position in which we place it there will be a final position of rest for all the needles into which they will in the end settle down, a general poise for the whole system. But even a slight displacement may set the whole assemblage of needles busily readjusting themselves.

One further complication. Suppose that while all the needles influence one another, some of them respond only to some of the outer magnets among which the system is moving. The reader can easily draw a diagram if his imagination needs a visual support.

The mind is not unlike such a system if we imagine it to be incredibly complex. The needles are our interests, varying in their importance, that is in the degree to which any movement they make involves movement in the other needles. Each new disequilibrium, which a shift of position, a fresh situation, entails, corresponds to a need: and the wagglings which ensue as the system rearranges itself are our responses, the impulses through which we seek to meet the need. Often the new poise is not found until long after the original disturbance. Thus states of strain can arise which last for years.

The child comes into the world as a comparatively simple arrangement. Few things affect him comparatively speaking, and his responses also are few and simple, but he very quickly becomes more complicated. His recurrent needs for food and for various attentions are constantly setting all his needles swinging. Little by little separate needs become departmentalized as it were, sub-systems are formed; hunger causes one set of responses, the sight of his toys another, loud noises yet another, and so on. But the sub-systems never become quite independent. So he grows up, becoming susceptible to ever more numerous and more delicate influences.

He grows more discriminating in some respects, he is thrown out of equilibrium by slighter differences in his situation. In other respects he becomes more stable. From time to time, through growth, fresh interests develop; sex is the outstanding example. His needs increase, he becomes capable of being upset by quite new causes, he becomes responsive to quite new aspects of the situation.

This development takes a very indirect course. It would be still more erratic if society did not mould and remould him at every stage, reorganizing him incompletely two or three times over before he grows up. He reaches maturity in the form of a vast assemblage of major and minor interests, partly a chaos, partly a system, with some tracts of his personality fully developed and free to respond, others tangled and jammed in all kinds of accidental ways. It is this incredibly complex assemblage of interests to which the printed poem has to appeal. Sometimes the poem is itself the influence which disturbs us, sometimes it is merely the means by which an already existing disturbance can right itself. More usually perhaps it is both at once.

We must picture then the stream of the poetic experience as the swinging back into equilibrium of these disturbed interests. We are reading the poem in the first place only because we are in some way interested in doing so, only because some interest is attempting to regain its poise thereby. And whatever happens as we read happens only for a similar reason. We understand the words (the intellectual branch of the stream goes on its way successfully) only because an interest is reacting through that means, and all the rest of the experience is equally but more evidently our adaptation working itself out.

The rest of the experience is made up of emotions and attitudes. Emotions are what the reaction, with its reverberations in bodily changes, feels like. Attitudes are the impulses towards one kind of behavior or another which are set ready by the response. They are, as it were, its outward going part.[2] Sometimes, as here in *Westminster Bridge,* they are very easily overlooked. But consider a simpler case—a fit of laughter which it is absolutely essential to conceal, in Church or during a solemn interview, for example. You contrive not to laugh; but there is no doubt about the activity of the impulses in their restricted form. The much more subtle and elaborate impulses which a poem excites are not different in principle. They do not show themselves as a rule, they do not come out into the open, largely because they are so complex. When they have adjusted themselves to one another and become organized into a coherent whole, the needs concerned may be satisfied. *In a fully developed man a state of readiness for action will take the place of action when the full appropriate situation for action is not present.* The essential peculiarity of poetry as of all the arts is that the full appro-

---

[2] For a further discussion of attitudes see the author's *Principles of Literary Criticism,* Chapter XV (International Library of Psychology).

priate situation is *not* present. It is an *actor* we are seeing upon the stage, not Hamlet. So readiness for action takes the place of actual behavior.

This is the main plan then of the experience. Signs on the retina, taken up by sets of needs (remember how many other impressions all day long remain entirely *unnoticed* because no interest responds to them); thence an elaborate agitation of impulses, one branch of which is *thoughts* of what the words mean, the other an emotional response leading to the development of *attitudes,* preparations, that is, for action which may or may not take place; the two branches being in intimate connection.

We must look now a little more closely at these connections. It may seem odd that we do not more definitely make the thoughts the rulers and causes of the rest of the response. To do just this has been in fact the grand error of traditional psychology. Man prefers to stress the features which distinguish him from monkey, and chief among these are his intellectual capacities. Important though they are, he has given them a rank to which they are not entitled. Intellect is an adjunct to the interests, a means by which they adjust themselves more successfully. Man is not in any sense primarily an intelligence; he is a system of interests. Intelligence helps man but does not run him.

Partly through this natural mistake, and partly because intellectual operations are so much easier to study, the whole traditional analysis of the working of the mind has been turned upside down. It is largely as a remedy from the difficulties which this mistake involves that poetry may have so much importance in the future. But let us look again more closely at the poetic experience.

In the first place, why is it essential in reading poetry to give the words their full imagined sound and body? What is meant by saying that the poet works with this sound and body? The answer is that even before the words have been intellectually understood and the thoughts they occasion formed and followed, the movement and sound of the words is playing deeply and intimately upon the interests. How this happens is a matter which has yet to be successfully investigated, but that it happens no sensitive reader of poetry doubts. A good deal of poetry and even some great poetry exists (e.g., some of Shakespeare's Songs and, in a different way, much of the best of Swinburne) in which the sense of the words can be *almost* entirely missed or neglected without loss. Never perhaps entirely without effort, however; though sometimes with advantage. But the plain fact that the relative importance of grasping the sense of the words may vary (compare Browning's *Before* with his *After*) is enough for our purpose here.

In nearly all poetry the sound and feel of the words, what is often called the *form* of the poem in opposition to its *content,* get to work first, and the sense in which the words are taken is subtly influenced by this fact. Most words are ambiguous as regards their plain sense, especially in poetry. We can take them as we please in a variety of senses. The sense we are pleased to choose is the one which most suits the impulses already stirred through the form of the verse. The same thing can be noticed in conversation. Not the strict logical sense of what is said, but the tone of voice and the occasion are the primary factors by which we interpret. Science, it is worth noting, endeavors with increasing success to bar out these factors. We believe a scientist because he can substantiate his remarks, not because he is eloquent or forcible in his enunciation. In fact, we distrust him when he seems to be influencing us by his manner.

In its use of words poetry is just the reverse of science. Very definite thoughts do occur, but not because the words are so chosen as logically to bar out all possibilities but one. No. But because the manner, the tone of voice, the cadence and the rhythm play upon our interests and make *them* pick out from among an indefinite number of possibilities the precise particular thought which they need. This is why poetical descriptions often seem so much more accurate than prose descriptions. Language logically and scientifically used cannot describe a landscape or a face. To do so it would need a prodigious apparatus of names for shades and nuances, for precise particular qualities. These names do not exist, so other means have to be used. The poet, even when, like Ruskin or De Quincey, he writes in prose, makes the reader pick out the precise particular sense required from an indefinite number of possible senses which a word, phrase or sentence may carry. The means by which he does this are many and varied. Some of them have been mentioned above, but the way in which he uses them is the poet's own secret, something which cannot be taught. He knows how to do it, but he does not himself know how it is done.

Misunderstanding and under-estimation of poetry is mainly due to over-estimation of the thought in it. We can see still more clearly that thought is not the prime factor if we consider for a moment not the experience of the reader but that of the poet. Why does the poet use these words and no others? Not because they stand for a series of thoughts which in themselves are what he is concerned to communicate. It is never what a poem *says* which matters, but what it *is*. The poet is not writing as a scientist. He uses these words because the interests which the situation calls into play combine to bring them, just in this form, into his consciousness *as a means of ordering, controlling and consolidating* the whole experience. The experience itself, the tide of impulses sweeping through the mind, is the source and the sanction of the words. They represent this experience itself, not any set of perceptions or reflections, though often to a reader who approaches the poem wrongly they will seem to be only a series of remarks about other things. But to a suitable reader the words—if they actually spring from experience and are not due to verbal habits, to the desire to be effective, to factitious excogitation, to imitation, to irrelevant contrivances, or to any other of the failings which prevent most people from writing poetry— the words will reproduce in his mind a similar play of interests putting him for the while into a similar situation and leading to the same response.

Why this should happen is still somewhat of a mystery. An extraordinarily intricate concourse of impulses brings the words together. Then in another mind the affair in part reverses itself, the words bring into being a similar concourse of impulses. The words which seem to be the effect of the experience in the first instance, seem to become the cause of a similar experience in the second. A very odd thing to happen, not exactly paralleled outside communication. But this description is not quite accurate. The words, as we have seen, are not simply the effect in one case, nor the cause in the other. In both cases they are the part of the experience which binds it together, which gives it a definite structure and keeps it from being a mere welter of disconnected impulses. They are *the key,* to borrow a useful metaphor from McDougall, for this particular combination of impulses. So regarded, it is less strange that what the poet wrote should reproduce his experience in the mind of the reader.

## 3. What Is Valuable?

Enough perhaps as to the kind of thing a poem is, as to the general structure of these experiences. Let us now turn to the further questions "Of what use is it?" "Why and how is it valuable?"

The first point to be made is that poetic experiences are valuable (when they are) in the same ways as any other experiences. They are to be judged by the same standards. What are these?

Extraordinarily diverse views have been held upon this point. Very naturally, since such very different ideas have been entertained as to what kind of thing an experience is. For our opinions as to the differences between good and bad experiences depend inevitably upon what we take an experience to be. As fashions have changed in psychology men's ethical theories have followed suit. When a created, simple and eternal soul was the pivotal point, Good was conformity with the will of the creator, Evil was rebellion. When the associationist psychologists substituted a swarm of sensations and images for the soul, Good became pleasure and Evil became pain, and so on. A long chapter of the history of opinions has still to be written tracing these changes. Now that the mind is seen to be a hierarchy of interests, what will for this account be the difference between Good and Evil?

It is the difference between free and wasteful organization, between fullness and narrowness of life. For if the mind is a system of interests, and if an experience is their play, the worth of any experience is a matter of the degree to which the mind, through this experience attains a complete equilibrium.

This is a first approximation. It needs qualifying and expanding if it is to become a satisfactory theory. Let us see how some of these amendments would run.

Consider an hour of any person's life. It holds out innumerable possibilities. Which of these are realized depends upon two main groups of factors:—the external situation in which he is living, his surroundings, including the other people with whom he is in contact; and, secondly, his psychological make-up. The first of these, the external situation, is sometimes given too much importance. We have only to notice what very different experiences different people undergo when in closely similar situations to recognize this fact. A situation which is dullness itself for one may be full of excitement for another. What an individual responds to is not the whole situation but a selection from it, and as a rule few people make the same selection. What is selected is decided by the organization of the individual's interests.

Now let us simplify the case by supposing that nothing which happens during this hour is going to have any further consequences either in our hypothetical person's life or in anyone else's. He is going to cease to exist when the clock strikes—but for our purposes he must be imagined not to know this—and no one is to be a whit better or worse whatever he thinks, feels or does during the hour. What shall we say it would be best for him, if he could, to do?

We need not bother to imagine the detail of the external situation or the character of the man. We can answer our question in general terms without doing so. The man has a certain definite instinctive make-up—the result of his past history, including his heredity. There will be many things which he cannot do which another man could, and many things which he cannot do in this situation, whatever it is, which he could do in other situations. But given this particular man in this particular situation, our question is, which of the possibilities open to him would be better than which others? How would we as friendly observers like to see him living?

Setting pain aside, we may perhaps agree that torpor would be the worst choice. Complete inertness, lifelessness, would be the sorriest spectacle—anticipating too nearly and unnecessarily what is to happen when the hour strikes. We can then perhaps agree, though here more resistance from preconceived ideas may be encountered, that the best choice would be the opposite of torpor, that is to say the fullest, keenest, most active and complete kind of life.

Such a life is one which brings into play as many as possible of the *positive* interests. We can leave out the negative interests. It would be a pity for our friend to be frightened or disgusted even for a minute of his precious hour.

But this is not all. It is not enough that many interests should be stirred. There is a more important point to be noted.

> The Gods approve
> The depth and not the tumult of the soul.

The interests must come into play and remain in play with as little conflict among themselves as possible. In other words, the experience must be organized so as to give all the impulses of which it is composed the greatest possible degree of freedom.[3]

It is in this respect that people differ most from one another. It is this which separates the good life from the bad. Far more life is wasted through muddled mental organization than through lack of opportunity. Conflicts between different impulses are the greatest evils which afflict mankind.

The best life then which we can wish for our friend will be one in which as much as possible of himself is engaged (as many of his impulses as possible). And this with as little conflict, as little mutual interference between different sub-systems of his activities as there can be. The more he lives and the less he thwarts himself, the better. That briefly is our answer as psychologists, as outside observers abstractly describing the state of affairs. And if it is asked, what does such life feel like, how is it to live through? the answer is that it feels like and is the experience of poetry.

There are two ways in which conflict can be avoided or overcome. By conquest and by conciliation. One or other of the contesting impulses can be suppressed, or they can come to a mutual arrangement, they can adjust themselves to one another. We owe to psycho-analysis—at present still a rather undisciplined branch of psychology—a great deal of striking evidence as to the extreme difficulty of suppressing any vigorous impulse. When it seems to be suppressed it is often found to be really as active as ever, but in some other form, generally a troublesome one. Persistent mental imbalances are the source of nearly all our troubles. For this reason, as well as for the simpler reason that suppression is wasteful of life, conciliation is always to be preferred to conquest. People who are always winning victories over themselves might equally well be described as always enslaving themselves. Their lives become unnecessarily narrow. The minds of many saints have been like wells; they should have been like lakes or like the sea.

Unfortunately, most of us, left to ourselves, have no option but to go in for extensive attempts at self-conquest. It is our only means of escape from chaos. Our impulses must have some order, some organization, or we do not live ten minutes without disaster. In the past, Tradition, a kind of Treaty of Versailles assigning frontiers and spheres of influence to the different interests, and based chiefly upon conquest, ordered our lives in a moderately satisfactory manner. But Tradition is weakening. Moral authorities are not as well backed by beliefs as they were; their sanctions are declining in force. We are in need of something to take the place of the old order. Not in need of a new balance of power, a new arrangement of conquests, but of a League of Nations for the moral ordering of the impulses; a new order based on conciliation, not on attempted suppression.

---

[3] See *The Foundations of Aesthetics* [1922], by C. K. Ogden, James Wood and the author, pp. 74–78, for a description of such experience.

Only the rarest individuals hitherto have achieved this new order, and never yet perhaps completely. But many have achieved it for a brief while, for a particular phase of experience, and many have recorded it for these phases.

Of these records poetry consists.

But before going on to this new point let us return for a moment to our hypothetical friend who is enjoying his last hour, and suppose this limitation removed. Instead of such an hour let us consider any hour, one which has consequences for his future and for other people. Let us consider any piece of any life. How far is our argument affected? Will our standards of good and evil be altered?

Clearly the case now is, in certain respects, different; it is much more complicated. We have to take these consequences into account. We have to regard his experience not in itself alone, but as a piece of his life and as a probable factor in other people's situations. If we are to approve of the experience, it must not only be full of life and free from conflict, but it must be likely to lead to other experiences, both his own and those of other people, also full of life and free from conflict. And often, in actual fact, it has to be less full of life and more restricted than it might be in order to ensure these results. A momentary individual good has often to be sacrificed for the sake of a later or a general good. Conflicts are often necessary in order that they should not occur later. The mutual adjustment of conflicting impulses may take time, and an acute struggle may be the only way in which they learn to co-operate peacefully in the future.

But all these complications and qualifications do not disturb the conclusion we arrived at through considering the simpler case. A good experience is still one full of life, in the sense which we have explained, or derivately one conducive to experiences full of life. An evil experience is one which is self-thwarting or conducive to stultifying conflicts. So far then, all is sound and shipshape in the argument, and we can go on to consider the poet.

## 4. The Command of Life

The chief characteristic of poets is their amazing *command* of words. This is not a mere matter of vocabulary, though it is significant that Shakespeare's vocabulary is the richest and most varied that any Englishman has ever used. It is not the quantity of words a writer has at his disposal, but the way in which he disposes them that gives him his rank as a poet. His sense of how they modify one another, how their separate effects in the mind combine, how they fit into the whole response, is what matters. As a rule the poet is not conscious of the reason why just these words and no others best serve. They fall into their place without his conscious control, and a feeling of rightness, of inevitability is commonly his sole conscious ground for his certainty that he has ordered them aright. It would as a rule be idle to ask him why he used a particular rhythm or a particular epithet. He might give reasons, but they would probably be mere rationalizations having nothing to do with the matter. For the choice of the rhythm or the epithet was not an intellectual matter (though it may be capable of an intellectual justification), but was due to an instinctive impulse seeking to confirm itself, or to order itself with its fellows.

It is very important to realize how deep are the motives which govern the poet's use of words. No study of other poets which is not an impassioned study will help him. He can learn much from other poets, but only by letting them influence him deeply, not by any superficial examination of their style. For the motives which shape a poem spring from the root of the mind. The poet's style is the direct outcome of the way in which his interests are organized. That amazing capacity of his for ordering speech is only a part of a more amazing capacity for ordering his experience.

This is the explanation of the fact that poetry cannot be written by cunning and study, by craft and contrivance. To a superficial glance the productions of the mere scholar, steeped in the poetry of the past, and animated by intense emulation and a passionate desire to place himself among the poets, will often look extraordinarily like poetry. His words may seem as subtly and delicately ordered as words can be, his epithets as happy, his transitions as daring, his simplicity as perfect. By every intellectual test he may succeed. But unless the ordering of the words sprang, not from knowledge of the technique of poetry added to a desire to write some, but from an actual supreme ordering of *experience*, a closer approach to his work will betray it. Characteristically its rhythm will give it away. For rhythm is no matter of tricks with syllables, but directly reflects personality. It is not separable from the words to which it belongs. Moving rhythm in poetry arises only from genuinely stirred impulses, and is a more subtle index than any other to the order of the interests.

Poetry, in other words, cannot be imitated; it cannot be faked so as to baffle the only test that ought ever to be applied. It is unfortunately true that this test is often very difficult to apply. And it is sometimes hard to know whether the test has or has not been applied. For the test is this—that only genuine poetry will give to the reader who approaches it in the proper manner a response which is as passionate, noble and serene as the experience of the poet, the master of speech because he is the master of experience itself. But it is easy to read carelessly and shallowly, and easy to mistake for the response something which does not properly belong to it at all. By careless reading we miss what is in the poem. And in some states of mind, for example, when intoxicated, the silliest doggerel may seem sublime. What happened was not due to the doggerel but to the drink.

With these general considerations in mind we may turn now from the question—What can the dawning science of psychology tell us about poetry?—to the allied questions—How is science in general, and the new outlook upon the world which it induces, already affecting poetry, and to what extent may science make obsolete the poetry of the past? To answer these questions we need to sketch some of the changes which have recently come about in our world-picture, and to consider anew what it is that we demand from poetry.

## 5. The Neutralization of Nature

The poets are failing us, or we them, if after reading them we do not find ourselves changed; not with a temporary change, such as luncheon or slumber will produce, from which we inevitably work back to the *status quo ante,* but with a permanent alteration of our possibilities as responsive individuals in good or bad adjustment to an all but overwhelming concourse of stimulations. How many living poets have the power to make such deep changes? Let us set aside youthful enthusiasm; there is a time in most lives when, rightly enough, Mr. Masefield, Mr. Kipling, Mr. Drinkwater, or even Mr. Noyes or Mr. Studdert Kennedy may profoundly affect the awakening mind; it is being introduced to poetry. Later on, looking back, we can see that any one of a hundred other poets would have served as well or better. Let us consider only the experienced, the fairly hardened reader, who is familiar with a great deal of the poetry of the past.

Contemporary poetry which will, accidents apart, modify the attitudes of this reader must be such as could not have been written in another age than our own. It must have sprung in part from the contemporary situation. It must correspond to needs, impulses, attitudes, which did not arise in the same fashion for poets in the past, and criticism also must take notice of the contemporary situation. Our attitudes to man, to nature, and to the universe change with every generation, and have changed with unusual violence in recent years. We cannot leave these changes out of account in judging modern poetry. When attitudes are changing neither criticism nor poetry can remain stationary. To those who realize what the poet is this will be obvious; but all literary history bears it out.

It would be of little use to give a list of the chief recent intellectual revolutions and to attempt to deduce therefrom what must be happening to poetry. The effects upon our attitudes of changes of opinion are too complex to be calculated so. What we have to consider is not men's current opinions but their attitudes—how they feel about this or that as part of the world; what relative importance its different aspects have for them; what they are prepared to sacrifice for what; what they trust, what they are frightened by, what they desire. To discover these things we must go to the poets. Unless they are failing us, they will show us just these things.

They will *show* them, but, of course, they will not state them. Their poetry will not be *about* their attitudes in the sense in which a treatise on anatomy is about the structure of the body. Their poetry will arise out of their attitudes and will evoke them in an adequate reader, but, as a rule, it will not mention any attitudes. We must, of course, expect occasional essays in verse upon psychological topics, but these should not mislead us. Most of the attitudes with which poetry is concerned are indescribable—because psychology is still in a primitive stage—and can only be named or spoken about as the attitude of this poem or that. The poem, the actual experience as it forms itself in the mind of the fit reader, controlling his responses to the world and ordering his impulses, is our best evidence as to how other men feel about things; and we read it, if we are serious, partly to discover how life seems to another, partly to try how his attitudes suit us, engaged as we also are in the same enterprise.

Although we cannot—for lack of a sufficient psychology—describe attitudes in terms which do not apply also to others which we are not considering, and although we cannot deduce a poet's attitudes from the general intellectual background, none the less, after reading his poetry, when his experience has become our own, we can sometimes profitably look round us to see why these attitudes should be so very different, in some ways, from those we find in the poetry of 100 or 1,000 years ago. In so doing we gain a means of indicating what these attitudes are, useful both for those who are constitutionally unable to read poetry (an increasing number), and for those victims of education who neglect modern poetry because they "don't know what to make of it."

What, then, has been happening to the intellectual background, to the world-picture, and in what ways may changes here have caused a reorganization of our attitudes?

The central dominant change may be described as the *Neutralization of Nature,* the transference from the Magical View of the world to the scientific, a change so great that it is perhaps only paralleled historically by the change, from whatever adumbration of a world-picture preceded the Magical View, to the Magical View itself. By the Magical View I mean, roughly, the belief in a world of Spirits and Powers which control events, and which can be evoked and, to some extent, controlled themselves by human practices. The belief in Inspiration and the beliefs underlying Ritual are representative parts of this view. It has been decaying slowly for some 300 years, but its definite overthrow has taken place only in the last 60. Vestiges and survivals of it prompt and direct a great part of our daily affairs, but it is no longer the world-picture which an informed mind most easily accepts. There is some evidence that Poetry, together with the other Arts, arose with this Magical View. It is a possibility to be seriously considered that Poetry may pass away with it.

The reasons for the downfall of the Magical View are familiar. It seems to have arisen as a consequence of an increase in man's knowledge of and command over nature (the discovery of agriculture). It fell through the extension of that knowledge of and command over nature. Throughout its (10,000 years?) reign its stability has been due to its capacity for satisfying men's emotional needs through its adequacy as an object for their attitudes. We must remember that human attitudes have developed always *inside* the social group; they are what a man feels, the mainsprings of his behavior towards his fellow-men, and they have only a limited field of applicability. Thus the Magical View, being an interpretation of nature in terms of man's own most intimate and most important affairs, very soon came to suit man's emotional make-up better than any other view possibly could. The attraction of the Magical View lay very little in the actual command over nature which it gave. That Galton was the first person to test the efficacy of prayer experimentally is an indication of this. What did give the Magical View its standing was the ease and adequacy with which the universe therein presented could be emotionally handled, the scope offered for man's love and hatred, for his terror as well as for his hope and his despair. It gave life a shape, a sharpness, and a coherence that no other means could so easily secure.

In its place we have the universe of the mathematician, a field for the tracing out of ever wider and more general uniformities. A field in which intellectual certainty is, almost for the first time, available, and on an unlimited scale. Also the despondencies, the emotional excitements accompanying research and discovery, again on an unprecedented scale. Thus a number of men who might in other times have been poets are today in bio-chemical laboratories—a fact of which we might avail ourselves, did we feel the need, in defense of an alleged present poverty in poetry. But apart from these thrills, what has the world-picture of science to do with human emotions? A god voluntarily or involuntarily subjected to the General Theory of Relativity does not make an emotional appeal. So this form of compromise fails. Various emergent deities have been suggested—by Mr. Wells, by Professors Alexander and Lloyd Morgan—but, alas! the reasons for suggesting them have become too clear and conscious. They are there to meet a demand, not to make one; they do not do the work for which they were invented.

The revolution brought about by science is, in short, too drastic to be met by any such half-measures. It touches the central principle by which the Mind has been deliberately organized in the past, and no alteration in beliefs, however great, will restore equilibrium while that principle is retained. I come now to the main purport of these remarks.

Ever since man first grew self-conscious and reflective he has supposed that his feelings, his attitudes, and his conduct spring from his knowledge. That as far as he could it would be wise for him to organize himself in this way, with knowledge[4] as the foundation on which should rest feeling, attitude, and behavior. In point of fact, he never has been so organized, knowledge having been until recently too scarce; but he has constantly been persuaded that he was built on this plan, and has

---

[4] I.e. thoughts which are both true and evidenced, in the narrower, stricter senses. For a discussion of some relevant senses of "truth" and "knowledge" see *Principles of Literary Criticim,* Chapters XXXIII and XXXIV.

endeavored to carry the structure further on these lines. He has sought for knowledge, supposing that it would itself *directly* excite a right orientation to existence, supposing that, if he only knew what the world was like, this knowledge in itself would show him how to feel towards it, what attitudes to adopt, and with what aims to live. He has constantly called what he found in this quest, "knowledge," unaware that it was hardly ever pure, unaware that his feelings, attitudes, and behavior were *already* orientated by his physiological and social needs, and were themselves, for the most part, the sources of whatever it was that he supposed himself to be knowing.

Suddenly, not long ago, he began to get genuine knowledge on a large scale. The process went faster and faster; it snow-balled. Now he has to face the fact that the edifices of supposed knowledge, with which he has for so long buttressed and supported his attitudes, will no longer stand up, and, at the same time, he has to recognize that pure knowledge is irrelevant to his aims, that it has no *direct* bearing upon what he should feel, or what he should attempt to do.

For science, which is simply our most elaborate way of *pointing* to things systematically, tells us and can tell us nothing about the nature of things in any *ultimate* sense. It can never answer any question of the form: *What* is so and so? It can only tell us *how* so and so behaves. And it does not attempt to do more than this. Nor, indeed, can more than this be done. Those ancient, deeply troubling, formulations that begin with "What" and "Why" prove, when we examine them, to be not questions at all; but requests—for emotional satisfaction. They indicate our desire not for knowledge but for assurance,[5] a point which appears clearly when we look into the "How" of questions and requests, of knowledge and desire. Science can tell us about man's place in the universe and his chances; that the place is precarious, and the chances problematical. It can enormously increase our chances if we can make wise use of it. But it cannot tell us what we are or what this world is; not because these are in any sense insoluble questions, but because they are not questions at all.[6] And if science cannot answer these pseudo-questions no more can philosophy or religion. So that all the varied answers which have for ages been regarded as the keys of wisdom are dissolving together.

The result is a biological crisis which is not likely to be decided without trouble. It is one which we can, perhaps, decide for ourselves, partly by thinking, partly by reorganizing our minds in other ways; if we do not it may be decided for us, not in the way we should choose. While it lasts it puts a strain on each individual and upon society, which is

---

[5] On this point the study of the child's questions included in *The Language and Thought of the Child* by J. Piaget (Kegan Paul, 1926), is illuminating.

[6] The remarks of Wittgenstein (*Tractatus Logico-Philosophicus*, 6.5, 6.52), which superficially resemble this, should be consulted, if only to show how important the *context* of a statement may be; for what is said above should lead not towards but away from all forms of mysticism.

part of the explanation of many modern difficulties, the difficulties of the poet in particular, to come back to our present subject. I have not really been far away.

## 6. Poetry and Beliefs

The business of the poet, as we have seen, is to give order and coherence, and so freedom, to a body of experience. To do so through words which act as its skeleton, as a structure by which the impulses which make up the experience are adjusted to one another and act together. The means by which words do this are many and varied. To work them out is a problem for psychology. A beginning has been indicated above, but only a beginning. What little can be done shows already that most critical dogmas of the past are either false or nonsense. A little knowledge is not here a danger, but clears the air in a remarkable way.

Roughly and inadequately, even in the light of our present knowledge, we can say that words work in the poem in two main fashions. As sensory stimuli and as (in the *widest* sense) symbols. We must refrain from considering the sensory side of the poem, remarking only that it is *not* in the least independent of the other side, and that it has for definite reasons prior importance in most poetry. We must confine ourselves to the other function of words in the poem, or rather, omitting much that is of secondary relevance, to one form of that function, let me call it *pseudo-statement*.

It will be admitted—by those who distinguish between scientific statement, where truth is ultimately a matter of verification as this is understood in the laboratory, and emotive utterance, where "truth" is primarily acceptability *by* some attitude, and more remotely is the acceptability *of* this attitude itself—that it is *not* the poet's business to make true statements. Yet poetry has constantly the air of making statements, and important ones; which is one reason why some mathematicians cannot read it. They find the alleged statements to be *false*. It will be agreed that their approach to poetry and their expectations from it are mistaken. But what exactly is the other, the right, the poetic, approach and how does it differ from the mathematical?

The poetic approach evidently limits the framework of possible consequences into which the pseudo-statement is taken. For the scientific approach this framework is unlimited. Any and every consequence is relevant. If any of the consequences of a statement conflicts with acknowledged fact then so much the worse for the statement. Not so with the pseudo-statement when poetically approached. The problem is—just how does the limitation work? The usual account is in terms of a supposed universe of discourse, a world of make-believe, of imagination, of recognized fictions common to the poet and his readers. A pseudo-statement which fits into this system of assumptions would be regarded as "poetically true"; one which does not, as "poetically false." This attempt to treat "poetic truth" on the model of general "coherence theories" is very natural for certain schools of logicians; but is inadequate, on the wrong lines from the outset. To mention two objections out of many; there is no means of discovering what the "universe of discourse" is on any occasion, and the kind of coherence which must hold within it, supposing it to be discoverable, is not an affair of logical relations. Attempt to define the system of propositions into which

### O Rose, thou art sick!

must fit, and the logical relations which must hold between them if it is to be "poetically true"; the absurdity of the theory becomes evident.

We must look further. In the poetic approach the relevant consequences are not logical or to be arrived at by a partial relaxation of logic. Except occasionally and by accident logic does not enter at all. They are the consequences which arise through our emotional organization. The acceptance which a pseudo-statement receives is entirely governed by its effects upon our feelings and attitudes. Logic only comes in, if at all, in subordination, as a servant to our emotional response. It is an unruly servant, however, as poets and readers are constantly discovering. A pseudo-statement is "true" if it suits and serves some attitude or links together attitudes which on other grounds are desirable. This kind of truth is so opposed to scientific truth that it is a pity to use so similar a word, but at present it is difficult to avoid the malpractice.[7]

This brief analysis may be sufficient to indicate the fundamental disparity and opposition between pseudo-statements as they occur in poetry and statements as they occur in science. A pseudo-statement is a form of words which is justified entirely by its effect in releasing or organizing our impulses and attitudes (due regard being had for the better or worse organizations of these *inter se*); a statement, on the other hand, is justified by its truth, i.e. its correspondence, in a highly technical sense, with the fact to which it points.

Statements true and false alike do of course constantly touch off attitudes and action. Our daily practical existence is largely guided by them. On the whole true statements are of more service to us than false ones. None the less we do not and, at present, cannot order our emotions and attitudes by true statements alone. Nor is there any probability that we ever shall contrive to do so. This is one of the great new dangers to which civilization is exposed. Countless pseudo-statements—about God, about the universe, about human nature, the relations of mind to mind, about the soul, its rank and destiny—pseudo-statements which are pivotal points in the organization of the mind, vital to its well-being, have suddenly become, for sincere, honest and informal minds, impossible to believe. For centuries they have been believed; now they are gone, irrecoverably; and the knowledge which has killed them is not of

---

[7] For an account of the various senses of truth and of the ways in which they may be distinguished in discussion cf. *The Meaning of Meaning*, by C. K. Ogden and the author, Chapters VII and X.

a kind upon which an equally fine organization of the mind can be based.

This is the contemporary situation. The remedy, since there is no prospect of our gaining adequate knowledge, and since indeed it is fairly clear that genuine knowledge cannot serve us here and can only increase our practical control of Nature, is to cut our pseudo-statements free from belief, and yet retain them, in this released state, as the main instruments by which we order our attitudes to one another and to the world. Not so desperate a remedy as may appear, for poetry conclusively shows that even the most important among our attitudes can be aroused and maintained without any belief entering in at all. Those of Tragedy, for example. We need no beliefs, and indeed we must have none, if we are to read *King Lear*. Pseudo-statements to which we attach no belief and statements proper such as science provides cannot conflict. It is only when we introduce illicit beliefs into poetry that danger arises. To do so is from this point of view a profanation of poetry.

Yet an important branch of criticism which has attracted the best talents from prehistoric times until today consists of the endeavor to persuade men that the functions of science and poetry are identical, or that the one is a "higher form" of the other, or that they conflict and we must choose between them.

The root of this persistent endeavor has still to be mentioned; it is the same as that from which the Magical View of the world arose. If we give to a pseudo-statement the kind of unqualified acceptance which belongs by right only to certified scientific statements, if we can contrive to do this, the impulses and attitudes with which we respond to it gain a notable stability and vigor. Briefly, if we can contrive to believe poetry, then the world *seems*, while we do so, to be transfigured. It used to be comparatively easy to do this, and the habit has become well established. With the extension of science and the neutralization of nature it has become difficult as well as dangerous. Yet it is still alluring; it has many analogies with drug-taking. Hence the endeavors of the critics referred to. Various subterfuges have been devised along the lines of regarding Poetic Truth as figurative, symbolic; or as more immediate, as a truth of Intuition, not of reason; or as a higher form of the same truth as reason yields. Such attempts to use poetry as a denial or as a corrective of science are very common. One point can be made against them all: they are never worked out in detail. There is no equivalent to Mill's Logic expounding any such view. The language in which they are framed is usually a blend of obsolete psychology and emotive exclamations.

The long-established and much-encouraged habit of giving to emotive utterances—whether pseudo-statements simple, or looser and larger wholes taken as saying something figuratively—the kind of assent which we give to established facts, has for most people debilitated a wide range of their responses. A few scientists, caught young and brought up in the laboratory, are free from it; but then, as a rule, they pay no *serious* attention to poetry. For most men the recognition of the neutrality of nature brings about—through this habit—a divorce from poetry. They are so used to having their responses propped up by beliefs, however vague, that when these shadowy supports are removed they are no longer able to respond. Their attitudes to so many things have been forced in the past, over-encouraged. And when the world-picture ceases to assist there is a collapse. Over whole tracts of natural emotional response we are today like a bed of dahlias whose sticks have been removed. And this effect of the neutralization of nature is only in its beginnings. Consider the probable effects upon love-poetry in the near future of the kind of enquiry into basic human constitution exemplified by psychoanalysis.

A sense of desolation, of uncertainty, of futility, of the groundlessness of aspirations, of the vanity of endeavor, and a thirst for a life-giving water which seems suddenly to have failed, are the signs in consciousness of this necessary reorganization of our lives.[8] Our attitudes and impulses are being compelled to become self-supporting; they are being driven back upon their biological justification, made once again sufficient to themselves. And the only impulses which seem strong enough to continue unflagging are commonly so crude that, to more finely developed individuals, they hardly seem worth having. Such people cannot live by warmth, food, fighting, drink and sex alone. Those who are least affected by the change are those who are emotionally least removed from the animals. As we shall see at the close of this essay, even a considerable poet may attempt to find relief by a reversion to primitive mentality.

It is important to diagnose the disease correctly and to put the blame in the right quarter. Usually it is some alleged "materialism" of science which is denounced. This mistake is due partly to clumsy thinking, but chiefly to relics of the Magical View. For even if the Universe were "spiritual" all through (whatever that assertion might mean; all such assertions are probably nonsense), that would not make it any more accordant to human attitudes. It is not what the universe is made of but how it works, the law it follows, which makes knowledge of it incapable of spurring on our emotional responses, and further the nature of knowledge itself makes it inadequate. The contact with things which we therein establish is too sketchy and indirect to help us. We are beginning to know too much about the bond which unites the mind to its object in knowledge for that old dream of a perfect knowledge which would guarantee perfect life to retain its sanction. What was thought

---

[8] To those familiar with Mr. Eliot's *The Waste Land,* my indebtedness to it at this point will be evident. He seems to me by this poem, to have performed two considerable services for this generation. He has given a perfect emotive description of a state of mind which is probably inevitable for a while to all meditative people. Secondly, by effecting a complete severance between his poetry and *all* beliefs, and this without any weakening of the poetry, he has realized what might otherwise have remained largely a speculative possibility, and has shown the way to the only solution of these difficulties. "In the destructive element immerse. That is the way."

to be pure knowledge, we see now to have been shot through with hope and desire, with fear and wonder, and these intrusive elements indeed gave it all its power to support our lives. In knowledge, in the "How?" of events, we can find hints by which to take advantage of circumstances in our favor and avoid mischances. But we cannot get from it a *raison d'être* or a justification of more than a relatively lowly kind of life.

The justification, or the reverse, of any attitude lies, not in the object, but in itself, in its serviceableness to the whole personality. Upon its place in the whole system of attitudes, which is the personality, all its worth depends. This is true equally for the subtle, finely compounded attitudes of the civilized individual as for the simpler attitudes of the child.

In brief, experience is its own justification; and this fact must be faced, although sometimes—by a lover, for example—it may be very difficult to accept. Once it is faced, it is apparent that all the attitudes to other human beings and to the world in all its aspects, which have been serviceable to humanity, remain as they were, as valuable as ever. Hesitation felt in admitting this is a measure of the strength of the evil habit we have described. But many of these attitudes, valuable as ever, are, now that they are being set free, more difficult to maintain, because we still hunger after a basis in belief.

## 7. Some Contemporary Poets

It is time to turn to those living poets through study of whose work these reflections have arisen. Mr. Hardy is for every reason the poet with whom it is most natural to begin. Not only does his work span the whole period in which what I have called the neutralization of nature was finally effected, but it has throughout definitely reflected that change. Short essays in verse are fairly frequent among his *Collected Poems,* essays almost always dealing with this very topic; but these, however suggestive, are not the ground for singling him out as the poet who has most fully and courageously accepted the contemporary background; nor are the poems which are most definitely *about* the neutrality of nature the ground for the assertion. There is an opportunity for a misunderstanding at this point. The ground is the tone, the handling and the rhythm of poems which treat other subjects, for example *The Self Unseeing, The Voice, A Broken Appointment,* and preeminently *After a Journey.* A poem does not necessarily accept the situation because it gives it explicit recognition, but only through the precise mutation of the attitudes of which it is composed. Mr. Middleton Murry, against whose recent positions parts of this essay may be suspected by the reader to be aimed, has best pointed out, in his *Aspects of Literature,* how peculiarly "adequate to what we know and have suffered" Mr. Hardy's poetry is. "His reaction to an episode has behind it and within it a reaction to the universe." This is not as I should put it were I making a statement; but read as a pseudo-statement, emotively, it is excellent; it makes us remember how we felt. Actually it describes just what Hardy, at his best, does not do. He makes no reaction to the universe, recognizing it as something to which no reaction is more relevant than another. Mr. Murry is again well inspired, this time both emotively and scientifically, when he says: "Mr. Hardy stands high above all other modern poets by the deliberate purity of his responsiveness. The contagion of the world's slow stain has not touched him; from the first he held aloof from the general conspiracy to forget in which not only those who are professional optimists take a part." These extracts (from a writer more agonizingly aware than others that some strange change has befallen man in this generation, though his diagnosis is, I believe, mistaken) indicate very well Mr. Hardy's place and rank in English poetry. He is the poet who has most steadily refused to be comforted. The comfort of forgetfulness, the comfort of beliefs, he has put both these away. Hence his singular preoccupation with death; because it is in the contemplation of death that the necessity for human attitudes, in the face of an indifferent universe, to become self-supporting is felt most poignantly. Only the greatest tragic poets have achieved an equally self-reliant and immitigable acceptance.

From Mr. Hardy to Mr. De la Mare may seem a large transition, though readers of Mr. De la Mare's later work will agree that there are interesting resemblances—in Who's That and in other poems in The Veil where Mr. De la Mare is notably less himself than when writing at his best. In his best poetry, in The Pigs and the Charcoal Burner, in John Mouldy, no intimation of the contemporary situation sounds. He is writing of, and from, a world which knows nothing of these difficulties, a world of pure phantasy for which the distinction between knowledge and feeling has not yet dawned. When in other poems, more reflective, in The Tryst, for example, Mr. De la Mare does seem to be directly facing the indifference of the universe towards "poor mortal longingness" a curious thing happens. His utterance, in spite of his words, becomes not at all a recognition of this indifference, but voices instead an impulse to turn away, to forget it, to seek shelter in the warmth of his own familiar thickets of dreams, not to stay out in the wind. His rhythm, that indescribable personal note which clings to all his best poetry, is a lulling rhythm, an anodyne, an opiate, it gives sleep and visions, phantasmagoria; but it does not give vision, it does not awaken. Even when he most appears to be contemplating the fate of the modern, "whom the words of the wise have made sad," the drift of his verse is still "seeking after that sweet golden clime" where the mental traveller's journey begins.

There is one exception to this charge (for in a sense it is an adverse criticism, though not one to be pressed except against a great poet), there is one poem in which there is no such reluctance to bear the blast —The Mad Prince's Song in Peacock Pie. But here the spirit of the poem, the impulse which gives it life, comes from a poet who more than most refused to take shelter; *The Mad Prince's Song* derives from *Hamlet*.

Mr. Yeats and Mr. Lawrence present two further ways of dodging those difficulties which come from being born into this generation rather than into some earlier age. Mr. De la Mare takes shelter in the dream-world of the child, Mr. Yeats retires into black velvet curtains and the visions of the Hermetist, and Mr. Lawrence makes a magnificent attempt to reconstruct in himself the mentality of the Bushman. There are other modes of escape open to the poet. Mr. Blundell, to name one other poet only, goes into the country, but few people follow him there in his spirit, whereas Mr. Yeats and Mr. Lawrence, whether they are widely read or not, do represent tendencies among the defeated which are only too easily observable.

Mr. Yeats' work from the beginning was a repudiation of the most active contemporary interests. But at first the poet of *The Wanderings of Usheen, The Stolen Child* and *Innisfree* turned away from contemporary civilization in favor of a world which he knew perfectly, the world of folk-lore as it is accepted, neither with belief nor disbelief, by the peasant. Folk-lore and the Irish landscape, its winds, woods, waters, islets, and seagulls, and for a while an unusually simple and direct kind of love poetry in which he became something more than a minor poet, these were his refuge. Later, after a drawn battle with the drama, he made a more violent repudiation, not merely of current civilization but of life itself, in favor of a supernatural world. But the world of the "eternal moods," of supernal essences and immortal beings is not, like the Irish peasant stories and the Irish landscape, part of his natural and familiar experience. Now he turns to a world of symbolic phantasmagoria about which he is desperately uncertain. He is uncertain because he has adopted as a technique of inspiration the use of trance, of dissociated phases of consciousness, and the revelations given in these dissociated states are insufficiently connected with normal experience. This, in part, explains the weakness of Mr. Yeats' transcendental poetry. A deliberate reversal of the natural relations of thought and feeling is the rest of the explanation. Mr. Yeats takes certain feelings—feelings of conviction attaching to certain visions—as evidence for the thoughts which he supposes his visions to symbolize. To Mr. Yeats the value of *The Phases of the Moon* lies not in any attitudes which it arouses or embodies but in the doctrine which for an initiate it promulgates.

The resort to trance, and the effort to discover a new world-picture to replace that given by science are the two most significant points for our purpose in Mr. Yeats' work. A third might be the singularly bitter contempt for the generality of mankind which occasionally appears.

The doctrinal problem arises again, but in a clearer form with Mr. Lawrence. But here (Mr. Yeats' promised treatise on the states of the soul has not yet appeared) we have the advantage of an elaborate prose exposition, *Phantasia of the Unconscious,* of the positions which so many of the poems advocate. It is not unfair to put the matter in this way, since there is little doubt possible that the bulk of Mr. Lawrence's published verse is prose, scientific prose too, jottings, in fact, from a psychologist's notebook, with a commentary interspersed. Due allowance being made for the extreme psychological interest of these observations, there remains the task of explaining how the poet who wrote the *Ballad of Another Ophelia* and *Aware,* and, above all, *The White Peacock,* should have wandered, through his own zeal misdirected, so far from the paths which once appeared to be his alone to open.

Mr. Lawrence's revolt against civilization seems to have been originally spontaneous, an emotional revulsion free from *ad hoc* beliefs. It sprang directly from experience. He came to abhor all the attitudes men adopt, not through the direct prompting of their instincts, but because of the supposed nature of the objects to which they are directed. The conventions, the idealizations, which come between man and man and between man and woman, which often queer the pitch for the natural responses, seemed to him the source of all evil. Part of his revolt was certainly justified. These idealizations—representative examples are the dogma of the equality of man and the doctrine that Love is primarily sympathy—are beliefs illicitly interpolated in order to support and strengthen attitudes in the manner discussed at length above. And Mr. Lawrence's original rejection of a morality not self-supporting but based upon beliefs, makes his work an admirable illustration of my main thesis. But two simple and avoidable mistakes deprived his revolt of the greater part of its value. He overlooked the fact that such beliefs commonly arise because the attitudes they support are already existent. He assumed that a bad basis for an attitude meant a bad attitude. In general, it does mean a forced attitude, but that is another matter. Secondly, he tried to cure the disease by introducing other beliefs of his own manufacture in place of the conventional beliefs and in support of very different attitudes.

The genesis of these beliefs is extremely interesting as an illustration of primitive mentality. Since the attitudes on which he fell back are those of a very early stage of human development, it is not surprising that the means by which he has supported them should be of the same era, or that the world-picture which he has worked out should be similar to that described in *The Golden Bough.* The mental process at work is schematically as follows: First, undergo an intense emotion, located with unusual definiteness in the body, which can be described as "a feeling *as though* the solar plexus were connected by a current of dark passional energy with another person." Those whose emotions tend to be localized will be familiar with such feelings. The second step is to say "I must trust my feelings." The third is to call the feeling an intuition. The last is to say "*I know* that my solar plexus is, etc." By this means we arrive at indubitable knowledge that the sun's energy is recruited from the life on the earth and that the astronomers are wrong in what they say about the moon, and so on.

The illicit steps in the argument are not quite so evident as they appear to be in this analysis. To distinguish an intuition *of* an emotion from an intuition *by* it is not always easy, nor is a description of an emotion always in practice distinguishable from an emotion. Certainly we must trust our feelings—in the sense of acting upon them. We have nothing else to trust. And to confuse this trusting with believing an emotive description of them is a mistake which all traditional codes of morality encourage us to commit.

The significance of such similar disasters in the work of poets so unlike and yet so greatly gifted as Mr. Yeats and Mr. Lawrence is noteworthy. For each the traditional scaffolding of conventional beliefs has proved unsatisfying, unworkable as a basis for their attitudes. Each has sought, in very different directions it is true, a new set of beliefs as a remedy. For neither has the world-picture of science seemed a possible substitute. And neither seems to have envisaged the possibility of a poetry which is independent of all beliefs, probably because, however much they differ, both are very serious poets. A great deal of poetry can, of course, be written for which total independence of all beliefs is an easy matter. But it is never poetry of the more important kind, because the temptation to introduce beliefs is a sign and measure of the importance of the attitudes involved. At present it is not primarily religious beliefs, in the stricter sense of the word, which are most likely to be concerned. Emphases alter surprisingly. University societies founded fifteen years ago, for example, to discuss religion, are usually found to be discussing sex today. And serious love poetry, which is independent of beliefs of one kind or another, traditional or eccentric, is extremely rare.

Yet the necessity for independence is increasing. This is not to say that traditional poetry, into which beliefs readily enter, is becoming obsolete; it is merely becoming more and more difficult to approach without confusion; it demands a greater imaginative effort, a greater purity in the reader.

We must distinguish here, however. There are many feelings and attitudes which, though in the past supported by beliefs now untenable, can survive their removal because they have other, more natural, supports and spring directly from the necessities of existence. To the extent to which they have been undistorted by the beliefs which have gathered round them they will remain as before. But there are other attitudes which are very largely the product of belief and have no other support. These will lapse if the changes here forecast continue. With their disappearance some forms of poetry—much minor devotional verse, for example—will become obsolete. And with the unravelling of the intellect *versus* emotion entanglement, there will be cases where even literature to which immense value has been assigned—the speculative portions of the work of Dostoevsky may be instanced—will lose much of its interest, except for the history of the mind. It was because he belonged to our age that Dostoevsky had to wrestle so terribly in these toils. A poet today, whose integrity is equal to that of the greater poets of the past, is inevitably plagued by the problem of thought and feeling as poets have never been plagued before.

A pioneer in modern research upon the origins of culture was asked recently whether his work had any bearing upon religion. He replied that it had, but that at present he was engaged merely in "getting the guns into position." The same answer might be given with regard to the probable consequences of recent progress in psychology, not only for religion but for the whole fabric of our traditional beliefs about ourselves. In many quarters there is a tendency to suppose that the series of attacks upon received ideas which began, shall we say, with Galileo and rose to a climax with Darwinism, has overreached itself with Einstein and Eddington, and that the battle is now due to die down. This view seems to be too optimistic. The most dangerous of the sciences is only now beginning to come into action. I am thinking less of Psychoanalysis or of Behaviorism than of the whole subject which includes them. It is very probable that the Hindenburg Line to which the defense of our traditions retired as a result of the onslaughts of the last century will be blown up in the near future. If this should happen a mental chaos such as man has never experienced may be expected. We shall then be thrown back, as Matthew Arnold foresaw, upon poetry. It is capable of saving us; it is a perfectly possible means of overcoming chaos. But whether man is capable of the reorientation required, whether he can loosen in time the entanglement with belief which now takes from poetry half its power and would then take all, is another question, and too large for the scope of this essay.

## HART CRANE

# General Aims and Theories

This brief essay by Hart Crane (1899–1932) was written in 1925 to explain the language and forms of his first volume of poems, *White Buildings* (1926). In it, Crane tries to come to terms with those aspects of "modernity" that are to be found both in the early poems and in the sequence, *The Bridge* (1930). The essay's relation to the group of pieces printed in this section lies in Crane's concern over the poetic treatment of a myth that is partly made up of classical borrowings, partly quite new. Crane warns against both enthusiastic modernism and unnecessary squeamishness over modern phenomena.

*W*hen I started writing Faustus & Helen* it was my intention to embody in modern terms (words, symbols, metaphors) a contemporary approximation to an ancient human culture or mythology that seems to have been obscured rather than illumined with the frequency of poetic allusions made to it during the last century. The name of Helen, for instance, has become an all-too-easily employed crutch for evocation whenever a poet felt a stitch in his side. The real evocation of this (to me) very real and absolute conception of beauty seemed to consist in a reconstruction in these modern terms of the basic emotional attitude toward beauty that the Greeks had. And in so doing I found that I was really building a bridge between so-called classic experience and many divergent realities of our seething, confused cosmos of today, which has no formulated mythology yet for classic poetic reference or for religious exploitation.

So I found "Helen" sitting in a street car; the Dionysian revels of her court and her seduction were transferred to a Metropolitan roof garden with a jazz orchestra; and the *katharsis* of the fall of Troy I saw approximated in the recent World War. The importance of this scaffolding may easily be exaggerated, but it gave me a series of correspondences between two widely separated worlds on which to sound some major themes of human speculation—love, beauty, death, renascence. It was a kind of grafting process that I shall doubtless not be interested in repeating, but which is consistent with subsequent theories of mine on the relation of tradition to the contemporary creating imagination.

It is a terrific problem that faces the poet today—a world that is so in transition from a decayed culture toward a reorganization of human evaluations that there are few common terms, general denominators of speech that are solid enough or that ring with any vibration or spiritual conviction. The great mythologies of the past (including the Church) are deprived of enough façade to even launch good raillery against. Yet much of their traditions are operative still—in millions of chance combinations of related and unrelated detail, psychological reference, figures of speech, precepts, etc. These are all a part of our common experience and the terms, or at least partially, of that very experience when it defines or extends itself.

The deliberate program, then, of a "break" with the past or tradition seems to me to be a sentimental fallacy. . . . The poet has a right to draw on whatever practical resources he finds in books or otherwise about him. He must tax his sensibility and his touchstone of experience for the proper selections of these themes and details, however,—and that is where he either stands, or falls into useless archeology.

I put no particular value on the simple objective of "modernity." The

---

* ["For the Marriage of Faustus and Helen," first published (aside from a fragment printed in a magazine) in *White Buildings* (New York: Boni and Liveright, 1926), pp. 37–44.—Ed.]

element of the temporal location of an artist's creation is of very secondary importance; it can be left to the impressionist or historian just as well. It seems to me that a poet will accidentally define his time well enough simply by reacting honestly and to the full extent of his sensibilities to the states of passion, experience and rumination that fate forces on him, first hand. He must, of course, have a sufficiently universal basis of experience to make his imagination selective and valuable. His picture of the "period," then, will simply be a by-product of his curiosity and the relation of his experience to a postulated "eternity."

I am concerned with the future of America, but not because I think that America has any so-called par value as a state or as a group of people. . . . It is only because I feel persuaded that here are destined to be discovered certain as yet undefined spiritual quantities, perhaps a new hierarchy of faith not to be developed so completely elsewhere. And in this process I like to feel myself as a potential factor; certainly I must speak in its terms and what discoveries I may make are situated in its experience.

But to fool one's self that definitions are being reached by merely referring frequently to skyscrapers, radio antennae, steam whistles, or other surface phenomena of our time is merely to paint a photograph. I think that what is interesting and significant will emerge only under the conditions of our submission to, and examination and assimilation of the organic effects on us of these and other fundamental factors of our experience. It can certainly not be an organic expression otherwise. And the expression of such values may often be as well accomplished with the vocabulary and blank verse of the Elizabethans as with the calligraphic tricks and slang used so brilliantly at times by an impressionist like Cummings.

It may not be possible to say that there is, strictly speaking, any "absolute" experience. But it seems evident that certain aesthetic experience (and this may for a time engross the total faculties of the spectator) can be called absolute, inasmuch as it approximates a formally convincing statement of a conception or apprehension of life that gains our unquestioning assent, and under the conditions of which our imagination is unable to suggest a further detail consistent with the design of the aesthetic whole.

I have been called an "absolutist" in poetry, and if I am to welcome such a label it should be under the terms of the above definition. It is really only a *modus operandi*, however, and as such has been used organically before by at least a dozen poets such as Donne, Blake, Baudelaire, Rimbaud, etc. I may succeed in defining it better by contrasting it with the impressionistic method. The impressionist is interesting as far as he goes—but his goal has been reached when he has succeeded in projecting certain selected factual details into his reader's consciousness. He is really not interested in the *causes* (metaphysical) of his materials, their emotional derivations or their utmost spiritual consequences. A kind of retinal registration is enough, along with a certain psychological stimulation. And this is also true of your realist (of the Zola type), and to a certain extent of the classicist, like Horace, Ovid, Pope, etc.

Blake meant these differences when he wrote:

> We are led to believe in a lie
> When we see *with* not *through* the eye.

The impressionist creates only with the eye and for the readiest surface of the consciousness, at least relatively so. If the effect has been harmonious or even stimulating, he can stop there, relinquishing entirely to his audience the problematic synthesis of the details into terms of their own personal consciousness.

It is my hope to go *through* the combined materials of the poem, using our "real" world somewhat as a spring-board, and to give the poem *as a whole* an orbit or predetermined direction of its own. I would like to establish it as free from my own personality as from any chance evaluation on the reader's part. (This is, of course, an impossibility, but it is a characteristic worth mentioning.) Such a poem is at least a stab at a truth, and to such an extent may be differentiated from other kinds of poetry and called "absolute." Its evocation will not be toward decoration or amusement, but rather toward a state of consciousness, an "innocence" (Blake) or absolute beauty. In this condition there may be discoverable under new forms certain spiritual illuminations, shining with a morality essentialized from experience directly, and not from previous precepts or preconceptions. It is as though a poem gave the reader as he left it a single, new *word,* never before spoken and impossible to actually enunciate, but self-evident as an active principle in the reader's consciousness henceforward.

As to technical considerations: the motivation of the poem must be derived from the implicit emotional dynamics of the materials used, and the terms of expression employed are often selected less for their logical (literal) significance than for their associational meanings. Via this and their metaphorical inter-relationships, the entire construction of the poem is raised on the organic principle of a "logic of metaphor," which antedates our so-called pure logic, and which is the genetic basis of all speech, hence consciousness and thought-extension.

These dynamics often result, I'm told, in certain initial difficulties in understanding my poems. But on the other hand I find them at times the only means possible for expressing certain concepts in any forceful or direct way whatever. To cite two examples:—when, in Voyages (II), I speak of "adagios of islands," the reference is to the motion of a boat through islands clustered thickly, the rhythm of the motion, etc. And it seems a much more direct and creative statement than any more logical employment of words such as "coasting slowly through the islands," besides ushering in a whole world of music. Similarly in Faustus and Helen (III) the speed and tense altitude of an aeroplane are much better suggested by the idea of "nimble blue plateaus"— *implying* the aeroplane and its speed against a contrast of stationary elevated earth. Although the statement is pseudo in relation to formal logic—it *is* completely logical in relation to the truth of the imagination, and there is expressed a concept of speed and space that could not be handled so well in other terms.

In manipulating the more imponderable phenomena of psychic motives, pure emotional crystallizations, etc. I have had to rely even more on these dynamics of inferential mention, and I am doubtless still very unconscious of having committed myself to what seems nothing but obscurities to some minds. A poem like Possessions really cannot be technically explained. It must rely (even to a large extent with myself) on its organic impact on the imagination to successfully imply its meaning. This seems to me to present an exceptionally difficult problem, however, considering the real clarity and consistent logic of many of the other poems.

I know that I run the risk of much criticism by defending such theories as I have, but as it is part of a poet's business to risk not only criticism—but folly—in the conquest of consciousness I can only say that I attach no intrinsic value to what means I use beyond their practical service in giving form to the living stuff of the imagination.

New conditions of life germinate new forms of spiritual articulation. And while I feel that my work includes a more consistent extension of traditional literary elements than many contemporary poets are capable of appraising, I realize that I am utilizing the gifts of the past as instruments principally; and that the voice of the present, if it is to be known, must be caught at the risk of speaking in idioms and circumlocutions sometimes shocking to the scholar and historians of logic. Language has built towers and bridges, but itself is inevitably as fluid as always.

PART II

# The 1930's

# THE SURVIVAL VALUES OF TRADITION

*introduction to*

I'LL TAKE MY STAND

This introductory statement should be seen in association with a number of essays by the twelve contributors, among them the essay that follows it, "Forms and Citizens" (from *The World's Body*, 1938). John Crowe Ransom (1888–    ), who wrote "Forms and Citizens," is largely responsible for the formulation of the following "Statement of Principles." The "Agrarian" volume of 1930 (*I'll Take My Stand*) states clearly, and not without some sharpness and hostility, the position of a number of Southern writers, economists, and historians. The lines of divergence and distinction are clearly drawn; there is no doubt of the polemical incentive. "Forms and Citizens" is, on the other hand, a critical essay, one of two on Milton's "Lycidas." Nevertheless, there are points in the latter which help to link the two pieces: particularly, Ransom's discussion of the "aesthetic" and the "economic" modes, his analysis of the purposes of the arts, and the statement concerning the "code" or "manners." The two essays should be considered as approaching similar issues (related to the question of a tradition) from two very different points of view.

*T*he authors contributing to this book are Southerners, well acquainted with one another and of similar tastes, though not necessarily living in the same physical community, and perhaps only at this moment aware of themselves as a single group of men. By conversation and exchange of letters over a number of years it had developed that they entertained many convictions in common, and it was decided to make a volume in which each one should furnish his views upon a chosen topic. This was the general background. But background and consultation as to the various topics were enough; there was to be no further collaboration. And so no single author is responsible for any view outside his own article. It was through the good fortune of some deeper agreement that the book was expected to achieve its unity. All the articles bear in the same sense upon the book's title-subject: all tend to support a Southern way of life against what may be called the American or prevailing way; and all as much as agree that the best terms in which to represent the distinction are contained in the phrase, Agrarian *versus* Industrial.

But after the book was under way it seemed a pity if the contributors, limited as they were within their special subjects, should stop short of showing how close their agreements really were. On the contrary, it seemed that they ought to go on and make themselves known as a group already consolidated by a set of principles which could be stated with a good deal of particularity. This might prove useful for the sake of future reference, if they should undertake any further joint publication. It was then decided to prepare a general introduction for the book which would state briefly the common convictions of the group. This is the statement. To it every one of the contributors in this book has subscribed.

Nobody now proposes for the South, or for any other community in this country, an independent political destiny. That idea is thought to have been finished in 1865. But how far shall the South surrender its moral, social, and economic autonomy to the victorious principle of Union? That question remains open. The South is a minority section that has hitherto been jealous of its minority right to live its own kind of life. The South scarcely hopes to determine the other sections, but it does propose to determine itself, within the utmost limits of legal action. Of late, however, there is the melancholy fact that the South itself has wavered a little and shown signs of wanting to join up behind the common or American industrial ideal. It is against that tendency that this book is written. The younger Southerners, who are being converted frequently to the industrial gospel, must come back to the support of the Southern tradition. They must be persuaded to look very critically at the advantages of becoming a "new South" which will be only an undistinguished replica of the usual industrial community.

But there are many other minority communities opposed to industrialism, and wanting a much simpler economy to live by. The communities and private persons sharing the agrarian tastes are to be found widely within the Union. Proper living is a matter of the intelligence and the will, does not depend on the local climate or geography, and is capable of a definition which is general and not Southern at all. Southerners have a filial duty to discharge to their own section. But their cause is precarious and they must seek alliances with sympathetic communities everywhere. The members of the present group would be happy to be counted as members of a national agrarian movement.

Industrialism is the economic organization of the collective American society. It means the decision of society to invest its economic resources in the applied sciences. But the word science has acquired a certain sanctitude. It is out of order to quarrel with science in the abstract, or even with the applied sciences when their applications are made subject to criticism and intelligence. The capitalization of the applied sciences has now become extravagant and uncritical; it has enslaved our human energies to a degree now clearly felt to be burdensome. The apologists of industrialism do not like to meet this charge directly; so they often take refuge in saying that they are devoted simply to science! They are really devoted to the applied sciences and to practical production. Therefore it is necessary to employ a certain skepticism even at the expense of the Cult of Science, and to say, It is an Americanism, which looks innocent and disinterested, but really is not either.

The contribution that science can make to a labor is to render it easier by the help of a tool or a process, and to assure the laborer of his perfect economic security while he is engaged upon it. Then it can be performed with leisure and enjoyment. But the modern laborer has not exactly received this benefit under the industrial regime. His labor is hard, its tempo is fierce, and his employment is insecure. The first principle of a good labor is that it must be effective, but the second principle is that it must be enjoyed. Labor is one of the largest items in the human career; it is a modest demand to ask that it may partake of happiness.

The regular act of applied science is to introduce into labor a labor-saving device or a machine. Whether this is a benefit depends on how far it is advisable to save the labor. The philosophy of applied science is generally quite sure that the saving of labor is a pure gain, and that the more of it the better. This is to assume that labor is an evil, that only the end of labor or the material product is good. On this assumption labor becomes mercenary and servile, and it is no wonder if many forms of modern labor are accepted without resentment though they are evidently brutalizing. The act of labor as one of the happy functions of human life has been in effect abandoned, and is practiced solely for its rewards.

Even the apologists of industrialism have been obliged to admit that some economic evils follow in the wake of the machines. These are such as overproduction, unemployment, and a growing inequality in the distribution of wealth. But the remedies proposed by the apologists are always homeopathic. They expect the evils to disappear when we have bigger and better machines, and more of them. Their remedial programs, therefore, look forward to more industrialism. Sometimes they see the system righting itself spontaneously and without direction: they are Optimists. Sometimes they rely on the benevolence of capital, or the militancy of labor, to bring about a fairer division of the spoils: they are

Coöperationists or Socialists. And sometimes they expect to find super-engineers, in the shape of Boards of Control, who will adapt production to consumption and regulate prices and guarantee business against fluctuations: they are Sovietists. With respect to these last it must be insisted that the true Sovietists or Communists—if the term may be used here in the European sense—are the Industrialists themselves. They would have the government set up an economic super-organization, which in turn would become the government. We therefore look upon the Communist menace as a menace indeed, but not as a Red one; because it is simply according to the blind drift of our industrial development to expect in America at last much the same economic system as that imposed by violence upon Russia in 1917.

Turning to consumption, as the grand end which justifies the evil of modern labor, we find that we have been deceived. We have more time in which to consume, and many more products to be consumed. But the tempo of our labors communicates itself to our satisfactions, and these also become brutal and hurried. The constitution of the natural man probably does not permit him to shorten his labor-time and enlarge his consuming-time indefinitely. He has to pay the penalty in satiety and aimlessness. The modern man has lost his sense of vocation.

Religion can hardly expect to flourish in an industrial society. Religion is our submission to the general intention of a nature that is fairly inscrutable; it is the sense of our rôle as creatures within it. But nature industrialized, transformed into cities and artificial habitations, manufactured into commodities, is no longer nature but a highly simplified picture of nature. We receive the illusion of having power over nature, and lose the sense of nature as something mysterious and contingent. The God of nature under these conditions is merely an amiable expression, a superfluity, and the philosophical understanding ordinarily carried in the religious experience is not there for us to have.

Nor do the arts have a proper life under industrialism, with the general decay of sensibility which attends it. Art depends, in general, like religion, on a right attitude to nature; and in particular on a free and disinterested observation of nature that occurs only in leisure. Neither the creation nor the understanding of works of art is possible in an industrial age except by some local and unlikely suspension of the industrial drive.

The amenities of life also suffer under the curse of a strictly-business or industrial civilization. They consist in such practices as manners, conversation, hospitality, sympathy, family life, romantic love—in the social exchanges which reveal and develop sensibility in human affairs. If religion and the arts are founded on right relations of man-to-nature, these are founded on right relations of man-to-man.

Apologists of industrialism are even inclined to admit that its actual processes may have upon its victims the spiritual effects just described. But they think that all can be made right by extraordinary educational efforts, by all sorts of cultural institutions and endowments. They would cure the poverty of the contemporary spirit by hiring experts to instruct it in spite of itself in the historic culture. But salvation is hardly to be encountered on that road. The trouble with the life-pattern is to be located at its economic base, and we cannot rebuild it by pouring in soft materials from the top. The young men and women in colleges, for example, if they are already placed in a false way of life, cannot make more than an inconsequential acquaintance with the arts and humanities transmitted to them. Or else the understanding of these arts and humanities will but make them the more wretched in their own destitution.

The "Humanists" are too abstract. Humanism, properly speaking, is not an abstract system, but a culture, the whole way in which we live, act, think, and feel. It is a kind of imaginatively balanced life lived out in a definite social tradition. And, in the concrete, we believe that this, the genuine humanism, was rooted in the agrarian life of the older South and of other parts of the country that shared in such a tradition. It was not an abstract moral "check" derived from the classics—it was not soft material poured in from the top. It was deeply founded in the way of life itself—in its tables, chairs, portraits, festivals, laws, marriage customs. We cannot recover our native humanism by adopting some standard of taste that is critical enough to question the contemporary arts but not critical enough to question the social and economic life which is their ground.

The tempo of the industrial life is fast, but that is not the worst of it; it is accelerating. The ideal is not merely some set form of industrialism, with so many stable industries, but industrial progress, or an incessant extension of industrialization. It never proposes a specific goal; it initiates the infinite series. We have not merely capitalized certain industries; we have capitalized the laboratories and inventors, and undertaken to employ all the labor-saving devices that come out of them. But a fresh labor-saving device introduced into an industry does not emancipate the laborers in that industry so much as it evicts them. Applied at the expense of agriculture, for example, the new processes have reduced the part of the population supporting itself upon the soil to a smaller and smaller fraction. Of course no single labor-saving process is fatal; it brings on a period of unemployed labor and unemployed capital, but soon a new industry is devised which will put them both to work again, and a new commodity is thrown upon the market. The laborers were sufficiently embarrassed in the meantime, but, according to the theory, they will eventually be taken care of. It is now the public which is embarrassed; it feels obligated to purchase a commodity for which it had expressed no desire, but it is invited to make its budget equal to the strain. All might yet be well, and stability and comfort might again obtain, but for this: partly because of industrial ambitions and partly because the repressed creative impulse must break out somewhere, there will be a stream of further labor-saving devices in all industries, and the cycle will have to be repeated over and over. The result is an increasing disadjustment and instability.

It is an inevitable consequence of industrial progress that production greatly outruns the rate of natural consumption. To overcome the disparity, the producers, disguised as the pure idealists of progress, must coerce and wheedle the public into being loyal and steady consumers, in order to keep the machines running. So the rise of modern advertising —along with its twin, personal salesmanship—is the most significant development of our industrialism. Advertising means to persuade the consumers to want exactly what the applied sciences are able to furnish them. It consults the happiness of the consumer no more than it consulted the happiness of the laborer. It is the great effort of a false economy of life to approve itself. But its task grows more difficult every day.

It is strange, of course, that a majority of men anywhere could ever as with one mind become enamored of industrialism: a system that has so little regard for individual wants. There is evidently a kind of thinking that rejoices in setting up a social objective which has no relation to the individual. Men are prepared to sacrifice their private dignity and happiness to an abstract social ideal, and without asking whether the social ideal produces the welfare of any individual man whatsoever. But this is absurd. The responsibility of men is for their own welfare and that of their neighbors; not for the hypothetical welfare of some fabulous creature called society.

Opposed to the industrial society is the agrarian, which does not stand in particular need of definition. An agrarian society is hardly one that has no use at all for industries, for professional vocations, for scholars and artists, and for the life of cities. Technically, perhaps, an agrarian society is one in which agriculture is the leading vocation, whether for wealth, for pleasure, or for prestige—a form of labor that is pursued with intelligence and leisure, and that becomes the model to which the other forms approach as well as they may. But an agrarian regime will be secured readily enough where the superfluous industries are not allowed to rise against it. The theory of agrarianism is that the culture of the soil is the best and most sensitive of vocations, and that therefore it should have the economic preference and enlist the maximum number of workers.

These principles do not intend to be very specific in proposing any practical measures. How may the little agrarian community resist the Chamber of Commerce of its county seat, which is always trying to import some foreign industry that cannot be assimilated to the life-pattern of the community? Just what must the Southern leaders do to defend the traditional Southern life? How may the Southern and the Western agrarians unite for effective action? Should the agrarian forces try to capture the Democratic party, which historically is so closely affiliated with the defense of individualism, the small community, the state, the South? Or must the agrarians—even the Southern ones—

abandon the Democratic party to its fate and try a new one? What legislation could most profitably be championed by the powerful agrarians in the Senate of the United States? What anti-industrial measures might promise to stop the advances of industrialism, or even undo some of them, with the least harm to those concerned? What policy should be pursued by the educators who have a tradition at heart? These and many other questions are of the greatest importance, but they cannot be answered here.

For, in conclusion, this much is clear: If a community, or a section, or a race, or an age, is groaning under industrialism, and well aware that it is an evil dispensation, it must find the way to throw it off. To think that this cannot be done is pusillanimous. And if the whole community, section, race, or age thinks it cannot be done, then it has simply lost its political genius and doomed itself to impotence.

## NORMAN FOERSTER

# Humanism in the Twentieth Century (Part II)

This excerpt from *Toward Standards* by Norman Foerster (1887–    ) is a summary of the Humanist position. The emphasis is upon moral standards, which are intended to suggest, or to be suggested by, both aesthetic and psychological values and effects. The modern Humanist interpretation of literature dates from the beginning of the century, but there was a concentration of its activities in 1930, as though the challenge of a decade of leftist criticism about to begin had stimulated a special effort on the part of other types of critics to define their purposes and aims.

*S*ome of the most cherished enthusiasms of the naturistic age, such as progress, romanticism, democracy, nationalism, have lost their warmth; the ultimate competence of science is questioned; realistic and naturalistic art appears to have entered upon disintegration and decadence. The great war has brought in its train a mood of disillusionment unfavorable to the reigning ideas of the century that culminated in the war, and a growing sense of the need for both social and intellectual reconstruction. The skepticism formerly applied to the wisdom of the ages is now frequently applied to the wisdom of our own age. Although much of this new skepticism is as puerile and wholesale as the old, more and more of it is drawing to the support of a genuinely critical movement that may be traced back, in this country, to Emerson and Lowell.

Emerson and Lowell were by no means wholly committed to the modern programme. Their vital memories reached far into the past, Lowell's to Dante and Emerson's to Plato. With an integrity equal to our own, they refused to accept anything on authority and submitted all tradition to free inquiry, seeking to disengage the permanent from the transitory elements in tradition and to reconcile the permanent elements with whatever appeared to be sound in the modern programme. Their task was continued by Charles Eliot Norton, and in the next generation by a number of critics and scholars who have been called "the new humanists."

These all attend to one or another phase of the cleavage between man's way and nature's way—a dualism which, whether it cut between man and external nature, or between the "natural man" and the "spiritual man" within; whether it emphasize the "inner check" in any of its various modes, or, as against the naturalistic "education of the senses," commend to man the study of his own humane tradition, and summon him to take up the racial torch and hand it on—in any case places man's hope not upon what nature, whether within or without, may do for him, but upon his making himself more completely human.[1]

This is a broad statement of a creed that has in recent years steadily acquired fresh adherents and fresh formulation.[2] The strength of this critical movement may be measured by the vehemence of the attacks upon it by the defenders of the old naturism. They object to the sharp clearness of the humanist creed, yet show their failure to understand it —condemning it, paradoxically, as both classical in its emphasis on form and romantic in its emphasis on imagination and also as both intellectualistic and moralistic ("puritanical"). If it is indeed all of these, it would seem to be immune from the charge which they press most violently of all: that it is rigid and narrow.

These attacks appeal to prejudices that have been fixed in our minds by naturistic modes of thought. A better way to consider the reconstruction proposed by the new humanism would be to examine its fundamental assumptions.

The first of these assumptions is that assumptions are inevitable, since every conception of life ultimately rests upon them. Absolute skepticism, if there were such a thing, would rest upon the assumption that unlimited doubt is necessary, a position that not even Anatole France was willing to take:

---

[1] *Cambridge History of American Literature*, IV, p. 491.
[2] The "new humanists" named in the *Cambridge History* are Paul Elmer More, Irving Babbitt, John Jay Chapman, and George Edward Woodberry. To these might be added W. C. Brownell, F. J. Mather, Jr., P. H. Frye, William F. Giese, Barry Cerf, Samuel Strauss, Stuart P. Sherman (especially in his earlier work), Robert Shafer, P. H. Houston, G. R. Elliott, and younger men whose names are less familiar.

I have feared those two words, full of a formidable sterility, "I doubt." So powerful are they that the mouth that has once pronounced them truly is for ever sealed, and can never reopen. If one doubts, one must keep silent; for, whatever one may discourse about, to speak is to affirm. Since I had not the courage for silence and renunciation, I willed to believe and did so. I at least believed in the relativity of things, and the succession of phenomena.[3]

Practically, silence is impossible, absolute skepticism is impossible. Practically, we live by belief, by faith, by that which we provisionally *know*: that which appears to us most nearly to correspond with reality, or rather with experience, or rather still with those portions of experience that we choose to value. Shrinking from the specter of sterility— that everlasting No—we make our affirmations, today no less than in the past, identifying our belief with the truth. Of this fact few naturists in our time seem to be aware. For the most part they dogmatically affirm that they can know and explain man and the universe, and patiently proceed to reduce everything in experience to a deterministic monism. In order to attain this conclusion, they assume, first, the final validity of reason, declaring their perfect faith in it, despite the testimony of the history of philosophy that faith in reason may lead to bewilderingly diverse doctrines. They therefore assume, secondly, that the reality to be explored by reason is the succession of phenomena, the realm of physical science; and thirdly, that whatever experience appears to conflict with this reality must be explained—if necessary, explained away— in terms of this natural reality. Such are the assumptions of our current naturistic thought that prides itself upon its avoidance of mere "faith"; such are the assumptions that underlie the great bulk of our so-called realistic and naturalistic literature, and of the criticism that interprets and encourages this literature. These assumptions we may now compare with the further assumptions of humanism.

Humanism assumes, secondly, that the essential elements of human experience are precisely those which appear to conflict with the reality explored by naturism. It recognizes, indeed, the service of naturism: the service of romanticism in showing the power of the natural man's impulses, the service of biology in showing the physical union of man with nature, the service of psychology in showing the instinctive processes that man shares with other forms of life; for thus has been demonstrated, if nothing else, the magnitude of the problem of morality. Yet exactly here, in the realm of the moral or specifically human, our modern faith is impotent. Nature, apparently blind and pitiless, indifferent to all that we value most, affords no light in our search for a *modus vivendi* in a state of society. In vain do we seek in her for standards of justice, self-restraint, moderation, gentleness; in vain for a principle of rational or spiritual guidance adequate for human life as we know it. The ethical problem cannot be illuminated by a naturistic philosophy which merely

[3] *On Life and Letters,* Third Series, xi. So, too, Plato had thought that a faithful sensationalism must be speechless.

affirms, optimistically or pessimistically, that man is motivated by natural instinct, or informs us, at best, how his moral habits may be "explained" by the process of evolution. In the motion picture of reality that science offers there are no values, but only quantitative measurements of force, mass, etc. Yet values are in fact the main concern of man, the perennial object of his ardent striving.[4]

Accordingly, the central assumption of humanism is that of a dualism of man and nature, as opposed to the monism assumed by naturism. Conceding, with Emerson, the possibility that the contrasting realms of the human and the natural might be reconciled if we could behold them both *ab extra*—that in the highest view the ancient maxim "Know Thyself" and the modern "Study Nature" may offer two approaches to the same reality—humanism is skeptical of all such speculation based upon the assumption of an underlying unity and is convinced that, practically, the rightful concern of man is his humanity, his world of value and quality that marks him off from a merely quantitative natural order.

In assuming this dualism, humanism appeals to the authority of the actual experience of mankind, past and present. Of the trend of past experience there can be no doubt; both of the old guiding traditions, the Greek and the Christian, however different outwardly, were absolutely at one in their sharp contrast between the human and the natural. Scarcely more doubtful is the trend of present experience; even in an age when the official philosophy is monistic, the working philosophy of the vast majority of mankind is still dualistic. Men are still conscious of an inner conflict, insusceptible of reconciliation, between the expression of natural desire and the will to conform to a standard of values. The failure of naturism to define new values has resulted in the continued application of the essentials of the classical and Christian traditions, even on the part of countless persons who profess the rejection of all tradition. Few indeed are those who are living "according to nature," expressing the "self" (that is, temperament) in disregard of convention without and inhibition within; most men are still living "according to society," patterning themselves in harmony with a general code and consequently restraining themselves. It is still the belief of most men (if by no means their invariable practice) that perfection is a worthy end, that it depends upon the control of the natural by the human, and that it necessitates loyalty to standards of truth and justice which cannot be conceived as

---

[4] Science measures what are significantly called *facts*, i.e., things done, phenomenal happenings viewed in retrospect. It believes that all the facts can be found, and that when they have been found, it will also be able to predict succeeding steps in evolution. These steps could then be measured quantitatively. A few less confident scientists, however, believe that, even if our knowledge of the past were complete, we could discern nothing in the past that would enable us to foresee the variations of the future. They thus point to a differentiating principle of pivotal importance, and confess their inability, as scientists, to deal with it.

natural but which are none the less binding. On the one side is the inclination of nature, sufficient for the conduct of the animal creation but insufficient for the conduct of man; on the other side, the authority of conscience (which remains a fact, even when "accounted for") and the authority of the laws, written and unwritten, that give direction to the activities of the conscience. These laws are the product of the convention-making power that man incessantly exerts, in revolutionary no less than in stable ages:

> As if his whole vocation
> Were endless imitation.

Of necessity, a natural, spontaneous action is rare, since, even when only once repeated, it is already in danger of moving toward a convention or social habit. Unconventionality itself quickly becomes conventional, as one may observe, in any period, among the young or the old who cultivate emancipation from conventions that do not please them. Thus do the most natural people bear witness to their humanity.

Finally, humanism assumes the freedom of the will to conform to a standard of values, as opposed to the deterministic assumption of naturism. While acknowledging that reason leads readily to a belief in necessity, whether that necessity be spiritual or mechanical, humanism is unwilling to follow reason when it proposes a conclusion at variance with the manifest facts of experience. It is a matter of universal experience that we assume our power to will our next actions; life appears to be impossible on other terms. Common sense, as well as intuition, dictates the assumption of choice. This is the precarious but ineluctable dignity of man, clearly affirmed by Greek humanism and by Christianity, confusedly promulgated by a romanticism that lost itself in nature, and still accepted in practice by a scientific age that rejects it in theory. We may believe, like Browning's Andrea, that we are in God's hand, or, like the behaviorist, that we are in Nature's hand, and yet actually we shall proceed to carry out the actions we have determined upon, in the conviction that they represent our own free choice. While the ultimate criterion of our actions may be God or Nature, in either case we assume, along with the Victorian Tennyson, that

> Our wills are ours, to make them thine,

and along with the mediæval Dante, that

> . . . la sua volontate è nostra pace.

In judging the acts of our fellows in the intercourse of daily life, we assume that they also are free to choose, or, as we prefer to say when their actions affect ourselves, that they are *responsible* for what they do. Our theoretical belief in the sovereignty of Providence or in the fatality of instinct and environment is forgotten in the practical experience of life.

Such have always been the assumptions of humanism. In opposition to the assumptions of naturism—first, that it makes no assumptions, secondly, that reason is the only sure guide, thirdly, that the reality found by reason consists of the phenomenal order, and fourthly, that no specifically human reality exists—humanism today, as in the past, assumes, first, that assumptions are unavoidable, secondly, that the essential reality of experience is not natural but ethical, thirdly, that there is a sharp dualism between man and nature, and fourthly, that man's will is free. Reflecting upon life in the light of these premises, humanism arrives at a doctrine and a discipline that may be briefly stated as follows:

1. An adequate human standard calls for *completeness;* it demands the cultivation of every part of human nature, including "natural" human nature. It suppresses nothing.

2. But it also calls for *proportion:* it demands the harmony of the parts with the whole. Instead of "accepting life" indiscriminately, it imposes a scale of values.

3. This complete, proportionate standard may be said to consist of the *normally or typically human.* It is concerned with the central and the universal, not the eccentric and the idiosyncratic. It is concerned with a permanently valid ethos, not with any temporary code of conventional society.

4. Although such an ethos has never existed, it has been approximated in the great ages of *the past,* to which humanism accordingly looks for guidance. It looks chiefly toward Greece, where it still finds its best examples (in sculpture, in Homer and Sophocles, in Plato and Aristotle); also toward Rome (Virgil, Horace), toward the Christian tradition (Jesus, Paul, Augustine, Francis of Assisi), toward the Orient (Buddha, Confucius), toward moderns like Shakespeare, Milton, and Goethe. Selecting the "constants" that appear to be worthy of preservation, humanism seeks to transcend the specialism that limits all ages in the past as well as the present age.

5. Unlike romanticism, which in its quest of a natural ethos repudiated the logical faculty, humanism is always true to its Hellenic origin in its faith in *reason.* It seeks to deal positively with the whole of experience, including those elements of experience that do not fall within the scope of what is termed science.

6. Unlike the conceptions of life that grow out of science, humanism seeks to press beyond reason by the use of *intuition* or *imagination,* following the example of the most poetical of Hellenic philosophers, who resorted again and again to symbol and myth, and the example of the foremost Christian poet when he forsook the guidance of Virgil in favor of that of Beatrice. Humanism holds that, after reason has brought us before the veil that shrouds truth, a power above the reason is needed to cope with what Goethe termed "the illusion of a higher reality." This power above the reason is the human or ethical imagina-

tion, as distinguished from the natural or pathetic imagination, which is below the reason.[5]

7. The ultimate ethical principle is that of *restraint* or *control*, indicated alike by practical experience and by the light of reason and the ethical imagination. There is a law for man and a law for thing. That which is law in nature becomes anarchy when surrendered to by man— the anarchy of wandering desires and blind impulses, the morbid ebb and flow of unhindered temperament, the restless oscillations of expansive pride and expansive sympathy. This anarchy is the product of romanticism and naturalism in their pure state, that is, when they do not wittingly or unwittingly draw upon the humanistic or religious tradition. As Coleridge perceived,

> The Sensual and the Dark rebel in vain,
> Slaves by their own compulsion!

Freedom and power and happiness cannot be won by those who practice the modern philosophy of what is loosely termed "self-expression." They can be won only when the energies of the instinctive self have been harnessed by the ethical self:

> The winged Courser, like a gen'rous Horse,
> Shows most true Mettle when you *check* his Course.

Humanism remembers, to be sure, that the Popean neo-classicists as well as the Puritans, instead of checking the steed, generally locked him in the stable, where he might indeed rebel in vain; it remembers always the need of freedom, which it defines as liberation from outer constraints and subjection to inner law. It asserts that this inner law of concentration, when it has eagerly expansive senses and emotional energies to command, is the true source of power, of character, of elevation, of happiness.[6]

---

[5] The excellence of Greek art may be said to lie in its success in achieving unified form while suggesting an ethical infinite. The romantic critics employed an insidious flattery when they credited Greek art with executing its humanistic aim "in the utmost perfection," in contrast with modern art, which "can only do justice to its endeavors after what is infinite by approximation." (A. W. Schlegel, *Dramatic Art and Literature*, Lecture 1; cf. Coleridge, *Works*, IV, p. 29, and Lowell, *Prose Works*, IV, pp. 232–35, *Poetical Works*, IV, pp. 45–46.) This contrast between the Greek perfection within fixed limits and the modern imperfection arising from infinite aspiration involves a twofold confusion: first, a confusion of the Christian aspiration toward the Infinite with the romantic yearning for the limitless and indefinite, the one quenching desire and the other exalting it; and secondly, a confusion of the classical aspiration toward an ethical infinite with the romantic yearning for the limitless and indefinite. The scholarship of the nineteenth century has made it clear that the Greeks, even in the "definite" forms of their sculpture, sought to express, as Professor Gardner says, an "inexhaustible idealism"— an endless approximation.

[6] H. S. Canby has well described (*Definitions*, 1922, pp. 165–66) the "anti-Puritans" of twentieth-century literature who, assuming that all things

8. This center to which humanism refers everything, this centripetal energy which counteracts the multifarious centrifugal impulses, this magnetic will which draws the flux of our sensations toward it while itself remaining at rest, is the reality that gives rise to religion. Pure humanism is content to describe it thus in physical terms, as an observed fact of experience; it hesitates to pass beyond its experimental knowledge to the dogmatic affirmations of any of the great religions. It cannot bring itself to accept a formal theology (any more than it can accept a romantic idealism) that has been set up in defiance of reason, for it holds that the value of supernatural intuition must be tested by the intellect. Again, it fears the asceticism to which religion tends in consequence of a too harsh dualism of the flesh and the spirit, for, as we have said, humanism calls for completeness, wishing to use and not annihilate dangerous forces. Unlike religion, it assigns an important place to the instruments of both science and art. Nevertheless, it agrees with religion in its perception of the ethical will as a power above the ordinary self, an impersonal reality in which all men may share despite the diversity of personal temperament and toward which their attitude must be one of subjection. This perception, immensely strengthened for us by Christianity, was already present in the humanism of the

---

have been proved false except their desires, make a philosophy of these desires. Their truth they derive from psychoanalysis, which they interpret to be a scientific justification of the frank expression of desires. They are quite unaware, however, that the traditional humanistic and religious values actually hold an important place in the popular books on psychotherapy. Dr. A. F. Riggs, for example, tells us that animals act "presumably without choice or without reason. On the other hand, the human being presides over the conflict of his own instincts, felt by him as a conflict of emotions. He presides over this conflict with intelligence and with a consciousness of the power and necessity of choice." "It is like guiding spirited horses—you guide, they obey, not their own impulse, but your will." "It is when intelligence and will are used to realize an ideal through an action which is contrary to instinctive demands, that animal behavior rises to the dignity of human conduct." (Just Nerves, 1922.) In another book Dr. J. A. Jackson and Helen M. Salisbury inform us that "Character is what we do with our instincts. . . . We may follow our primal desires, we may deny their existence, or we may use them for ends which are in harmony with our lives as we want them to be." "What Paul calls the law of his members warring against the law of his mind is simply what we call today the instinctive desires coming into conflict with our conscious ideal." (Outwitting Our Nerves, 1922.) In a third book we may read that Jesus, the perfect man, illustrates "the right expression of power. He exerts it over himself, and on behalf of others. His self-mastery is complete, so that the claims of body and mind are acceded to or denied at will." He is contrasted with "the primitive man, whose instinctive energy pushes forth to destroy rather than to build up." (G. Coster, Psychoanalysis for Normal People, 1926.) All of these books call to us, with the ancient Greek sage, "Know Thyself," and exhort us to conversion, which they term sublimation, and to the quest of salvation, which they term mental and physical health (mens sana in corpore sano). Their psychology is new, after all, chiefly in showing the power and the subtlety of that instinctive life the control of which renders man human. The humanist may be grateful for this new light on the appetitive principle in the Aristotelian ethics; the religionist, for this new light on the devil.

Greeks, who saw that the unpardonable sin is insolence or presumption, an overweening pride of passion or reason, a failure to be mindful of the Nemesis that lies in wait for disproportionate self-assertion. Humanism, no less than religion, enjoins the virtue of *humility*.

From what has been said, it should be clear that humanism, like Greek philosophy, "begins with science and not with religion," and that it is "a serious endeavor to understand the world and man, having for its chief aim the discovery of the right way of life and the conversion of people to it." [7]

### YVOR WINTERS

## Preliminary Problems

This statement of critical problems by Yvor Winters (1900– ) originally headed the volume *The Anatomy of Nonsense* (1943) and was designed principally to defend and explain Winters' practice of evaluation, which he has demonstrated throughout his career. The key words are "rational" and "control," applied both to the criticism and to the creation of poetry. Winters believes that the creative act is above all a moral act, one which demonstrates in form and diction the balance, or lack of it, of the poet, and his view of the human condition. What distinguishes Winters from the Humanists is that he actually does attend to formal problems, while the Humanists rarely do, being satisfied to rely on several critical metaphors to sustain their judgments of the moral values in literature.

### First Problem

*I*s it possible to say that Poem A (one of Donne's *Holy Sonnets,* or one of the poems of Jonson or of Shakespeare) is better than Poem B (Collins' *Ode to Evening*) or vice versa?

If not, is it possible to say that either of these is better than Poem C (*The Cremation of Sam Magee,* or something comparable)?

If the answer is no in both cases, then any poem is as good as any other. If this is true, then all poetry is worthless; but this obviously is not true, for it is contrary to all our experience.

If the answer is yes in both cases, then there follows the question of

[7] Such is J. Burnet's characterization of the central spirit of Greek philosophy, *The Legacy of Greece,* p. 58.

whether the answer implies merely that one poem is better than another for the speaker, or whether it means that one poem is intrinsically better than another. If the former, then we are impressionists, which is to say relativists; and are either mystics of the type of Emerson, or hedonists of the type of Stevens and Ransom. If the latter, then we assume that constant principles govern the poetic experience, and that the poem (as likewise the judge) must be judged in relationship to those principles. It is important, therefore, to discover the consequences of assuming each of these positions.

If our answer to the first question is no and to the second yes, then we are asserting that we can distinguish between those poems which are of the canon and those which are not, but that within the canon all judgment is impossible. This view, if adopted, will require serious elucidation, for on the face of it, it appears inexplicable. On the other hand, one cannot deny that within the canon judgment will become more difficult, for the nearer two poems may be to the highest degrees of excellence, the harder it will be to choose between them. Two poems, in fact, might be so excellent that there would be small profit in endeavoring to say that one was better, but one could arrive at this conclusion only after a careful examination of both.

## Second Problem

If we accept the view that one poem can be regarded as better than another, the question then arises whether this judgment is a matter of inexplicable intuition, or whether it is a question of intuition that can be explained, and consequently guided and improved by rational elucidation.

If we accept the view that the judgment in question is inexplicable, then we are again forced to confess ourselves impressionists and relativists, unless we can show that the intuitions of all men agree at all times, or that the intuitions of one man are invariably right and those of all others wrong whenever they differ. We obviously can demonstrate neither of these propositions.

If we start, then, with the proposition that one poem may be intrinsically superior to another, we are forced to account for differences of opinion regarding it. If two critics differ, it is possible that one is right and the other wrong, more likely that both are partly right and partly wrong, but in different respects: neither the native gifts nor the education of any man have ever been wholly adequate to many of the critical problems he will encounter, and no two men are ever the same in these respects or in any others. On the other hand, although the critic should display reasonable humility and caution, it is only fair to add that few men possess either the talent or the education to justify their being taken very seriously, even of those who are nominally professional students of these matters.

But if it is possible by rational elucidation to give a more or less clear account of what one finds in a poem and why one approves or disapproves, then communication between two critics, though no doubt imperfect, becomes possible, and it becomes possible that they may in some measure correct each other's errors and so come more near to a true judgment of the poem.

## Third Problem

If rational communication about poetry is to take place, it is necessary first to determine what we mean by a poem.

A poem is first of all a statement in words.

But it differs from all such statements of a purely philosophical or theoretical nature, in that it has by intention a controlled content of feeling. In this respect, it does not differ from many works written in prose, however.

A poem differs from a work written in prose by virtue of its being composed in verse. The rhythm of verse permits the expression of more powerful feeling than is possible in prose when such feeling is needed, and it permits at all times the expression of finer shades of feeling.

A poem, then, is a statement in words in which special pains are taken with the expression of feeling. This description is merely intended to distinguish the poem from other kinds of writing; it is not offered as a complete description.

## Fourth Problem

What, however, are words?

They are audible sounds, or their visual symbols, invented by man to communicate his thoughts and feelings. Each word has a conceptual content, however slight; each word, exclusive, perhaps, of the particles, communicates vague associations of feeling.

The word *fire* communicates a concept; it also connotes very vaguely certain feelings, depending on the context in which we happen to place it—depending, for example, on whether we happen to think of a fire on a hearth, in a furnace, or in a forest. These feelings may be rendered more and more precise as we render the context more and more precise; as we come more and more near to completing and perfecting our poem.

## Fifth Problem

But if the poem, as compared to prose, pays especial attention to feeling, are we to assume that the rational content of the poem is unimportant to its success?

The rational content cannot be eliminated from words; consequently the rational content cannot be eliminated from poetry. It is there. If it is unsatisfactory in itself, a part of the poem is unsatisfactory; the poem is thus damaged beyond argument. If we deny this, we must surely explain ourselves very fully.

If we admit this, we are faced with another problem: is it conceivable that rational content and feeling-content may both be perfect, and yet that they may be unrelated to each other, or imperfectly related? To me this is inconceivable, because the emotional content of words is generated by our experience with the conceptual content, so that a relationship is necessary.

This fact of the necessity of such relationship may fairly return us for a moment to the original question: whether imperfection of rational content damages the entire poem. If there is a necessary relationship between concept and feeling, and concept is unsatisfactory, then feeling must be damaged by way of the relationship.

## Sixth Problem

If there is a relationship between concept and feeling, what is the nature of that relationship?

To answer this, let us return to the basic unit, the word. The concept represented by the word motivates the feeling which the word communicates. It is the concept of fire which generates the feelings communicated by the word, though the sound of the word may modify these feelings very subtly, as may other accidental qualities, especially if the word be used skillfully in a given context. The accidental qualities of a word, however, such as its literary history, for example, can only modify, cannot essentially change, for these will be governed ultimately by the concept; that is, *fire* will seldom be used to signify *plum-blossom,* and so will have few opportunities to gather connotations from the concept, *plum-blossom.* The relationship, in the poem, between rational statement and feeling, is thus seen to be that of motive to emotion.

## Seventh Problem

But has not this reasoning brought us back to the proposition that all poems are equally good? For if each word motivates its own feeling, because of its intrinsic nature, will not any rational statement, since it is composed of words, motivate the feeling exactly proper to it?

This is not true, for a good many reasons, of which I shall enumerate only a few of the more obvious. In making a rational statement, in purely theoretical prose, we find that our statement may be loose or exact, depending upon the relationships of the words to each other. The precision of a word depends to some extent upon its surroundings. This is true likewise with respect to the connotations of words. Two words, each of which has several usably close rational synonyms, may reinforce and clarify each other with respect to their connotations or they may not do so.

Let me illustrate with a simple example from Browning's *Serenade at the Villa:*

> So wore night; the East was gray,
> White the broad-faced hemlock flowers.

The lines are marred by a crowding of long syllables and difficult consonants, but they have great beauty in spite of the fault. What I wish to point out, for the sake of my argument, is the relationship between the words *wore* and *gray.* The verb *wore* means literally that the night passed, but it carries with it connotations of exhaustion and attrition which belong to the condition of the protagonist; and grayness is a color which we associate with such a condition. If we change the phrase to read: "Thus night passed," we shall have the same rational meaning, and a meter quite as respectable, but no trace of the power of the line: the connotation of *wore* will be lost, and the connotation of *gray* will remain merely in a state of ineffective potentiality. The protagonist in seeing his feeling mirrored in the landscape is not guilty of motivating his feeling falsely, for we know his general motive from the poem as a whole; he is expressing a portion of the feeling motivated by the total situation through a more or less common psychological phenomenon. If the poem were such, however, that we did not know why the night *wore* instead of *passed,* we should have just cause for complaint; in fact, most of the strength of the word would probably be lost. The second line contains other fine effects, immediately with reference to the first line, ultimately with reference to the theme; I leave the reader to analyze them for himself, but he will scarcely succeed without the whole poem before him.

Concepts, as represented by particular words, are affected by connotations due to various and curious accidents. A word may gather connotations from its use in folk-poetry, in formal poetry, in vulgar speech, or in technical prose: a single concept might easily be represented by four words with these distinct histories; and any one of the words might prove to be proper in a given poetic context. Words gain connotation from etymological accidents. Something of this may be seen in the English word *outrage,* in which is commonly felt, in all likelihood, something associated with *rage,* although there is no rage whatever in the original word. Similarly the word *urchin,* in modern English, seldom connotes anything related to hedgehogs, or to the familiars of the witches, by whose intervention the word arrived at its modern meaning and feeling. Yet the connotation proper to any stage in the history of such a word might be resuscitated, or a blend of connotations effected, by skillful use. Further, the connotation of a word may be modified very strongly by its function in the metrical structure, a matter which I shall discuss at length in connection with the theories of Ransom.

This is enough to show that exact motivation of feeling by concept is not inherent in any rational statement. Any rational statement will govern the general possibilities of feeling derivable from it, but the task of the poet is to adjust feeling to motive precisely. He has to select words containing not only the right relationships within themselves, but the right relationships to each other. The task is very difficult; and this is no doubt the reason why the great poetry of a great poet is likely to be very small in bulk.

## Eighth Problem

Is it not possible, however, to escape from this relationship of motive to emotion by confining ourselves very largely to those words which denote emotion: love, envy, anger, and the like?

This is not possible, for these words, like others, represent concepts. If we should confine ourselves strictly to such a vocabulary, we should merely write didactic poetry: poetry about love in general, or about anger in general. The emotion communicated would result from our apprehension of the ideas in question. Such poetry is perfectly legitimate, but it is only one kind of poetry, and it is scarcely the kind which the Romantic theorist is endeavoring to define.

Such poetry has frequently been rendered particular by the use of allegory. The playful allegorizing of minor amoristic themes which one encounters in the Renaissance and which is possibly descended from certain neo-Platonic elements in medieval poetry may serve as illustration. Let us consider these and the subsequent lines by Thomas Lodge:

> Love in my bosom like a bee
>   Doth suck his sweet;
> Now with his wings he plays with me,
>   Now with his feet.

Love itself is a very general idea and might include many kinds of experience; the idea is limited by this allegory to the sentimental and sensual, but we still have an idea, the subdivision of the original idea, and the feeling must be appropriate to the concept. The concept is rendered concrete by the image of Cupid, whose actions, in turn, are rendered visible by comparison to the bee: it is these actions which make the poem a kind of anticipatory meditation on more or less sensual love, a meditation which by its mere tone of expression keeps the subject in its proper place as a very minor one. Sometimes the emphasis is on the mere description of the bee, sometimes on the description of Cupid, sometimes on the lover's feeling; but the feeling motivated in any passage is governed by this emphasis. The elements, once they are united in the poem, are never really separated, of course. In so far as the poet departs from his substantial theme in the direction of mere bees and flowers, he will achieve what Ransom calls irrelevance; but if there is much of this the poem will be weakened. Whether he so departs or not, the relation of motive to emotion must remain the same, within each passage. I have discussed this problem in my essay on Ransom.

A common romantic practice is to use words denoting emotions, but to use them loosely and violently, as if the very carelessness expressed emotion. Another is to make a general statement, but seem to refer it to a particular occasion, which, however, is never indicated: the poet thus seems to avoid the didactic, yet he is not forced to understand the particular motive. Both these faults may be seen in these lines from Shelley:

> Out of the day and night
> A joy has taken flight;
> Fresh spring, and summer, and winter hoar,
> Move my faint heart with grief, but with delight
> No more—oh, never more.

The poet's intention is so vague, however, that he achieves nothing but stereotypes of a very crude kind.

The Romantics often tried other devices. For example, it would be possible to write a poem on fear in general, but to avoid in some measure the effect of the purely didactic by illustrating the emotion along the way with various experiences which might motivate fear. There is a danger here, though it is merely a danger, that the general idea may not dominate the poem, and that the poem may thus fall apart into a group of poems on particular experiences. There is the alternative danger, that the particular quality of the experiences may be so subordinated to the illustrative function of the experiences, that within each illustration there is merely a stereotyped and not a real relationship of motive to feeling: this occurs in Collins' *Ode to Fear*, though a few lines in the Epode come surprisingly to life. But the methods which I have just described really offer no semblance of an escape from the theory of motivation which I am defending.

Another Romantic device, if it is conscious enough to be called a device, is to offer instead of a defensible motive a false one, usually culled from landscape. This kind of writing represents a tacit admission of the principle of motivation which I am defending, but a bad application of the principle. It results in the kind of writing which I have called pseudo-reference in my volume, *Primitivism and Decadence*. One cannot believe, for example, that Wordsworth's passions were charmed away by a look at the daffodils, or that Shelley's were aroused by the sight of the leaves blown about in the autumn wind. A motive is offered, and the poet wants us to accept it, but we recognize it as inadequate. In such a poem there may be fragments of good description, which motivate a feeling more or less purely appropriate to the objects described, and these fragments may sustain our liking for the poem: this happens in Collins' *Ode to Evening*; but one will find also an account of some kind of emotion essentially irrelevant to the objects described, along with the attempt, more or less explicit, to deduce the emotion from the object.

There remains the method of the Post-Romantics, whether French Symbolists or American Experimentalists: the method of trying to extinguish the rational content of language while retaining the content of association. This method I have discussed in *Primitivism and Decadence,* and I shall discuss it again in this book.

## Ninth Problem

The relationship in the poem of rational meaning to feeling we have seen to be that of motive to emotion; and we have seen that this must be a satisfactory relationship. How do we determine whether such a relationship is satisfactory? We determine it by an act of moral judgment. The question then arises whether moral judgments can be made, whether the concept of morality is or is not an illusion.

If morality can be considered real, if a theory of morality can be said to derive from reality, it is because it guides us toward the greatest happiness which the accidents of life permit: that is, toward the fullest realization of our nature, in the Aristotelian or Thomistic sense. But is there such a thing, abstractly considered, as full realization of our nature?

To avoid discussion of too great length, let us consider the opposite question: is there such a thing as obviously unfulfilled human nature? Obviously there is. We need only turn to the feeble-minded, who can not think and so cannot perceive or feel with any clarity; or to the insane, who sometimes perceive and feel with great intensity, but whose feelings and perceptions are so improperly motivated that they are classed as illusions. At slightly higher levels, the criminal, the dissolute, the unscrupulously selfish, and various types of neurotics are likely to arouse but little disagreement as examples.

Now if we are able to recognize the fact of insanity—if in fact we are forced to recognize it—that is, the fact of the obvious maladjustment of feeling to motive, we are forced to admit the possibility of more accurate adjustment, and, by necessary sequence, of absolutely accurate adjustment, even though we admit the likelihood that most people will attain to a final adjustment but very seldom indeed. We can guide ourselves toward such an adjustment in life, as in art, by means of theory and the critical examination of special instances; but the final act of judgment is in both life and art a unique act—it is a relationship between two elements, the rational understanding and the feeling, of which only one is classificatory and of which the other has infinite possibilities of variation.

## Tenth Problem

If the final act of adjustment is a unique act of judgment, can we say that it is more or less right, provided it is demonstrably within the general limits prescribed by the theory of morality which has led to it? The answer to this question is implicit in what has preceded; in fact the answer resembles exactly that reached at the end of the first problem examined. We can say that it is more or less nearly right. If extreme deviation from right judgment is obvious, then there is such a thing as right judgment. The mere fact that life may be conducted in a fairly satisfactory manner, by means of inaccurate judgment within certain limits, and that few people ever bother to refine their judgment beyond the stage which enables them to remain largely within those limits, does not mean that accurate judgment has no reality. Implicit in all that has preceded is the concept that in any moral situation, there is a right judgment as an ultimate possibility; that the human judge, or actor, will approximate it more or less nearly; that the closeness of his approximation will depend upon the accuracy of his rational understanding and of his intuition, and upon the accuracy of their interaction upon each other.

## Eleventh Problem

Nothing has thus far been said about human action, yet morality is supposed to guide human action. And if art is moral, there should be a relationship between art and human action.

The moral judgment, whether good, bad, or indifferent, is commonly the prelude and instigation to action. Hastily or carefully, intelligently or otherwise, one arrives at some kind of general idea of a situation calling for action, and one's idea motivates one's feeling: the act results. The part played by will, or the lack of it, between judgment and act, the possibility that action may be frustrated by some constitutional or habitual weakness or tendency, such as cowardice or a tendency to anger, in a person of a fine speculative or poetic judgment, are subjects for a treatise on ethics or psychology; a treatise on poetry stops with the consideration of the speculative judgment, which reaches its best form and expression in poetry. In the situations of daily life, one does not, as a rule, write a poem before acting: one makes a more rapid and simple judgment. But if the poem does not individually lead to a particular act, it does not prevent action. It gives us a better way of judging representative acts than we should otherwise have. It is thus a civilizing influence: it trains our power of judgment, and should, I imagine, affect the quality of daily judgments and actions.

## Twelfth Problem

What, then, is the nature of the critical process?

It will consist (1) of the statement of such historical or biographical knowledge as may be necessary in order to understand the mind and method of the writer; (2) of such analysis of his literary theories as we may need to understand and evaluate what he is doing; (3) of a rational critique of the paraphrasable content (roughly, the motive) of the poem; (4) of a rational critique of the feeling motivated—that is, of the details of style, as seen in language and technique; and (5) of the final act of judgment, a unique act, the general nature of which can be indicated, but which cannot be communicated precisely, since it consists in receiving from the poet his own final and unique judgment of his matter and in judging that judgment. It should be noted that the purpose of the first four processes is to limit as narrowly as possible the region in which the final unique act is to occur.

In the actual writing of criticism, a given task may not require all of these processes, or may not require that all be given equal emphasis; or it may be that in connection with a certain writer, whether because of the nature of the writer or because of the way in which other critics have treated him previously, one or two of these processes must be given so much emphasis that others must be neglected for lack of space. These are practical matters to be settled as the occasions arise.

## 5

# THE LEFTIST IMPERATIVE

*CHRISTOPHER CAUDWELL*

## D. H. Lawrence*

   This study by the British leftist, Christopher Caudwell (Christopher St. John Sprigg, 1907–1937), perhaps the most intelligent of modern Marxist critics, ought to be considered in relation to the two that follow it in this collection. The three together describe the range of leftist perception of and attitude toward literature. Caudwell's analysis deals largely with the social implications of language and with the tensions set up between individual instincts and social obligations. While Caudwell's criticism is often independent of any Marxist directives (as Mike Gold's is not), clues to his position can be found, particularly in his treatment of Lawrence's plea for the release of instinct as a "bourgeois" protest rather than a socially orientated indictment of capitalist restraints. The essay points up especially the degree to which a leftist criticism can be serious, restrained, and without the polemical urgency that characterizes so much of its contemporaries.

   *W*hat is the function of the artist? Any artist such as Lawrence, who aims to be "more than" an artist, necessarily raises this question. It is supposed to be the teaching of Marxism that art for art's sake is an illusion and that art must be propaganda. This is, however, making the usual bourgeois simplification of a complex matter.

   Art is a social function. This is not a Marxist demand, but arises from the very way in which art forms are defined. Only those things

———————
* The spelling in this selection has been Americanized by the editor.

161

are recognized as art forms which have a conscious social function. The phantasies of a dreamer are not art. They only become art when they are given music, forms or words, when they are clothed in socially recognized symbols, and of course in the process there is a modification. The phantasies are modified by the social dress; the language as a whole acquires new associations and context. No chance sounds constitute music, but sounds selected from a socially recognized scale and played on socially developed instruments.

It is not for Marxism therefore to demand that art play a social function or to attack the conception of "art for art's sake," for art only *is* art, and recognizable as such, in so far as it plays a social function. What is of importance to art, Marxism and society is the question: *What social function is art playing?* This in turn depends on the type of society in which it is secreted.

In bourgeois society social relations are denied in the form of relations between men, and take the form of a relation between man and a thing, a property relation, which, because it is a dominating relation, is believed to make man free. But this is an illusion. The property relation is only a disguise for relations which now become unconscious and therefore anarchic but are still between man and man and in particular between exploiter and exploited.

The artist in bourgeois culture is asked to do the same thing. He is asked to regard the art work as a finished commodity and the process of art as a relation between himself and the work, which then disappears into the market. There is a further relation between the art work and the buyer, but with this he can hardly be immediately concerned. The whole pressure of bourgeois society is to make him regard the art work as hypostatized and his relation to it as primarily that of a producer for the market.

This will have two results.

(i) The mere fact that he has to earn his living by the sale of the concrete hypostatized entity as a property right—copyright, picture, statue—may drive him to estimate his work as an artist by the market chances which produce a high total return for these property rights. This leads to the commercialization or vulgarization of art.

(ii) But art is not in any case a relation to a thing, it is a relation between men, between artist and audience, and the art work is only like a machine which they must both grasp as part of the process. The commercialization of art may revolt the sincere artist, but the tragedy is that he revolts against it still within the limitations of bourgeois culture. He attempts to forget the market completely and concentrate on his relation to the art work, which now becomes still further hypostatized as an entity-in-itself. Because the art work is now completely an end-in-itself, and even the market is forgotten, the art process becomes an extremely individualistic relation. The social values inherent in the art form, such as syntax, tradition, rules, technique, form, accepted tonal scale, now seem to have little value, for the art work more and more exists for the individual alone. The art work is necessarily always the product of a tension between old conscious social formulations—the art "form"—and new individual experience made conscious—the art "content" or the artist's "message." This is the synthesis, the specifically hard task of creation. But the hypostatization of the art work as the goal makes old conscious social formulations less and less important, and individual experience more and more dominating. As a result art becomes more and more formless, personal, and individualistic, culminating in Dadaism, surrealism and "Steining."

Thus bourgeois art disintegrates under the tension of two forces, both arising from the same feature of bourgeois culture. On the one hand there is production for the market—vulgarization, commercialization. On the other there is hypostatization of the art work as the goal of the art process, and the relation between art work and individual as paramount. This necessarily leads to a dissolution of those social values which make the art in question a social relation, and therefore ultimately results in the art work's ceasing to be an art work and becoming a mere private phantasy.

All bourgeois art during the last two centuries shows the steady development of this bifurcation. As long as the social values inherent in an art form are not disintegrated—e.g. up to say 1910—the artist who hypostatizes the art form and despises the market can produce good art. After that, it becomes steadily more difficult. Needless to say, the complete acceptance of the market, being a refusal to regard any part of the art process as a social process, is even more incompetent to produce great art. Anything which helps the artist to escape from the bourgeois trap and become conscious of social relations inherent in art, will help to delay the rot. For this reason the novel is the last surviving literary art form in bourgeois culture, for in it, for reasons explained elsewhere, the social relations inherent in the art process are overt. Dorothy Richardson, James Joyce, and Proust, all in different ways are the last blossoms of the bourgeois novel, for with them the novel begins to disappear as an objective study of social relations and becomes a study of the subject's experience in society. It is then only a step for the thing experienced to disappear and, as in Gertrude Stein, for complete "me-ness" to reign.

It is inevitable that at this stage the conception of the artist as a pure "artist" must cease to exist. For commercialized art has become intolerably base and negated itself. And equally art for art's sake (that is, the ignoring of the market and concentration on the perfect art work as a goal in itself) has negated itself, for the art form has ceased to exist, and what was art has become private phantasy. It is for this reason that sincere artists, such as Lawrence, Gide, Romain Rolland, Romains and so on, cannot be content with the beautiful art work, but seem to desert the practice of art for social theory and become novelists of ideas, literary prophets and propaganda novelists. They represent the efforts of bourgeois art, exploded into individualistic phantasy and commercialized muck, to become once more a social process and so be reborn. Whether such art is or can be great art is beside the point, since it is inevitably the pre-requisite for art becoming art again, just as it is beside the point whether the transition from bourgeoisdom to communism is itself smooth or happy or beautiful or free, since it is the inevitable step if bourgeois anarchy and misery is to be healed and society to become happy and free.

But what is art as a social process? What is art, not as a mere art work or a means of earning a living, but in itself, the part it plays in society? I have dealt fully with this point elsewhere, and need only briefly recapitulate now.

The personal phantasy or day-dream is not art, however beautiful. Nor is the beautiful sunset. Both are only the raw material of art. It is the property of art that it makes mimic pictures of reality which we accept as illusory. We do not suppose the events of a novel really happen, that a landscape shown on a painting can be walked upon—yet it has a measure of reality.

The mimic representation, by the technique appropriate to the art in question, causes the social representation to sweat out of its pores an affective emanation. The emanation is *in* us, *in* our affective reaction with the elements of the representation. Given in the representation are not only the affects, but, simultaneously, their organization in an affective *attitude* towards the piece of reality symbolized in the mimicry. This affective attitude is bitten in by a general heightening of consciousness and increase in self-value, due to the non-motor nature of the innervations aroused, which seems therefore all to pass into an affective irradiation of consciousness. This affective attitude is not permanent, as is the intellectual attitude towards reality aroused by a cogent scientific argument, but still—because of the mnemic characteristics of an organism—it remains as an *experience* and must, therefore, in proportion to the amount of conscious poignancy accompanying the experience and the nature of the experience, modify the subject's general attitude towards life itself. This modification tends to make life more interesting to the organism, hence the survival value of art. But viewed from society's standpoint, art is the fashioning of the affective consciousness of its members, the conditioning of their instincts.

Language, simply because it is the most general instrument for communicating views of reality, whether affective and cognitive, has a particularly fluid range of representations of reality. Hence the suppleness and scope of literary art; the novel, the drama, the poem, the short story, and the essay. It can draw upon all the symbolic pictures of reality made by scientific, historical and discursive intellectual processes. Art can only achieve its purpose if the pictures themselves are made simultaneously to produce affect and organization. Then, even as the artist holds up to us the piece of reality, it seems already glowing with affective coloring.

Reality constitutes for us our environment; and our environment, which is chiefly social, alters continuously—sometimes barely perceptibly, sometimes at dizzy speeds. The socially accepted pictures we make in words of reality cannot change as if they were reflections in a mirror. An object is reflected in a mirror. If the object moves the reflection moves. But in language reality is symbolized in unchanging words, which give a false stability and permanence to the object they represent. Thus they instantaneously photograph reality rather than reflect it. This frigid character of language is regrettable but it has its utilitarian purposes. It is probably the only way in which man, with his linear consciousness, can get a grip of fluid reality. Language, as it develops, shows more and more of this false permanence, till we arrive at the Platonic Ideas, Eternal and Perfect Words. Their eternity and perfection is simply the permanence of print and paper. If you coin a word or write a symbol to describe an entity or event, the word will remain "eternally" unchanged even while the entity has changed and the event is no longer present. This permanence is part of the inescapable nature of symbolism, which is expressed in the rules of logic. It is one of the strange freaks of the human mind that it has supposed that reality must obey the rules of logic, whereas the correct view is that symbolism by its very nature has certain rules, expressed in the laws of logic, and these have nothing to do with the process of reality, but represent the nature of the symbolic process itself.

The artist experiences this discrepancy between language and reality as follows: he has had an intense experience of a rose and wishes to communicate his experience to his fellows in words. He wishes to say, "I saw a rose." But "rose" has a definite social meaning, or group of meanings, and we are to suppose that he has had an experience with the rose which does not correspond to any of society's previous experiences of roses, embodied in the word and its history. His experience of the rose is therefore the negation of the word "rose," it is "not-rose" —all that in his experience which is not expressed in the current social meaning of the word "rose." He therefore says—"I saw a rose like"— and there follows a metaphor, or there is an adjective—"a heavenly rose," or a euphemism—"I saw a flowery blush," and in each case there is a synthesis, for his new experience has become socially fused into society's old experiences and both have been changed in the process. His own experience has taken color from all past meanings of the word "rose," for these will be present in men's minds when they read his poem, and the word "rose" will have taken color from his individual experience, for his poem will in future be in men's minds when they encounter the word "rose."

But why was the poet's experience different from society's tradition? Because that cross-section of his environment which we call his individual life-experience was different. But if we take all society's art as a whole, i.e. the sum of individual cross-sections, we get on the one hand the whole experience of the environment averaged out, and also the average man, or average genotype. Now the constant genesis of new art must mean that the environment is changing, so that man's individual experiences are changing, and he is constantly finding inherited social conscious formulations inadequate and requiring resynthesis. Thus if art forms remain unchanged and traditional, as in Chinese civilization, it is evident that the environment—social relations—are static. If they decay the environment is on the down-grade, as with current bourgeois culture. If they improve, the reverse is the case. But the artist's value is not in *self*-expression. If so, why should he struggle to achieve the synthesis in which old social formulations are fused with his individual experience? Why not disregard social formalities and express himself direct as one does by shouting, leaping, and cries? Because, to begin with, it is the old bourgeois illusion to suppose there is such a thing as pure individual expression. It is not even that the artist nobly forces his self-expression into a social mould for the benefit of society. Both attitudes are simply expressions of the old bourgeois fallacy that man is free in freely giving vent to his instincts. In fact the artist does not express himself in art forms, he finds himself therein. He does not adulterate his free self-expression to make it socially current, he finds free self-expression only in the social relations embodied in art. The value of art to the artist then is this, that it makes him free. It appears to him of value as a self-expression, but in fact it is not the expression of a self but the discovery of a self. It is the creation of a self. In synthesizing experience with society's, in pressing his inner self into the mould of social relations, he not only creates a new mould, a socially valuable product, but he also moulds and creates his own self. The mute inglorious Milton is a fallacy. Miltons are made not born.

The value of art to society is that by it an emotional adaptation is possible. Man's instincts are pressed in art against the altered mould of reality, and by a specific organization of the emotions thus generated, there is a new attitude, an *adaptation*.

All art is produced by this tension between changing social relations and outmoded consciousness. The very reason why new art is created, why the old art does not satisfy either artist or appreciator, is because it seems somehow out of gear with the present. Old art always has meaning for us, because the instincts, the source of the affects, do not change, because a new system of social relations does not exclude but includes the old, and because new art too includes the traditions of the art that has gone before. But it is not enough. We must have new art.

And new art results from tension. This tension takes two forms. (i) One is productive—the evolutionary form. The tension between productive relations and productive forces secures the advance of society as a whole, simply by producing in an even more pronounced form the contradiction which was the source of the dynamism. Thus bourgeois culture by continually dissolving the relations between men for relations to a thing, and thus hypostatizing the market, procured the growth of industrial capitalism. And, in the sphere of art it produced the increasing individualism which, seen at its best in Shakespeare, was a positive value, but pushed to its limit finally spelt the complete breakdown of art in surrealism, Dadaism and Steinism.

(ii) The tension now becomes revolutionary. For productive relations are a brake on productive forces and the tension between them, instead of altering productive relations in the direction of giving better outlet to productive forces, has the opposite effect. It drives productive relations on still further into negation, increases the tension, and prepares the explosion which will shatter the old productive relations and enable them to be rebuilt anew—not arbitrarily, but according to a pattern which will itself be given by the circumstances of the tension. Thus in art the tension between individualism and the increasing complexity and catastrophes of the artist's environment, between the free following of dream and the rude blows of anarchic reality, wakes the artist from his dream and forces him in spite of himself to look at the world, not merely as an artist, but also as a man, as a citizen, as a sociologist. It forces him to be interested in things not strictly germane to art; politics, economics, science, and philosophy, just as it did during the early bourgeois Renaissance, producing "all-round men" like Leonardo da Vinci. Whether this is good for art or not is beside the point. Bourgeois art like bourgeois culture is moribund and this process is an inevitable concomitant of the stage proceeding art's rebirth. And because of this intervening period, the new art when it emerges will be art more conscious of itself as part of the whole social process, will be *communist* art. This explains why all modern artists of any significance such as Lawrence, Gide, Aragon, Dos Passos, Eliot and so on, cannot be content to be "pure" artists, but must also be prophets, thinkers, philosophers, and politicians, men interested in life and social reality as a whole. They are conscious of having a message. This is the inevitable effect on art of a revolutionary period, and it is not possible to escape from it into "pure" art, into the ivory tower, for now there is no pure art; that phase is either over or not yet begun.

But at a revolution two paths are possible. So indeed they are in evolution—one can either stay still and be classical, academic and null, or go forward. But at a time of revolution it is not possible to stay still, one must either go forward, or back. To us this choice appears as a choice between Communism and Fascism, either to create the future or to go back to old primitive values, to mythology, racialism, nationalism, hero-worship, and *participation mystique*. This Fascist art is like the regression of the neurotic to a previous level of adaptation.

It is Lawrence's importance as an artist that he was well aware of the fact that the pure artist cannot exist to-day, and that the artist must inevitably be a man hating cash relationships and the market, and profoundly interested in the relations between persons. Moreover, he must be a man not merely profoundly interested in the relations between persons as they are, but interested in changing them, dissatisfied with them as they are, and wanting newer and fuller values in personal relationships.

But it is Lawrence's final tragedy that his solution was ultimately Fascist and not Communist. It was regressive. Lawrence wanted us to return to the past, to the "Mother." He sees human discontent as the yearning of the solar plexus for the umbilical connection, and he demands the substitution for sharp sexual love of the unconscious fleshy identification of foetus with mother. All this was symbolic of regression, of neurosis, of the return to the primitive.

Lawrence felt that the Europe of to-day was moribund; and he turned therefore to other forms of existence, in Mexico, Etruria and Sicily, where he found or thought he found systems of social relations in which life flowed more easily and more meaningfully. The life of Bourgeois Europe seemed to him permeated with possessiveness and rationalizing, so that it had got out of gear with the simple needs of the body. In a thousand forms he repeats this indictment of a civilization which consciously *and just because it is conscious*—sins against the instinctive currents which are man's primal source of energy. It is a mistake to suppose that Lawrence preaches the gospel of sex. Bourgeois Europe has had its bellyful of sex, and a sex cult would not now attract the interest and emotional support which Lawrence's teaching received. Lawrence's gospel was purely sociological. Even sex was too conscious for him.

Anybody who calls my novel (Lady Chatterley's Lover) a dirty sexual novel, is a liar. It's not even a sexual novel: it's a phallic. Sex is a thing that exists in the head, its reactions are cerebral, and its processes mental. Whereas the phallic reality is warm and spontaneous———

Again he wrote:

What ails me is the absolute frustration of my primitive societal instinct. . . . I think societal instinct much deeper than the sex instinct —and societal repression much more devastating. There is no repression of the sexual individual comparable to the repression of the societal man in me, by the individual ego, my own and everybody else's. I am weary even of my own individuality, and simply nauseated by other people's.

One more analysis by him of the evil in bourgeois culture: (In the Cornish people)—

the old race is still revealed, a race which believed in the darkness, in magic, and in the magic transcendency of one man over another which is fascinating. Also there is left some of the old sensuousness of the darkness and warmth and passionateness of the blood, sudden, incalculable. Whereas they are like insects, gone cold, living only for money, for *dirt*. They are foul in this. They ought to die.

Now here is a clear artistic, i.e. *emotional*, analysis of the decay of bourgeois social relations. They live for money, the societal instinct is repressed, even the sex relations have become cold and infected. Survivals of barbaric social relations between men (the "magic transcendency" of man over man) stand out as valuable in a culture where these relations have become relations between man and a thing, *man and dirt*.

But Lawrence does not look for a cause in social relations themselves, but in man's consciousness of them. The solution of the individual's needs is then plainly to be found in a return to instinctive living. But how are we to return to instinctive living? By casting off consciousness; we must return along the path we have come. But intellectualism consists in this, that we give either linguistically, plastically, or mentally, a symbolic projection to portions of reality, and consciousness or thinking consists simply in shuffling these images or verbal products. If therefore we are to cast off intellectualism and consciousness we must abandon all symbolism and rationalization *tout court,* we must *be,* and no longer think, even in images. Yet on the contrary Lawrence again and again *consciously* formulates his creed in intellectual terms or terms of imagery. But this is self-contradiction, for how can we be led intellectually and consciously *back* from consciousness? It is our consciousness that Lawrence attempts to extend and heighten even at the moment he urges us to abandon it.

Consciousness can only be abandoned in action, and the first action of Fascism is the crushing of culture and the burning of the books. It is impossible therefore for an artist and thinker to be a consistent Fascist. He can only be like Lawrence, a self-contradictory one, who appeals to the consciousness of men to abandon consciousness.

There is a confusion here due to equating consciousness with thinking and unconsciousness with feeling. This is wrong. Both are conscious. No one ever had or could have an unconscious affect or emotion. Feeling indeed is what makes the unconscious memory-traces conscious, and heats them into thoughts. All of us, in times of deep feeling, whether artistic or emotional feeling, are aware of heightened consciousness almost like a white light in us so intense and clear is it. But Lawrence never clearly saw this, and constantly equates unconsciousness with feeling and consciousness with intellect. For example:

My great religion is a belief in the blood, in the flesh, as being wiser than the intellect. We can go wrong in our minds. But what our blood feels and believes and says is always true. The intellect is only a bit and a bridle. What do I care about knowledge? All I want is to answer to my blood, direct, without fumbling intervention of mind, or moral, or what not. I conceive a man's body as a kind of flame, like a candle flame forever upright and yet flowing: and the intellect is just the light that is shed on the things around, coming God knows how from out of practically nowhere, and being *itself,* whatever there is around it that it lights up. We have got so ridiculously mindful, that we never know that we ourselves are anything—we think there are only the objects we shine upon. And there the poor flame goes on burning ignored, to produce this light. And instead of chasing the mystery in the fugitive, half-lighted things outside us, we ought to look at ourselves and say, "My God, I am myself!" That is why I like to live in Italy. The people are so unconscious. They only feel and want, they don't know. We know too much. No, we only *think* we know such a lot. A flame isn't a flame because it lights up two, or twenty objects on a table. It's a flame because it is itself. And we have forgotten ourselves.

Feeling and thinking play into each other's hands and heighten each other. Man feels more deeply than the slug because he thinks more. Why did Lawrence make this error of supposing them essentially exclusive, and equate feeling with unconsciousness? Once again, the answer is in the nature of current society. All feeling and all thinking must contain something of each other to form part of consciousness at all. But it is possible to distinguish certain conscious phenomena as chiefly feeling, or vice versa. "Pure" feelings, any more than "Pure" thoughts, do not exist at all, since the first would be a mere instinctive tendency, the second nothing but a mnemic trace. Both would be unconscious and evidenced therefore only in behavior. Lawrence might mean that feeling has wilted under modern conditions and that we must expand the feeling basis of our consciousness.

We know this of feelings (and affects generally) that they come into consciousness associated with innate responses or—more loosely—that they seem to be born of the modification, by experience and in action of the "instincts." Instinct going out in unmodified action, in mechanical response to a stimulus, is without *feeling*, it is pure automatism. Only when it becomes modified by memory-traces or stifled by action does it become conscious and appear as feeling. The more intelligent the animal, the more its behavior is modifiable by experience, the more feeling it displays. This extra display of feeling is *because* it is more intelligent, more conscious, less swayed by heredity, more subject to personal experience. Modification of innate responses by experience simply implies that previous behavior leaves a mnemic trace on the neurones, chiefly of the cortex. These when innervated produce a new pattern, whose modification takes in the cortical sphere the form of thoughts and, in the visceral and thalamic sphere, the form of feelings or emotional dynamism. The different proportion of the components decides whether we call them thoughts or feelings. Even the simplest thought is irradiated with affect, and even the simplest emotion is accompanied by a thought, not necessarily verbalized but of some such character as "I am hurt," or "A pain." It is because thought and feeling arise from the same modification of innate responses, by experience, that the growth of intelligence, i.e. of the *capacity* for modification of behavior by experience, is accompanied by a steadily increasing emotional complexity, richness, and deepness. It is plain that the growth of civilization in *Homo Sapiens* has been accompanied by a steady increase in sensibility to pain and pleasure. This is the famous "sensitiveness" of civilized man, the "luxury" of high cultures, which is also manifested in their art and their vocabulary. Primitive peoples on the other hand show a marked deficiency in their sensibility, not only to refined emotions but even the cruder ones. The extremely erotic character of savage dances is not due, as some observers naïvely suppose, to the emotional erethism of the natives, but to the reverse, that in them the erotic impulses, owing to their deficient sensibility, can only be aroused by violent stimulation, whereas a slight stimulus will set off the hair-trigger emotions of civilized people. The same phenomenon is shown in primitive insensibility to pain. Consequently if we are to return down the path we have come from, back to primitiveness, to the blood, to the flesh, it is not only to less and cruder thought but also to less and cruder feeling, to a lessened consciousness in which feeling and thought, precisely because they are less rich and complex, will be more intimately mingled, until finally, as they both blend completely and become one, they vanish and nothing is left but unconscious *behavior*. But how can this goal be of value to an artist, save on condition he denies himself the very law of his being? Art is not unconscious behavior, it is conscious feeling.

It is, however, possible to broaden feeling without altering thought or losing consciousness, by altering the ratio between them in modern civilization. That is precisely the purpose of art, for the artist makes use always of just those verbal or pictorial images of reality which are more charged with feeling than cognition, and he organizes them in such a way that the affects re-inforce each other and fuse to a glowing mass. Consequently, he who believes that at all costs the feeling element must be broadened in present-day consciousness, must preach and secure, not the contraction of all consciousness, but the widening of feeling consciousness. This is art's mission. Art is the technique of affective manipulation in relation to reality. Lawrence was doing what I suppose him to have wished to do, just when he was artist pure and simple, sensitively recording the spirit of a place or the emotions of real people —in his early work. In proportion as he became a prophet, preaching a gospel intellectually, he departed from that goal.

How did he come to make first the initial *sortie* in favor of feeling, and then the contradictory error, deserting art for preaching? He came to the first conclusion because feeling is impoverished by modern bourgeois culture. Social relations, by ceasing to be between man and man and adhering to a thing, become emptied of tenderness. Man feels himself deprived of love. His whole instinct revolts against this. He feels a vast maladaptation to his environment. Lawrence perceives this clearly when he talks about the repression of the societal instinct.

But things have gone so far that no tinkering with social relations, no adaptation of the instincts to the environment by means of art, will cure this. Social relations themselves must be rebuilt. The artist is bound for the sake of his integrity to become thinker and revolutionary. Lawrence therefore was bound not to be content with pure art, with widening feeling consciousness in the old circle. He had to try and recast social relations and proceed to a solution. But there is only one revolutionary solution. Social relations must be altered, not so as to contract consciousness but so as to widen it. The higher feeling must be found, not in a lower but as always in a higher level of culture.

Naturally consciousness seems in bourgeois culture now, as in all periods of decay, full of defects with which being struggles, and this seems like unconsciousness crippled by consciousness. Those defects in bourgeois social relations all arise from the cash nexus which replaces all other social ties, so that society seems held together, not by mutual love or tenderness or obligation, but simply by profit. Money makes the bourgeois world go round and this means that selfishness is the hinge on which bourgeois society turns, for money is a dominating relation to an owned thing. This commercialization of all social relations invades the most intimate of emotions, and the relations of the sexes are affected by the differing economic situations of man and woman. The notion of private property, aggravated by its importance and overwhelming power in bourgeois relations, extends to love itself. Because economic relations in capitalism are simply each man struggling for himself in the impersonal market, the world seems torn apart with the black forces of envy, covetousness and hate, which mix with and make ambivalent even the most "altruistic" emotions.

But it is simplifying the drama to make it a struggle between contemporary consciousness and old being. It is a conflict between productive relations and productive powers, between the contemporary formulations of consciousness, and all the possibilities of future being including consciousness latent in society and struggling to be released from their bonds. Bourgeois defects are implicit in bourgeois civilization and therefore in bourgeois consciousness. Hence man wants to turn against the intellect, for it seems that the intellect is his enemy, and indeed it is, if by intellect we mean the bourgeois intellect. But it can only be fought with intellect. To deny intellect is to assist the forces of conservatism. In hundreds of diverse forms we see to-day the useless European revolt against intellectualism.

In any civilization the rôle of consciousness is to modify instinctive responses so that they flow smoothly into the mill of social relations and turn it. Instinct not money really turns the social mill, though in the bourgeois world instinctive relations can only operate along the money channel. Hence when social relations come to be a brake on society's forces, there is felt a conflict between the social relations and the instincts. It seems as if the feelings were out of gear, as if the world was uncomfortable and hurt the feelings and repressed them. It seems as if the instincts, and the feelings, those products of the instincts, were being penalized by the environment, and that, therefore, the instincts and feelings must be "given their due," must be exalted even if it means breaking up and abandoning the civilized environment for a more primitive one. To-day this exaltation of the instincts is seen in all demands for a return to deeper "feeling" as with Lawrence, and in all worships of unconscious "mentation," as with the surrealists, Hemingways, and Fascists. In individuals this mechanism is infantile regression, seen in its pathological form in the neuroses.

Now these mechanisms involve the discovery of a real defect. Social being *is* held back by social consciousness; the instincts *are* thwarted and the feelings *are* made poor by the environment. But the remedy is wrong. The neurotic cannot, as we know, be cured by infantile regression. All it does for him is to secure him unconsciousness and take from him painful thoughts, at the price of a lowering of consciousness and an impoverishing of values. Civilization cannot be cured by going back along the path to the primitive, it can only become at a lower level more unconscious of its decay. Just as the neurotic's return to childhood solutions of problems is unhealthier than childhood, so a civilization's return to a primitive solution is unhealthier than primitive life itself. The very history between makes such solutions unreal. To the primitive these problems have never existed. To the regressive they have existed but he has repressed them. It is into the wilderness these people would lead us. They preach, not new vigor, but old decadence.

What then is the cure? We know that both in the case of the neurotic and the civilization, the cure is a more strenuous and creative act than the invalid's relapse into the womb of that unconsciousness from which we emerged. Our task is to be performed, not in an air heavy and fetid with mysteries and dead symbolism like that of a cavern used for old obscene rites, but in the open air.

We are not to return to the old but it is into the new we must go; and the new does not exist, we must bring it into being. The child would love to return to the womb, but it must become adult and face the strenuous and bracing tasks of life. We are not to abandon consciousness but to expand it, to deepen and purge feeling and break up and recast thought, and this new consciousness does not exist in any thing's keeping either Mexicans or Yogis or the "blood" but we must make it ourselves. In this struggle with reality in which instincts, feeling and thought all partake and interact, the instincts themselves will be changed, and emerging in consciousness as new thought and new feeling, will once again feel themselves in harmony with the new environment they have created. Social relations must be changed so that love returns to the earth and man is not only wiser but more full of emotion. This is not a task which one prophet can perform in one Gospel, but since the whole fabric of social relations is to be changed, every human being must in some sort participate in the change, be either for it or against it, and be victorious if he is for it and be defeated if he is against it.

Why did Lawrence, faced with the problem, fail of a solution? He failed because while hating bourgeois culture he never succeeded in escaping from its limitations. Here in him, too, we see the same old lie. Man is "free" in so far as his "free" instincts, the "blood," the "flesh," are given an outlet. Man is free not through but *in spite of* social relations.

If one believes this—which, as we have seen, is the deepest and most ineradicable bourgeois illusion, all others are built on this—one must, if one is hurt by bourgeois social relations, see security and freedom only in casting them off, and returning to a primitive state with less "constraints." One must necessarily believe freedom and happiness can be found by one's own individual action. One will not believe freedom and happiness can only be found through social relations, by co-operating with others to change them, but there is always something one can do, fly to Mexico, find the right woman or the right friends, and so discover salvation. One will never see the truth, that one can only find salvation for oneself by finding it for all others at the same time.

Lawrence therefore could never escape from this essential selfishness —not a petty selfishness but the selfishness which is the pattern of bourgeois culture and is revealed in pacifism, Protestantism, and all varieties of salvation obtained by individual action. The world to which Lawrence wished to return is not really the world of primitives who are in fact bound by more rigid relations than those of bourgeois Europe. It is the old bourgeois pastoral heaven of the "natural man" born everywhere in chains, which does not exist. It does not exist because it is self-contradictory, and because it is self-contradictory the bourgeois world in striving for it more clearly produces the opposite, as in moving towards an object in a mirror we move away from the real object. Lawrence's gospel therefore only forms part of the self-destructive element in bourgeois culture.

Lawrence for all his gifts suffered from the old *petit bourgeois* errors. Like Wells, he strove to climb upwards into the world of bourgeois culture; being more artistic than Wells and born in a later era, it could not be the security and power of that already sick class that appealed to him. It was their cultural values. He succeeded in entering that world and drinking deeply of all its tremendous intellectual and aesthetic riches, only to find them riches turning into dust. The shock of that disillusion, added to the pain endured in that climb, filled him finally with a hatred for bourgeois values. He could criticize them relentlessly and bitterly, but he could provide no solution for the whole set of his life; all that long difficult climb of his into the bourgeois sunshine ensured that he remained a bourgeois. His was always bourgeois culture, conscious of its decay, criticizing itself and with no solution except to go back to a time when things were different and so undo all the development that had brought bourgeois culture to this pass.

Had he been born later, had that sunlit world never appealed to him so irresistibly, he might have seen that it was the proletariat—to whom he was so near at the start of his climb—that was the dynamic force of the future. Not only would he then have had a standpoint outside bourgeois culture from which to criticize it, but from that position he would have been able to find the true solution—in the future, not the past. But Lawrence remained to the end a man incapable of that subordination of self to others, of co-operation, of solidarity as a class, which is the characteristic of the proletariat. He remained the individualist, the bourgeois revolutionary angrily working out his own salvation, critical of all, alone in possession of grace. He rid himself of every bourgeois illusion but the important one. He saw finally neither the world nor himself as it really was. He saw the march of events as a bourgeois tragedy, which is true but unimportant. The important thing, which was absolutely closed to him, was that it was also a proletarian renaissance.

Everywhere to-day will be found the conscious or unconscious followers of Lawrence—the pacifists, the snug little hedonists, the conscientious sexualists, the well-meaning Liberals, the idealists, all seeking the impossible solution, salvation through the free act of the individual will amid decay and disaster. They may find a temporary solution, a momentary happiness, although I judge Lawrence to have found neither. But it is of its nature unstable, for external events to which they have regressively adjusted themselves, beget incessantly new horrors and undreamed-of disasters. What avails such pinchback constructs during the screaming horror of a War? One may stop one's ears and hide oneself in Cornwall like Lawrence, but the cry of one's millions of suffering fellow-humans reaches one's ears and tortures one. And, the War at last survived, there come new horrors. The eating disintegration of the slump. Nazism outpouring a flood of barbarism and horror. And what next? Armaments piling up like an accumulating catastrophe, mass neurosis, nations like mad dogs. All this seems gratuitous, horrible, cosmic to such people, unaware of the causes. How can the bourgeois still pretend to be free, to find salvation individually? Only by sinking himself in still cruder illusions, by denying art, science, emotion, even ultimately life itself. Humanism, the creation of bourgeois culture, finally separates from it. Against the sky stands Capitalism without a rag to cover it, naked in its terror. And humanism, leaving it, or rather, forcibly thrust aside, must either pass into the ranks of the proletariat or, going quietly into a corner, cut its throat. Lawrence did not live to face this final issue, which would necessarily make straw of his philosophy and his teaching.

*MICHAEL GOLD*

# Wilder: Prophet of the Genteel Christ*

In order to understand the inclusion of this essay as a "perspective" on modern literature, two things are necessary: (1) comparison and contrast with the essay that precedes it and the one that follows; and (2) an appreciation of the circumstances of its publication. When the fall literary issue of the *New Republic* appeared in 1930, the effects of the Wall Street crash of October, 1929, were beginning seriously to be felt. Mike Gold (1896– ), who served as an editor of the *New Masses* from 1926 to 1933, was beginning to feel his power as a spokesman for the

---

* *The Cabala, The Bridge of San Luis Rey, The Woman of Andros, The Angel That Troubled the Waters,* by Thornton Wilder.

"right" (which is to say, the left) point of view. This review of
Wilder's fiction, therefore, set up the terms according to which
much journalistic criticism was written in the thirties. Controversy
over it raged in the pages of the *New Republic* for two years, until
its editors refused to print any more correspondence on the subject. Edmund Wilson pointed out finally (*New Republic*, May 4,
1932) that "the Gold-Wilder row marked definitely the eruption
of the Marxist issues out of the literary circles of the radicals into
the field of general criticism. . . ." What was to follow was a
mixture of serious considerations of the "new social responsibility"
with the wildest kind of charge and countercharge. Gold's naïve
nativism and his narrow view that literature should concern itself
with only one kind of morality, and with the present, are only an
extreme example of American criticism of the left.

*H*ere's a group of people losing sleep over a host of notions
that the rest of the world has outgrown several centuries ago: one
duchess's right to enter a door before another; the word order in a dogma
of the Church; "the divine right of Kings, especially of Bourbons."

In these words Thornton Wilder describes the people in his first book,
*The Cabala*. They are some eccentric old aristocrats in Rome, seen
through the eyes of a typical American art "pansy" who is there as a
student.

Marcantonio is the sixteen-year-old son of one of the group; he is
burned out with sex and idleness, and sexualizes with his sister, and
then commits suicide. Another character is a beautiful, mad Princess,
who hates her dull Italian husband, falls in love with many Nordics,
and is regularly rejected by them. Others are a moldy old aristocrat
woman who "believes," and a moldy old Cardinal who doesn't, and
some other fine worm-eaten authentic specimens of the rare old Italian
antique.

Wilder views these people with tender irony. He makes no claim as
to their usefulness to the world that feeds them; yet he hints that their
palace mustiness is a most important fact in the world of today. He
writes with a brooding seriousness of them as if all the gods were watch-
ing their little lavender tragedies. The style is a diluted Henry James.

Wilder's second novel was *The Bridge of San Luis Rey*. This famous
and vastly popular yarn made a bold leap backward in time. Mr. Wilder,
by then, had evidently completed his appraisal of our own age. The
scene is laid in Lima, Peru; the time is Friday noon, July 20, 1714.
In this volume Wilder perfected the style which is now probably permanent with him; the diluted and veritable Anatole France.

Among the characters of San Luis Rey are: (1) A sweet old duchess
who loves her grown daughter to madness, but is not loved in return;
(2) A beautiful unfortunate genius of an actress who after much sex-
ualizing turns nun; (3) Her tutor, a jolly old rogue, but a true wor-
shipper of literature; (4) Two strange brothers who love each other

with a passion and delicacy that again brings the homosexual bouquet into a Wilder book, and a few other minor sufferers.

Some of the characters in this novel die in the fall of a Bridge. Our author points out the spiritual lessons imbedded in this Accident; viz.: that God is Love.

The third novel is the recent *The Woman of Andros*. This marks a still further masterly retreat into time and space. The scene is one of the lesser Greek islands, the hour somewhere in B.C.

The fable: a group of young Greeks spend their evenings in alternate sexual bouts and lofty Attic conversations with the last of the Aspasias. One young man falls in love with her sister, who is "pure." His father objects. Fortunately, the Aspasia dies. The father relents. But then the sister dies, too. Wistful futility and sweet soft sadness of Life. Hints of the coming of Christ: "and in the East the stars shone tranquilly down upon the land that was soon to be called Holy and that even then was preparing its precious burden."

Then Mr. Wilder has published some pretty, tinkling, little three-minute playlets. These are on the most erudite and esoteric themes one could ever imagine: all about Angels, and Mozart, and King Louis, and Fairies, and a Girl of the Renaissance, and a whimsical old Actress (1780) and her old Lover; Childe Harold to the Dark Tower Came; Proserpina and the Devil; The Flight into Egypt; a Venetian Prince and a Mermaid; Shelley, Judgment Day, Centaurs, God, The Woman in the Chlamys, Christ; Brigomeide, Leviathan, Ibsen; every waxwork in Wells's Outline, in fact, except Buffalo Bill.

And this, to date, is the garden cultivated by Mr. Thornton Wilder. It is a museum, it is not a world. In this devitalized air move the wan ghosts he has called up, each in "romantic" costume. It is an historic junkshop over which our author presides.

Here one will not find the heroic archæology of a Walter Scott or Eugene Sue. Those men had social passions, and used the past as a weapon to affect the present and future. Scott was the poet of feudalism. The past was a glorious myth he created to influence the bourgeois anti-feudal present. On every page of history Eugene Sue traced the bitter, neglected facts of the working-class martyrdom. He wove these into an epic melodrama to strengthen the heart and hand of the revolutionary workers, to inspire them with a proud consciousness of their historic mission.

That is how the past should be used: as a rich manure, as a springboard, as a battle cry, as a deepening, clarifying, and sublimation of the struggles in the too-immediate present. But Mr. Wilder is the poet of the genteel bourgeoisie. They fear any such disturbing lessons out of the past. Their goal is comfort and status quo. Hence, the vapidity of these little readings in history.

Mr. Wilder, in a foreword to his book of little plays, tells himself and us the object of his æsthetic striving:

"I hope," he says, "through many mistakes, to discover that spirit that is not unequal to the elevation of the great religious themes, yet which does not fall into a repellent didacticism. Didacticism is an attempt at the coercion of another's free mind, even though one knows that in these matters, beyond logic, beauty is the only persuasion. Here the schoolmaster enters again. He sees all that is fairest in the Christian tradition made repugnant to the new generations by reason of the diction in which it is expressed. . . . So that the revival of religion is almost a matter of rhetoric. The work is difficult, perhaps impossible (perhaps all religions die out with the exhaustion of the language), but it at least reminds us that Our Lord asked us in His work to be not only gentle as doves, but as wise as serpents."

Mr. Wilder wishes to restore, he says, through Beauty and Rhetoric, the Spirit of Religion in American Literature. One can respect any writer in America who sets himself a goal higher than the usual racketeering. But what is this religious spirit Mr. Wilder aims to restore? Is it the crude self-torture of the Holy Rollers, or the brimstone howls and fears of the Baptists, or even the mad, titanic sincerities and delusions of a Tolstoy or Dostoievsky?

No, it is that newly fashionable literary religion that centers around Jesus Christ, the First British Gentleman. It is a pastel, pastiche, dilettante religion, without the true neurotic blood and fire, a daydream of homosexual figures in graceful gowns moving archaically among the lilies. It is Anglo-Catholicism, that last refuge of the American literary snob.

This genteel spirit of the new parlor-Christianity pervades every phrase of Mr. Wilder's rhetoric. What gentle theatrical sighs! what lovely, well composed deaths and martyrdoms! what languishings and flutterings of God's sinning doves! what little jewels of Sunday-school wisdom, distributed modestly here and there through the softly flowing narrative like delicate pearls, diamonds, and rubies on the costume of a meek, wronged Princess gracefully drowning herself for love (if my image is clear).

Wilder has concocted a synthesis of all the chambermaid literature, Sunday-school tracts, and boulevard piety there ever were. He had added a dash of the prep-school teacher's erudition, then embalmed all this in the speciously glamorous style of the late Anatole France. He talks much of art, of himself as Artist, of style. He is a very conscious craftsman. But his is the most irritating and pretentious style pattern I have read in years. It has the slick, smug finality of the lesser Latins; that shallow clarity and tight little good taste that remind one of nothing so much as the conversation and practice of a veteran cocotte.

Mr. Wilder strains to be spiritual; but who could reveal any real agonies and exaltations of spirit in this neat, tailormade rhetoric? It is a great lie. It is Death. Its serenity is that of the corpse. Prick it, and it will bleed violet ink and *apéritif*. It is false to the great stormy music of Anglo-Saxon speech. Shakespeare is crude and disorderly beside Mr.

Wilder. Milton, Fielding, Burns, Blake, Byron, Chaucer or Hardy could never receive a passing mark in Mr. Wilder's classroom of style.

And is this the style with which to express America? Is this the speech of a pioneer continent? Will this discreet French drawingroom hold all the blood, horror, and hope of the world's new empire? Is this the language of the intoxicated Emerson? Or the clean, rugged Thoreau, or vast Whitman? Where are the modern streets of New York, Chicago, and New Orleans in these little novels? Where are the cotton mills, and the murder of Ella May and her songs? Where are the child slaves of the beet fields? Where are the stockbroker suicides, the labor racketeers, or passion and death of the coal miners? Where are Babbitt, Jimmy Higgins, and Anita Loos's Blonde? Is Mr. Wilder a Swede or a Greek, or is he an American? No stranger would know from these books he has written.

But is it right to demand this "nativism" of him? Yes, for Mr. Wilder has offered himself as a spiritual teacher; therefore one may say: Father, what are your lessons? How will your teaching help the "spirit" trapped in American capitalism? But Wilder takes refuge in the rootless cosmopolitanism which marks every *émigré* trying to flee the problems of his community. Internationalism is a totally different spirit. It begins at home. Mr. Wilder speaks much of the "human heart" and its eternal problems. It is with these, he would have us believe, that he concerns himself; and they are the same in any time and geography, he says. Another banal evasion. For the human heart, as he probes it in Greece, Peru, Italy, and other remote places, is only the "heart" of a small futile group with whom few Americans have the faintest kinship.

For to repeat, Mr. Wilder remains the poet of a small sophisticated class that has recently arisen in America—our genteel bourgeoisie. His style is their style; it is the new fashion. Their women have taken to wearing his Greek chlamys and faintly indulge themselves in his smart Victorian pieties. Their men are at ease in his Paris and Rome.

America won the War. The world's wealth flowed into it like a red Mississippi. The newest and greatest of all leisure classes was created. Luxury-hotels, golf, old furniture, and Vanity Fair sophistication were some of their expressions.

Thorstein Veblen foretold all this in 1899, in an epoch-making book that every American critic ought to study like a Bible. In *The Theory of the Leisure Class* he painted the hopeless course of most American culture for the next three decades. The grim, ironic prophet has been justified. Thornton Wilder is the perfect flower of the new prosperity. He has all the virtues Veblen said this leisure class would demand: the air of good breeding, the decorum, priestliness, glossy high finish as against intrinsic qualities, conspicuous inutility, caste feeling, love of the archaic, etc. . . .

All this is needed to help the parvenu class forget its lowly origins in American industrialism. It yields them a short cut to the aristocratic emotions. It disguises the barbaric sources of their income, the billions wrung from American workers and foreign peasants and coolies. It lets them feel spiritually worthy of that income.

Babbitt made them ashamed of being crude American climbers. Mr. Wilder, "gentle as the dove and wise as the serpent," is a more constructive teacher. Taking them patiently by the hand, he leads them into castles, palaces, and far-off Greek islands, where they may study the human heart when it is nourished by blue blood. This Emily Post of culture will never reproach them; or remind them of Pittsburgh or the breadlines. He is always in perfect taste; he is the personal friend of Gene Tunney.

"For there is a land of the living and a land of the dead, and the bridge is love, the only survival, the only meaning." And nobody works in a Ford plant, and nobody starves looking for work, and there is nothing but Love in God's ancient Peru, Italy, Greece, if not in God's capitalist America 1930!

Let Mr. Wilder write a book about modern America. We predict it will reveal all his fundamental silliness and superficiality, now hidden under a Greek chlamys.

*KENNETH BURKE*

## Revolutionary Symbolism in America

The first of three American Writers' Congresses was held in April, 1935. The report of it indicates a wide variety of points of view, so that one may correctly infer that leftist criticism was neither unified nor clear as to the precise direction it should take. The statements ranged from Edwin Seaver's, that the only important criterion is "the present class loyalty of the author," to the plea made by Kenneth Burke (1897–    ), in the piece reprinted here, that the critic try to employ "as many imaginative, aesthetic, and speculative fields as hc can handle. . . ." Burke has, of course, published much more sophisticated and intricate criticism than this statement. In fact, one might almost say that it is not at all representative of his critical mind, were it not for its emphasis upon a variety of social perspectives upon literature. This was advice he was himself to take quite seriously and thoroughly in his later work. His Writers' Congress speech is used here as a third type of leftist strategy in criticism, somehow mediating between the wild and naïve denunciation of Gold's review and the intricate psychologizing of Caudwell's analysis. For a discussion of the first Writers' Congress, see Walter Rideout's brilliant book,

The *Radical Novel in the United States, 1900–1954* (Boston: Harvard University Press, 1956), pp. 167–69.

*W*hen considering how people have coöperated, in either conservative or revolutionary movements of the past, we find that there is always some unifying principle about which their attachments as a group are polarized. I do not refer to such mere insignia as tri-color, hammer and sickle, swastika, crucifix, or totem pole—but to the subtle complex of emotions and attitudes for which such insignia are little more than the merest labels.

From a strictly materialistic point of view, such symbols are pure nonsense. Food, tools, shelter, productive technique—these things are the "realest" part of our vocabulary; they correspond to objects that can be seen and felt, and to operations that can be clearly and obviously performed. But the communal relationships by which a group is bound, do not possess such primary reality. However vital they are in promoting historic processes, they are "myths," quite as the gods of Homer were myths. To search for them critically is to dissolve them, while a few rudimentary "realities" take their place. If you find a man attached to some cause, and keep pressing him with questions, he will not be able to point out the nature of his attachment in the way he might if you asked him to point to his house. Yet for all the illusive character of his attachment, we know that it may be a genuine social motive behind his actions.

"Myths" may be wrong, or they may be used to bad ends—but they cannot be dispensed with. In the last analysis, they are our basic psychological tools for working together. A hammer is a carpenter's tool; a wrench is a mechanic's tool; and a "myth" is the social tool for welding the sense of interrelationship by which the carpenter and the mechanic, though differently occupied, can work together for common social ends. In this sense a myth that works well is as real as food, tools, and shelter are. As compared with the reality of material objects, however, we might say that the myth deals with a *secondary* order of reality. Totem, race, godhead, nationality, class, lodge, guild—all such are the "myths" that have made various ranges and kinds of social coöperation possible. They are not "illusions," since they perform a very real and necessary social function in the organizing of the mind. But they may look illusory when they survive as fossils from the situations for which they were adapted into changed situations for which they are not adapted.

Lasswell holds that a revolutionary period is one in which the people drop their allegiance to one myth, or symbol, and shift to another in its place. However, when a symbol is in the process of losing its vitality as a device for polarizing social coöperation, there are apt to be many rival symbols competing to take its place. A symbol probably loses its vitality when the kinds of coöperation it promotes—and with which its destiny is united—have ceased to be serviceable. The symbol of bourgeois nationalism is in such a state of decay to-day, for instance—hence the attempt of Communists to put the symbol of class in its place. Similarly the Technocrats, attempting to profit by the prestige which the technological expert enjoys in the contemporary framework of values, would polarize allegiance around the symbol of the engineer. A project like the Douglas Social Credit plan, whatever its economic feasibility may or may not be, has no such symbol—hence, movements of this sort become objects of popular allegiance only when some distinct personality arises to champion them, and to polarize group allegiance about himself as an *individual*. In this category fall the procedures of men like Huey Long and Father Caughlin—and I need not examine, before a pro-Communist audience, the tendency of such individual polarizations to trick the allegiance of the people by deflecting their attention from the principal faults of their system. It is wholesome to give allegiance, even to a crook—but the mere fact that the tendency is wholesome is no guaranty that the people will not suffer for their wholesomeness.

The Communists generally focus their scheme of allegiance about the symbol of the worker, which they would put in the place of a misused nationalism as the polarizing device about which our present attempts at historic coöperation should cluster. Accordingly, my paper will discuss this symbol, and to what extent it fulfills the conditions of attachment. I should also emphasize the fact that I shall consider this matter *purely from the standpoint of propaganda*. It may be that the needs of the propagandist are not wholly identical with the needs of the organizer. Insofar as a writer really is a propagandist, not merely writing work that will be applauded by his allies, convincing the already convinced, but actually moving forward like a pioneer into outlying areas of the public and bringing them the first favorable impressions of his doctrine, the nature of his trade may give rise to special symbolic requirements. Accordingly, it is the *propaganda* aspect of the symbol that I shall center upon—considering the symbol particularly as a device for spreading the areas of allegiance.

In the first place, I assume that a symbol must embody an *ideal*. The symbol appeals to us as an incentive because it suggests traits which we should like to share. Yet there are few people who really want to work, let us say, as a human cog in an automobile factory, or as gatherers of vegetables on a big truck farm. Such rigorous ways of life enlist our *sympathies*, but not our *ambitions*. Our ideal is as far as possible to *eliminate* such kinds of work, or to reduce its strenuousness to a minimum. Some people, living overly sedentary lives, may like to read of harsh physical activity (as they once enjoyed Wild West fiction)—but Hollywood knows only too well that the people engaged in such kinds of effort are vitalized mainly by some vague hope that they may some day escape it. "Adult education" in capitalist America to-day is centered in the efforts of our economic mercenaries (our advertising men and sales organizations) to create a maximum desire for commodities consumed under expensive conditions—and Hollywood appeals to the worker mainly by picturing the qualities of life in which this commercially stimulated desire is gratified. The question arises: Is the symbol of the worker accurately attuned to us, as so conditioned by the reactionary forces in control of our main educational channels?

I tentatively suggest that it is not. By this I do not mean that a proletarian emphasis should be dropped from revolutionary books. The rigors of the worker must certainly continue to form a major part of revolutionary symbolism, if only for the reason that here the worst features of capitalist exploitation are concentrated. But the basic symbol, it seems to me, should be focused somewhat differently. Fortunately, I am not forced to advocate any great change—though I do think that the shift I propose, while minor in itself, leads in the end to quite different emphases in our modes of propaganda. The symbol I should plead for, as more basic, more of an ideal incentive, than that of the worker, is that of "the people." In suggesting that "the people," rather than "the worker," rate highest in our hierarchy of symbols, I suppose I am suggesting fundamentally that one cannot extend the doctrine of revolutionary thought among the lower middle class without using middle-class values—just as the Church invariably converted pagans by making the local deities into saints. I should also point out that we are very close to this symbol of "the people" in our term "the masses," which is embodied in the title of the leading radical magazine. But I think that the term "the people" is closer to our folkways than is the corresponding term, "the masses," both in spontaneous popular usage and as stimulated by our political demagogues. I should add that, in an interview published recently in the New York *World-Telegram,* Clarence Hathaway frequently used a compound of the two in the form: "the masses of the people."

The symbol of "the people," as distinct from the proletarian symbol, also has the tactical advantage of pointing more definitely in the direction of unity (which in itself is a sound psychological tendency, for all that it is now misused by nationalists to mask the conditions of disunity). It contains the *ideal,* the ultimate *classless* feature which the revolution would bring about—and for this reason seems richer as a symbol of allegiance. It can borrow the advantages of nationalistic conditioning, and at the same time be used to combat the forces that hide their class prerogatives behind a communal ideology.

The acceptance of "the people" as the basic symbol also has the great virtue that it makes for less likelihood of schematization on the part of our writers. So far at least, the *proletarian* novel has been over-simplified, leading to a negative symbol (that enlists our sympathies) rather than to a positive symbol (that incorporates our ideals). The symbol of "the people" should make for greater breadth in a writer's allegiance. By informing his work mainly from the standpoint of this positive symbol, he would come to see, I believe, that a poet does not sufficiently glorify his political cause by pictures of suffering and revolt. Rather, a poet makes his soundest contribution in this wise: He shows himself alive to all the aspects of contemporary effort and thought (in contrast with a certain anti-intellectualist, semi-obscurantist trend among some of the strictly *proletarian* school, who tend to imply that there is some disgrace attached to things of the mind). I can understand how such resistance arises, since the many channels of thought are in control of reactionaries —but to turn against thought for such a reason would be like advocating illiteracy because people that read are exposed to the full force of our newspapers and magazines. The complete propagandist, it seems to me, would take an interest in as many imaginative, aesthetic, and speculative fields as he can handle—and into this breadth of his concerns he would interweave a general attitude of sympathy for the oppressed and antipathy towards our oppressive institutions. In this way he would ally his attitudes with everything that is broadest and fullest in the world to-day. And he would argue for his political sympathies, not literally and directly, but by the intellectual company he keeps.

Much explicit propaganda must be done, but that is mainly the work of the pamphleteer and political organizer. In the purely imaginative field, the writer's best contribution to the revolutionary cause is *implicit*. If he shows a keen interest in every manifestation of our cultural development, and at the same time gives a clear indication as to where his sympathies lie, this seems to me the most effective long-pull contribution to propaganda he can make. For he thus indirectly links his cause with the kinds of intellectual and emotional engrossment that are generally admired. He speaks in behalf of his cause, not in the ways of a lawyer's brief, but by the sort of things he associates with it. In a rudimentary way, this is what our advertisers do when they recommend a particular brand of cigarette by picturing it as being smoked under desirable conditions; it is the way in which the best artists of the religious era recommended or glorified their Faith; and I imagine it would be the best way of proceeding to-day. Reduced to a precept, the formula would run: Let one encompass as many desirable features of our cultural heritage as possible—and let him make sure that his political alignment figures prominently among them. . . .* And I am suggesting that an approach based upon the positive symbol of "the people," rather than upon the negative symbol of "the worker," makes more naturally for this kind of identification whereby one's political alignment is fused with broader cultural elements.

I might also note that the symbol of "the people" (which, I repeat, is already tacitly approved in the analogous term, "the masses") suggests *

---

* "The author says that, somewhere along the line, a paragraph of his paper was omitted, without his being consulted. The paragraph was to this effect: One must bear in mind the great difference between such attitudes here and in Russia. In the USA they are 'revolutionary'; but in the USSR they are 'conservative.' His memory is that the omission occurred at the point where these three dots are inserted." (Kenneth Burke, letter to the editor, August 25, 1961.)

partial fallacy in too strict adherence to the doctrine of "antithetical moralities" ("proletarian" as antithetical to "bourgeois"). We convince a man by reason of the values which we and he hold *in common*. Propaganda (the extension of one's recruiting into ever widening areas) is possible only insofar as the propagandizer and the propagandized have *kindred* values, share the *same* base of reference. If you and I agree on a criterion of justice, I may turn you against a certain institution, such as capitalism, by showing that it makes for injustice. But no matter how well put together my arguments might be, they would be pointless in this case unless you were relatively in agreement with me as to the desirability of justice. Particularly as regards the specific problems of propaganda, the emphasis upon the *antithetical* tends to incapacitate a writer for his task as a *spreader* of doctrine by leading him too soon into antagonistic modes of thought and expression. It gives him too much authority to *condemn*—and however human this desire to grow wrathful may be, and however justified it is by the conditions all about us, the fact remains that his specific job as a propagandist requires him primarily to wheedle or cajole, to practice the arts of ingratiation. As a propagandizer, it is not his work to convince the convinced, but to plead with the unconvinced, which requires him to use *their* vocabulary, *their* values, *their* symbols, insofar as this is possible.

For we must remember that among the contradictions of capitalism we must also include the contradictions of anti-capitalist propaganda. Marxism is war to the ends of peace, heresy to the ends of unity, organization to the ends of freedom, glorification of toil to the ends of greater leisure, revolution in the interests of conservation, etc. Such a confusion cannot be settled once and for all. It is our particular "burden" at this particular stage of history. In the last analysis, art strains towards *universalization*. It tends to overleap imaginatively the class divisions of the moment and go after modes of thought that would apply to a society freed of class divisions. It seeks to consider the problems of *man,* not of *classes of men*. We are agreed that the current situation militates against this tendency, which is all the more reason for artists to enlist in the work of changing it. For a totally universalized art, if established in America to-day, would simply be the spiritual denial of an underlying economic disunity (the aesthetic of fascism). The strictly proletarian symbol has the useful advantage of emphasizing the temporary antagonism—but it has the disadvantage of not sufficiently embodying within its connotations the ideal incentive, the eventual state of unification that is expected to flow from it.

For this contradiction there is no wholly satisfactory solution. The closest to a satisfactory solution I can think of is simply to suggest that the imaginative artist show, in a general way, a wholesome alignment of attitudes, both political and nonpolitical. Some may and should deal specifically with strikes, lock-outs, unemployment, unsavory working conditions, organized resistance to the police, etc.—but an attempt to focus all their imaginative range within this orbit must produce an over-simplified and impoverished art, which would defeat its own purposes, failing even as propaganda, since it did not invigorate audiences by incorporating sufficient aspects of cultural glorification in its material.

I believe that the symbol of "the people" makes more naturally for such *propaganda by inclusion* than does the strictly proletarian symbol (which makes naturally for a *propaganda by exclusion,* a tendency to eliminate from one's work all that does not deal specifically with the realities of the workers' oppression—and which, by my thesis, cannot for this reason engage even the full allegiance of the workers themselves). And since the symbol of "the people" contains connotations both of oppression and of unity, it seems better than the exclusively proletarian one as a psychological bridge for linking the two conflicting aspects of a transitional, revolutionary era, which is Janus-faced, looking both forwards and back. I recognize that my suggestion bears the telltale stamp of my class, the petty bourgeoisie. And I should not dare to make it, except for a belief that it is vitally important to enlist the allegiance of this class. But I should point out, in closing, that there are really two features in my present paper, and although I think that they *tend* to be interconnected, they may not *necessarily* be. I make this point because I hope that, even if my hearers may resist my first suggestion (and I see many just grounds for their doing so), they may still accept the second. The first was that we take "the people" rather than "the worker" as our basic symbol of exhortation and allegiance. The second was that the imaginative writer seek to propagandize his cause by surrounding it with as full a cultural texture as he can manage, thus thinking of propaganda not as an over-simplified, literal, explicit writing of lawyer's briefs, but as a process of broadly and generally associating his political alignment with cultural awareness in the large. I consider the first suggestion important primarily because the restricted proletarian symbol *tends* to militate against the full use of propaganda by inclusion. But I should not like to make your acceptance of the second absolutely dependent upon your acceptance of the first. Some writers may be able to dissociate them, and to surround the strictly proletarian symbol with sufficient richness of cultural ideals to make it appealing even as a symbol of allegiance for people who do not think of themselves primarily within the proletarian framework. But I still insist that their function as propagandists will not be complete unless they do thus propagandize by inclusion, not confining themselves to a few schematic situations, but engaging the entire range of our interests, even such interests as we might have at a time of industry and peace.

# PART III

# The Postwar Scene

# 6

# THE "ETERNAL VERITIES"

*WILLIAM FAULKNER*

## The Stockholm Address

This famous address by William Faulkner (1897–    ) is here reprinted, not as a foil but as a contrast to the three that follow it, which conclude this volume of *Perspectives*. Despite Faulkner's frequent reiteration of the need to preserve the "verities," in a number of talks and interviews that followed his elevation to Nobel distinction, the fact is that "verities" did not often receive in the fifties the kind of somber and single-minded treatment they are here given. His address was, therefore, more like a farewell to an age that was passing than the beginning of a new era. For a discussion of the rhetoric and the influence of this address, see the Introduction to *William Faulkner: Three Decades of Criticism*, edited by F. J. Hoffman and O. W. Vickery (Lansing, Mich.: Michigan State University Press, 1960), pp. 26–42.

*I* feel that this award was not made to me as a man but to my work—a life's work in the agony and sweat of the human spirit, not for glory and least of all for profit, but to create out of the materials of the human spirit something which did not exist before. So this award is only mine in trust. It will not be difficult to find a dedication for the money part of it commensurate with the purpose and significance of its origin. But I would like to do the same with the acclaim too, by using this moment as a pinnacle from which I might be listened to by the young men and women already dedicated to the same anguish and travail, among whom is already that one who will some day stand here where I am standing.

Our tragedy today is a general and universal physical fear so long sustained by now that we can even bear it. There are no longer problems of the spirit. There is only the question: When will I be blown up? Because of this, the young man or woman writing today has forgotten the problems of the human heart in conflict with itself which alone can make good writing because only that is worth writing about, worth the agony and the sweat.

He must learn them again. He must teach himself that the basest of all things is to be afraid; and, teaching himself that, forget it forever, leaving no room in his workshop for anything but the old verities and truths of the heart, the old universal truths lacking which any story is ephemeral and doomed—love and honor and pity and pride and compassion and sacrifice. Until he does so, he labors under a curse. He writes not of love but of lust, of defeats in which nobody loses anything of value, of victories without hope and, worst of all, without pity or compassion. His griefs grieve on no universal bones, leaving no scars. He writes not of the heart but of the glands.

Until he relearns these things, he will write as though he stood alone and watched the end of man. I decline to accept the end of man. It is easy enough to say that man is immortal simply because he will endure; that when the last ding-dong of doom has clanged and faded from the last worthless rock hanging tideless in the last red and dying evening, that even then there will still be one more sound: that of his puny inexhaustible voice, still talking. I refuse to accept this. I believe that man will not merely endure: he will prevail. He is immortal, not because he alone among creatures has an inexhaustible voice but because he has a soul, a spirit capable of compassion and sacrifice and endurance. The poet's, the writer's, duty is to write about these things. It is his privilege to help man endure by lifting his heart, by reminding him of the courage and honor and hope and pride and compassion and pity and sacrifice which have been the glory of his past. The poet's voice need not merely be the record of man, it can be one of the props, the pillars to help him endure and prevail.

# THE REVOLT AGAINST IDEOLOGY

*DANIEL BELL*

## The Mood of Three Generations

This essay, from one of the most stimulating recent books written by cultural sociologists, *The End of Ideology,* is actually a composite review of two significant books and a magazine: Murray Kempton's *Part of Our Time* (New York: Simon and Schuster, 1955); Dwight Macdonald's *Memoirs of a Revolutionist* (New York: Farrar, Straus, and Cudahy, 1957); and Irving Howe's *Dissent,* beginning with the Winter issue, 1954. Each provides a commentary upon one of the three generations of intellectuals; and Bell's comment upon them helps to arrange a perspective upon the culture of the fifties. It is largely a perspective derived from politics, economics, and the questions of loyalties and commitment these usually raise. Bell's portrayal is not complete; it needs at least to be supplemented by the two essays that follow it. But it is packed with the kinds of information and insight that are necessary to the evaluation of a decade so close to us as the years immediately preceding our present time.

## A. The Once-Born, the Twice-Born, and the After-Born

> *We get the belief in the old age of mankind, the belief at all times harmful, that we are late survivals, mere Epigoni.—*
> NIETZSCHE

*I*t is difficult for me to know if I am, or am not, of the "young generation." I came to political awareness in the Depression and joined

191

the Young People's Socialist League in 1932, at the precocious age of thirteen. At the age of fifteen I was writing resolutions on the "road to power." At C.C.N.Y., in the late thirties, I was already a veteran of many factional wars. Since graduating, in 1938, I have worked for twenty years, half my life, as a writer or teacher—a respectable period, yet whenever biographical details are printed, I am, almost inescapably, referred to as a *young* American sociologist, or a *young* American writer. And so are others of my generation of the same age or slightly older. To take some random examples: Harvey Swados, now thirty-nine, is still called a promising "young" writer although he has published three novels; Richard Hofstadter, who, at the age of forty-two, has published four first-rate historical interpretations, is called a young American scholar; James Wechsler, over forty, a young editor; Saul Bellow, over forty, a young American novelist; Leslie Fiedler, aged forty-three, a young American critic; Alfred Kazin, aged forty-four, a young American critic, etc., etc.

Two generations ago, a man of forty would not have been considered young. The Founding Fathers of the American Republic were largely in their thirties when the country was formed; so, too, were the leaders of the Russian Revolution. But this is an older man's world, and in the lengthening of the "shadow line" a damper is put on the younger generations.

But, beyond the general change in the tone of the culture, there is a more specific reason why the college generation of "the thirties" has been until now, at bay. This is because those who dominated "the thirties" were young themselves when they became established, and, until recently, have held major sway in the culture. *Partisan Review,* for example, is twenty-three years old, yet its editors, William Phillips and Philip Rahv, are not "old" men (say, fifty, give or take a year). Our intellectual nestors—Lionel Trilling, Sidney Hook, Edmund Wilson, Reinhold Niebuhr, John Dos Passos, Newton Arvin, F. W. Dupee, James T. Farrell, Richard Wright, Max Lerner, Elliott Cohen— were in their late twenties and early thirties when they made their mark as a new generation. The reason why there has been no revolt against them, as they, in asserting a radical politics, had ousted their elders, is that they led their own "counter-revolt." They had both iliad and odyssey, were iconistic and iconoclastic. They were intense, horta- tory, naive, simplistic, and passionate, but, after the Moscow Trials and the Soviet-Nazi pact, disenchanted and reflective; and from them and their experiences we have inherited the key terms which dominate discourse today: irony, paradox, ambiguity, and complexity.

Curiously, though they—and we—are sadder and perhaps wiser than the first political generations of the century, we are not better or greater. There are few figures today, or of the last twenty years, and few books, that can match the stature and work of Dewey, Beard, Holmes, Veblen, Brandeis. But to read these men today is to be struck by their essential optimism (even Veblen: read his *Engineers and the Price System,* and its technocratic vision of the future), which was based upon an ultimate faith in the rationality or common sense of men. Ours, a "twice-born" generation, finds its wisdom in pessimism, evil, tragedy, and despair. So we are both old and young "before our time."

The remarkable fact about the recent post-college generation, as one of its spokesmen, Norman Podhoretz, has pointed out, is its sober, matter-of-fact, "mature" acceptance of the complexities of politics and existence; but also, as he concludes, an underlying restlessness, a feeling of being cheated out of adventure, and a search for passion. There is a hankering for the misspent life that was never misspent. (But, I suspect, there has been, along with the strong emphasis on estheticism, homosexuality, and the like, a greater *sub-rosa* exploration of the decadent than Mr. Podhoretz admits.) And, among the more serious-minded, a longing for "a cause to believe in," although the self-conscious awareness of the desire for "a cause" itself is self-defeating.

Yet no generation can be denied an experience, even a negative one. Previously sane periods have seen such efflorescences as the "Yellow Book estheticism" of England in the nineties, or the mysticism and debauchery of Russian intellectuals (cf. Artzybesheff's *Sanine*) in the 1910's. In England today, in Kingsley Amis's *Lucky Jim* or John Osborne's *Look Back in Anger*, we have the flowering of what Christopher Sykes has called "redbrickism, provincialism, and all this belly-aching"—meaning a revolt against the cultural inbreeding of Oxford and Cambridge, and the grayness of the Welfare State. What will happen in the United States is difficult to foresee, for all expressions of revolt, whether it be Zen, or abstract expressionism, or Jungianism, or progressive jazz, quickly become modish and flat.[1] In the Christian trials of conversion (i.e., a genuine experience that transformed one's life) one had to be lost to be saved. Today, experiences are transposed from the moral to the psychological level, and to become "ecstatic" (literally, "ex-stasis," or outside one's self) one has to "let go" completely. But consciousness of self has become so inbred that even an impulse to "let go" becomes self-conscious; and so there is, almost, an infinite regress.

But the problem for the generation is less, as Mr. Podhoretz says, the "fear of experience" than an inability to define an "enemy." One can have causes and passions only when one knows against whom to fight. The writers of the twenties—Dadaist, Menckenian, and nihilist—scorned bourgeois mores. The radicals of the thirties fought "capitalism," and later, fascism, and for some, Stalinism. Today, intellectually, emotionally, who is the enemy that one can fight?

---

[1] This was written before the Beatnik fad unfolded, and dealt with the complaint of Mr. Podhoretz that his generation had found it difficult to adopt a radical political stance. Jack Kerouac, the "spokesman" of the Beat Generation, is, it should be pointed out, thirty-seven years old—a curious reversal of role, since the effort of the Beats is, like Peter Pan, the denial of growing up. It is, of course, an apolitical movement. See the essay by Norman Podhoretz, "The Know-Nothing Bohemians," *Partisan Review*, Spring, 1958.

The paradox is that the generation wants to live a "heroic" life but finds the image truly "quixotic." This is, as for Cervantes' Don, the end of an age. For the younger generation, as for all intellectuals, there is this impasse. It is part of the time which has seen the end of ideology.

The ideologist—Communist, existentialist, religionist—wants to live at some extreme, and criticizes the ordinary man for failing to live at the level of grandeur. One can try to do so if there is the genuine possibility that the next moment could be, actually, a "transforming moment" when salvation or revolution or genuine passion could be achieved. But such chiliastic moments are illusions. And what is left is the unheroic, day-to-day routine of living.

Max Weber, more than forty years ago, in a poignant essay entitled "Politics as a Vocation," posed the problem as one of accepting the "ethics of responsibility" or the "ethics of ultimate ends." For the latter —the "true believer"—all sacrifices, all means, are acceptable for the achievement of one's belief. But for those who take on responsibility, who forego the sin of pride, of assuming they know how life should be ordered or how the blueprint of the new society should read, one's role can be only to reject all absolutes and accept pragmatic compromise. As Edmund Wilson once described Theodore Roosevelt's attitude, politics, in a society where there is a shared consensus, becomes a "matter of adapting oneself to all sorts of people and situations, a game in which one may score but only by accepting the rules and recognizing one's opponents, rather than a moral crusade in which one's stainless standard must mow the enemy down."

In this sense, the generation of the thirties, whose representative men are Lionel Trilling and Reinhold Niebuhr, were prodigal sons who, in terms of American culture, had returned home. But one can't tread the same road twice. And a generation that knows it has to be "moral" and "responsible" is a generation that is destined to stay home.

## B. The Loss of Innocence in the Thirties

For a small group, the thirties have a special meaning. These are the individuals who went through the radical movement and who bear, as on invisible frontlets, the stamp of those years on their foreheads. The number is small. Of the four million college and high-school youths, less than twenty thousand, or one-half of one per cent, took part in radical activity. But, like the drop of dye that suffuses the cloth, this number gave the decade its coloration.

A radical is a prodigal son. For him, the world is a strange place whose contours have to be explored according to one's destiny. He may eventually return to the house of his elders, but the return is by choice, and not, as of those who stayed behind, because of unblinking filial obedience. A resilient society, like a wise parent, understands this ritual, and, in meeting the challenge to tradition, grows.

But in the thirties, the fissures were too deep. Seemingly, there was no home to return to. One could only march forward. Everybody seemed to be tramping, tramping, tramping. *Marching, Marching* was the title of a prize-winning proletarian novel.* There were parades, picketing, protests, farm holidays, and even a general strike in San Francisco. There was also a new man, the Communist. Not just the radical—always alien, always testing, yet open in his aims—but a hidden soldier in a war against society.

In a few short years, the excitement evaporated. The labor movement grew fat and bureaucratized. The political intellectuals became absorbed into the New Deal. The papier-mâché proletarian novelists went on to become Hollywood hacks. And yet it is only by understanding the fate of the prodigal sons and the Communists that one can understand the loss of innocence that is America's distinctive experience of the thirties.

Murray Kempton, in his book *Part of Our Time,* has looked at the small band who dreamed, and who—because of having a dream "possessed no more of doubting"—sought to impress that dream into action. But in action, one defines one's character. In some, the iron became brittle, in some it became hard; others cast the iron away, and still others were crushed. In the end, almost all had lost the dream and the world was only doubt.

The story opens, naturally enough, with Alger Hiss and Whittaker Chambers. Kempton retells the familiar story, but with a special nuance. What united the strange pair was their symbiotic relation to Baltimore, a mildewed city which was Kempton's home and whose musty character he captures so well. Hiss, from a shabby, genteel Baltimore family, fled its faded elegance to meet Chambers, the tortured man from the underground, who settled gratefully into its Victorian dust. Each found, in the secret craving of the other, the lives they were rejecting, until, locked in defeat, they both sank beneath the waters.

The story spreads out and touches on the writers attracted by the myth of the revolutionary collective, the "rebel girls," the militant labor leaders, the youth movement, and others who were riding the crest of history's waves. It is not a formal history of the left, but a series of novellas. What gives it its special cast and enormous appeal is the elegiac mood, the touch of adolescent ache in the writing.

A descendant of an old Southern family, James Murray Mason Ambler Kempton carries many bloodlines in his full name. In the thirties, he was, briefly a college Communist, went to sea, became a Socialist, and, fleeing the deracinated talk of New York intellectuals, enlisted and found a community, for a while, in the fighting platoons of New Guinea. Like all utopian moments, this communion had vitality only in memory, rather than enduring reality, and Kempton returned to New York, where, for the past six years, as a widely read columnist on the New York *Post,* he has been another Brann the iconoclast.

There are no villains in the book—none so wholly black that some

---

* [By Clara Weatherwax. Published by John Day in 1935.—Ed.]

degree of pity does not remain—only the pathos of those who, by living a lie, became consumed by it: John Howard Lawson, whose nervous *Processional* promised a new style in the American theater, but who, as a Hollywood commissar, played at revolution by smuggling lines of "progressive dialogue" into banal movies; Lee Pressman, the taut, brilliant labor lawyer, who chose Henry Wallace and the Progressives over Phil Murray and the C.I.O., and found, too late, that he had made the wrong choice; Ann Moos Remington, the prototype of the "rebel girl," who would only marry ardent William Remington if he would join the Young Communist League, but later, as his ex-wife, testified against him in a perjury trial.

There are heroes, for, unlike many disenchanted, Kempton has some —that radical breed, who, though patronized by the later "realists" who equated revolution with tough-mindedness, retained their kindness and idealism: James T. Farrell, an unpolished novelist, perhaps, but one whose bullheaded grasp of truth sent him rampaging against the Communist writer fronts; Gardener (Pat) Jackson, who organized the Sacco-Vanzetti defense but ran afoul of the Communist amoralists; Mary Heaton Vorse, who wrote of labor not as an abstract collective but as individuals; Edmund Wilson, whose canons of criticism kept him on an inviolate path of honesty.

There are many others: the incredible J. B. Matthews, a political Reverend Davidson, who, having slept with the red Sadie Thompsons, got lascivious contrition in exposing them; John Dos Passos, who found the Communist manipulations too frightening for his anarchist impulses and turned Republican; Joe Curran, who in going from park bench to labor leader became trapped by the dilemmas of responsibility and was forced to sweep aside his old rebel cohorts; the Reuther boys, uncomplicated by bohemian trappings, who soberly have sought to instill a sense of social discipline in America. And many others—the middle-class Vassar girls, the boy who died in Spain, the Negroes who rebuffed the Communists and obtained a new dignity. Like Malcolm Cowley's *Exile's Return* or Vincent Sheean's *Personal History*, Kempton's book is the story of a generation, and if it sometimes lacks the personal element of those accounts of the twenties, it has a sweep and power fired by the ache for the lost Arcadia.

In the end, the generation failed. Not because the idealistic impulses became exhausted; this is the inevitable trajectory, perhaps, of any radical generation. Not because events had belied the predictions; this is a healthier America. But because this may well have been the *last* radical generation for a time—the last because it was the first that tasted power and became corrupt. (Yet it is not only that power corrupts, for, as Alex Comfort once said, corrupt men seek power.) But the seed of the corruption was the *hubris* of the "possessed." Generous of impulse, it sought the end of injustice, but in the single vision the dogmatism grew hard and the moral sense cynical, so that, when reality proved the vision false, all that was left was the hardness, or the despair.

## C. *Politics* in the Forties

Dwight Macdonald made his political debut in 1937 by writing a five-page letter to the *New Republic* protesting Malcolm Cowley's pusillanimous review of the official transcripts of the Moscow trials; after considerable haggling, the *New Republic* printed one-third of the letter. Earlier, he had formed an exclusive club at Phillips Exeter Academy under the revolutionary motto of *Pour Epater les Bourgeois*. Following uneventful, non-revolutionary years at Yale, he worked briefly, during the opening of the Depression, at Macy's, as a member of its Executive Training Squad (in reaction to which, I suppose, he acquired the habit of wearing the loud pink-and-black striped shirts he now sports), and subsequently, like Jacob for Laban, he worked seven years on *Fortune*. For two years, Macdonald was a Trotskyite, making his exit from organized politics in 1940, when the Schachtmanites printed only 4,000 words of a 30,000-word study characterizing Nazi society as a new social form, that of bureaucratic collectivism. Writing an 8,000-word letter to the Political Committee, Macdonald made as a "minimum demand" for his continued collaboration the publication of an additional 4,000 words of his article. When the committee collectively and bureaucratically refused, he resigned. Reflecting on the incident, he declared that the party was not seriously "engaged in politics, but in metapolitics." (More seriously, it would seem to have been micropolitics.) Macdonald now concentrated his attention on *Partisan Review*, but resigned in 1943, when his pacifism led to growing disagreement with his co-editors. In 1944, Macdonald founded his monthly, later quarterly, periodical, *Politics*, an extraordinary achievement in personal journalism. In 1949, exhausted by these efforts, Macdonald surrendered *Politics* and politics, and turned to the more genteel pastures of the *New Yorker*.

This, then, is the career which unfolds in the lead essay of *The Memoirs of a Revolutionist*. These "memoirs," subtitled "Essays in Political Criticism," are not, apart from the introductory essay, autobiographical or reflective. They are, fifty selections in all, *aperçus*, editorials, reviews, the majority of them from *Politics*, the shorter and often insubstantial chips from the writer's block. The book does not contain Macdonald's most celebrated essay, on Popular Culture, or his most ambitious, "The Root Is Man," or (except for the profile of the latter-day Franciscan, Dorothy Day) any of the longer pieces from the *New Yorker*, e.g., the demolition of Mortimer Adler's *Syntopicon*, the do-it-yourself craze, etc.

And yet, these *cosettes* reveal Macdonald at his best—lively, witty, versatile—and at his worst—sardonic, superior, irritating. Macdonald is what may be called "an inconstant dogmatist." At any particular moment, he is completely cocksure of his position and unmerciful to an opponent. (When he is doing a literary demolition job, of which he is a master, woe to the writer who uses clumsy metaphors or commits stylistic gaucheries.) But then, like Heisenberg's particle, he is off in the next historical moment on a new, erratic tack, and often as dogmatic in the new stance as in the old.

There are several—saving—reasons why one is not annoyed at these inconstancies (apart from the grace of Macdonald's own good humor and his willingness to laugh at his own faults). Macdonald is a journalist-*cum*-intellectual, not a social scientist or a philosopher. The intellectual takes as a starting point his *self* and relates the world to his own sensibilities; the scientist accepts an existing field of knowledge and seeks to map out the unexplored terrain. The impulse of the journalist is to be novel, yet to relate his curiosities to the urgencies of the moment; the philosopher seeks what he conceives to be true, regardless of the moment. The changing nature of experience, thus, always seduces the intellectual. That is why Macdonald, temperamentally, is not really interested in ideas but in moral posture, and his is a constant search for inconstant verities.

These impulses, plus a remarkable devotion to his craft, did lead him for a moment to a unique place in American intellectual history. For when we come to look more closely at the forties, as our curiosities are now turned to the earlier decades, we may see that *Politics* was the only magazine that was aware of and insistently kept calling attention to, changes that were taking place in moral temper, the depths of which we still incompletely realize.

The singular theme of *Politics* was the event of depersonalization: the denigration of the individual through the impersonality of killing; the role of terror and extreme situations; how things happen to people and people became "things," the turning of society into a mechanism. The theme of depersonalization has now been made abstract and objectified, almost a literary commodity, by existentialism, Tillich's theology, and the popular sociology of the mass society. But in *Politics* it was there, palpable, in concrete detail, and illustrated in the ways in which individuals lost their humanness.

The best essays in the book, unfortunately only a fifth of the total, are those written during the war, when Macdonald, with his remarkable eye for significant detail, illuminated the psychology of killing, the pathetic attempts to expiate guilt, the mock bravado of war. Perhaps the most extraordinary article that *Politics* ever published was the abridgment of Bruno Bettelheim's account, from the *Journal of Abnormal and Social Psychology*, of "Behavior in Extreme Situations." The sense of fear that it evoked arose not from the descriptions of sadism in the concentration camps, but from the horrifying awareness that a victim, out of the deep, infantile, regressive aspects in one's own nature, would willingly take on the hideous mask, stance, and code of the brutes. Whatever we have heard subsequently about confessions, brainwashing, and the like, hardly matched the awesome revelation of those first disclosures.

Macdonald was more sensitive to these concerns because, as a pacifist, he was more alive to and horrified by these changes than those who justified the war; he was also influenced by Nicola Chiaramonte and other refugees who had first-hand contact with these sickening events.

Yet, more fundamentally, this awareness derived from a singular innocence about politics. One of the accusations that Ortega y Gasset brought against liberalism, as Mrs. Judith Shklar reminds us in her interesting book *After Utopia,* is that it forgot the violence inherent in politics. Ortega's indictment derived from the liberal's inability to understand the "fierce nature of the State," which, owing to the Hobbesian need to maintain order, must rule by threat against all. (And it followed for Ortega that all political activity was degrading, especially for the intellectual, whose vocation—the desire for truth—brought him into opposition to the politician, with his need for expediency, compromise, and myths.) Macdonald's fall from innocence came in the horrifying realization that violence—and the drive for domination—was a craving in man, and, following Hannah Arendt, that modern society had become a bureaucratized apparatus for periodically, and necessarily, evoking and suppressing such violence. And since the indictment of innocence could be leveled against radicalism as well, politics—and *Politics* —had to come to an end.

There remains the difficult question—far beyond the scope of this essay—of how true such a theory is. These political images are conceptions that derive from "heroic" and ultimately romantic images of life and man's place in it. To see politics on the more mundane, and civil, level of reconciling diverse interests may be naive. But this has been the British experience and, McCarthy apart, that of America, too. We do not live "at extremes" (and when we do, as in popular culture, this represents vicarious violence, not real experience, and is perhaps a useful displacement). That is why, perhaps, we have avoided some of the extreme ideological conflicts that wrecked Europe.

Apart from the apathy of the fat fifties, one reason, perhaps, why *Politics* could not last is that it drew from alien experiences. Is the fabric of American life strong enough to resist such rents as occurred in Europe? Did the war really leave us unmarked? It is the merit of Dwight Macdonald's *Memoirs* that he forces us once again to confront such desperate questions.

## D. *Dissent* in the Fifties

*Dissent* is one of the few cultural periodicals in the United States avowedly socialist in politics and radical in its criticism of contemporary culture. It is, like *Universities and Left Review* in England and *Arguments* in France, at odds with the doctrinaire interpretation of orthodox Marxism, and at one with the search for a new socialist humanism. But in important respects the differences are greater than the similarities. *Universities and Left Review* arose out of the ferment in the Communist world following the Khrushchev admissions that the Stalin regime had criminally murdered thousands of innocent Communists. *Arguments* came into being after the 1956 events in Poland and Hungary, and, in its intense philosophical absorption, reflects the revisionist discussions that have taken place in Eastern Europe. *Dissent,* five years older than the other two, was founded largely by individuals who had left the Trotskyite movement a few years before (the "class of 1950"), and who were long schooled in the doctrinal debates of Marxist exegetics.

The difference in origin accounts for the differences in tone and content. The first two are products of the fifties, cut off from the past by the war and the tales of their tired elders; the latter is an echo of the thirties, repeating, in mournful anger, the concerns and debates of the past. *Universities and Left Review* and *Arguments* represent a new generation with all the earnestness and questing freshness of the young; *Dissent* is a magazine of the epigone, the after-born, jejune, and weary. *Universities and Left Review* and *Arguments* are intense, frenetic, naive, bursting out with a new sense of auto-didact wonder about theoretical issues that had been wrangled over by the Left twenty years before; *Dissent* is querulous, scornful, magisterial, sectarian, yet infinitely more sophisticated.

These differences in style caricature, as extreme statements are wont to do, the gulf between European and American radicalism. It is not only that America has become an affluent society, offering place (in the universities and in the publishing houses) and prestige (if not in the society as a whole, certainly in the universities and the publishing houses) to the onetime radicals—and it is interesting to note that the two chief editors of *Dissent,* Irving Howe and Lewis Coser, are university professors—but American radicalism had, intellectually, long ago disposed of the very questions that rack the serious European Left today. It is that fact—as well as the one that American society, through the modifications introduced by Roosevelt and Truman, belied Marxist predictions of "fascism and collapse"—which explains much of the difference in intellectual atmosphere between the two continents.

This is a seeming paradox. Europe, in legend, has always been the home of subtle philosophical discussion; America was the land of grubby pragmatism. Questions laid to rest in Europe found their reincarnation (an old quip had it) twenty years later in the United States. Whatever the truth of the remark once, the reverse is true today. Take any of the questions that in the last five years have preoccupied Sartre and Camus in France, Wolfgang Harich in East Germany, Kolakowski in Poland— the questions of ends and means, of class truth, the meaningfulness of dialectic materialism as a scientific construct, the definition of a workers' State, party democracy, the nature of bureaucracy, the relationship of literature to propaganda, the mixed economy—and you will find that these were thrashed out more than twenty years ago by Sidney Hook, Ernest Nagel, Lewis Corey, Edmund Wilson, Philip Rahv, John Dewey, and dozens of others in the pages of *Partisan Review,* the *New International,* and the *New Leader.* It is not that these men had greater theoretical acumen than Marxists in Europe, many of whom, individually (most notably Ignazio Silone, in *Bread and Wine*), had explored these same problems. But while in Europe only a small number of intellectuals left the Communist orbit before the war, in the United States almost the entire group of serious intellectuals who had been attracted to Marxism had broken with the Communist party by 1940. Thus, as an intellectual problem, Bolshevism disappeared from the American scene almost twenty years ago.

The sociological reasons for these differences in behavior are varied. Being 3,000 miles from Europe, the American radicals were not caught up in the immediate political struggles of fascism—and the possibility of having to become refugees—so there was less reason to suppress the political doubts which had been fired by the Moscow Trials and the Nazi-Soviet Pact. In the United States, moreover, the Communist party never had a large following in the labor movement, so there was no emotional force the party could use to hold the intellectuals. And, being free-floating intellectuals, rather than functionaries or officials who had to swing a large political movement with them, the discussions were more "irresponsible," yet by the same token freer and more intense.

As a result of such free-spiritedness, the basic political drift of the former Left intelligentsia in the United States in the forties and fifties has been anti-ideological—that is to say, skeptical of the rationalistic claim that socialism, by eliminating the economic basis of exploitation, would solve all social questions; and to a great extent this anti-rationalism is the source of the intellectual vogue of Freudianism and neo-orthodox theology (i.e., Reinhold Niebuhr and Paul Tillich), with their anti-rational stoicism. Moreover, the American intellectuals found new virtues in the United States because of its pluralism, the acceptance of the Welfare State, the spread of education, and the expanding opportunities for intellectual employment. And, in the growing Cold War, they accepted the fact that Soviet Russia was the principal threat to freedom in the world today. These political attitudes were reflected largely in the pages of *Partisan Review, Commentary,* and the *New Leader,* the three magazines, and the writers grouped around them, that originally made up the core of the American Committee for Cultural Freedom. On the academic level, these re-evaluations called into question the populist basis of American radicalism and argued that the political conflicts of the fifties, such as McCarthyism, were more fruitfully explained by sociological concepts such as "status anxiety" than by the more conventional notions of class or interest group conflicts. The changes in intellectual temper can be seen in Lionel Trilling's *The Liberal Imagination,* Richard Hofstadter's *The Age of Reform,* Edward Shils' *The Torment of Secrecy,* and the various essays on "McCarthyism" in *The New American Right,* edited by this writer.

It was in this context of the breakup of the old Left, and in reaction to these re-evaluations, that *Dissent* arose. Its targets were those who were calling the old radical clichés into question, and the internal debate was carried on, as it has usually been in the United States, in that large, exotic cauldron that is the New York intellectual world. While *Dissent* talked of the conformism of American society, and the need for "new ideas," there was little path-breaking thought on radicalism. "What Shall We Do?" asks one of the editors, Lewis Coser, in a programmatic essay. "Above all, it would seem to me," says editor Coser, the radical "must be concerned with maintaining, encouraging, fostering the growth of the species 'radical.' If it becomes extinct, our culture will inevitably ossify from want of challenge." But challenge to what? Radical about what? *Dissent* attacked *Partisan Review* and *Commentary* for not being radical. But, other than attacking these magazines, there was little in *Dissent* itself that was new; it never exemplified what it meant by radicalism; and it has not been able, especially in politics, to propose anything new.

For actually *Dissent* has been hoist, as has been the Left as a whole, on the meaninglessness of the term. In the past, radicalism had vitality because it was a form of *apocalyptic* thought—it wanted to wash away an entire society in one tidal wave. ("I went to Cuba," writes Livio Stecchini in a recent issue of *Dissent,* in an article which expresses in extraordinary fashion the romantic pathos of the magazine, "because over the years I have become disappointed with revolutionary ideas and experience. Selfishly I wanted to share the exhilaration that comes from living by hope and desire *before the dawn of reality.*") But where the problems are, as Karl Popper put it, of "piecemeal technology," of the prosaic, yet necessary questions, of school costs, municipal services, the urban sprawl, and the like, bravura radicalism simply becomes a hollow shell.

If *Dissent* has had a single unifying idea—and this is what gives any radical magazine its character—it is its conceptualization of America as a *mass society,* and its attack on the grotesque elements of such a society. And here *Dissent* begins to merge in identity with *Universities and Left Review,* and other new voices of the Left which attack modern society. The concept of the *mass society,* however, has a peculiar amorphousness. Those who used the older vocabulary of radicalism could attack "the capitalists" or even "the bourgeoisie," but in the *mass society* one simply flails out against "the culture," and it is hard to discover who, or what, is the enemy. This is not true of the older group of writers who first employed the idea of the mass society, principally Ortega y Gasset, Joseph Pieper, Karl Jaspers, and T. S. Eliot. They have had an aristocratic, or Catholic, or elite conception of culture, and for them the standards of taste and excellence, once set by the educated and the cultivated, have been torn down by the mass. They stood against equalitarianism and industrial society. In effect, they did not want to give the masses "cultural voting rights." But it is difficult for the "young radical" to adopt this stance. Nor can they easily absorb, intellectually, though many have done so without seeing the contradiction, the pastoral-romantic image (which derives from German sociology)—that the roots of the old *Gemeinschaft* have been torn up by the impersonal, mechanized society. This protest has always been the cry of the rural society against the rootlessness, anonymity—yet privacy and freedom— of the city. (But the young radicals are not rural idiots.) I believe the image of the mass society, as used by *Dissent* and *Universities and Left Review,* to be misleading. The bringing of the "mass" *into* a society from which they have been excluded is, as Edward Shils has been argu- ing, a long and difficult process. Yet against the "traditional society," in which people led the same dull, rote, often brutalized lives (Saul Padover, in a study of France, has pointed out that a large number of Frenchmen have never traveled, belonged to a voluntary association, or even seen the inside of a museum), modern society, with its possibilities for mobility, occupational choice, theater, books, and museums, is more differentiated, variegated, and life-enhancing.

The pages of *Dissent* and *Universities and Left Review* are full of attacks against advertising, the debaucheries of mass culture, and the like. And, often, phrasing these criticisms in the language of the early Marx, particularly in terms of alienation, gives these attacks a seeming political content. But the point is that these problems are essentially cultural and not political, and the problem of radical thought today is to reconsider the relationship of culture to society. Certainly few per- sons will assume the relationships of culture to politics to be as direct as Marxist critics assumed them to be twenty-five years ago. And when, with the lesson of totalitarianism and bureaucracy in mind, one comes to accept—in the mixed economy and political pluralism—moderation in social politics, specifying the content of "cultural radicalism" becomes even more difficult. The paradox is that whatever is deemed radical in culture is quickly accepted, and whatever calls itself avant-garde, be it abstract expressionism or Beatnik poetry, is quickly acclaimed. When the products of high culture, from Schönberg to Matisse to *l'école de New York,* become best-selling cultural items, the problem of locating the source of the "corruption" of standards becomes a difficult one. The acceptance of the avant-garde has become so vexing that Hilton Kramer (an editor of *Arts*), writing in *Dissent,* was moved to say, "The fact of the matter is that since 1945 bourgeois society has tightened its grip on all the arts by allowing them a freer rein." (And, one might say, a freer reign.)

In part, some of this is due to the desire for novelty and sensation in American life. But on a more serious level, these changes are also a feature of the absorption of radicalism into the society. Just as mana- gerial authority is shared, in part, by the unions, and political power is shared, in part, with the ethnic and labor groups, so the culture, too, in part, has been transformed. Many of the new cultural arbiters (Clem- ent Greenberg and Harold Rosenberg in painting, Lionel Trilling and Alfred Kazin in literature) were part of the *ancien* Left, and their tastes have affected not only the serious painters and novelists but the standards of the larger public as well. One other important consideration must be noted. The cultural elite—to the extent that there is one, and I believe there is—is primarily a university culture, that of Harvard, Columbia, Berkeley, and other large centers; and, in contrast to fifty years ago, it is a "liberal culture," receptive to ideas, critical in its outlook, and encouraging of (and sometimes nostalgic for) dissent. To that extent, and this is the final paradox, even *Dissent* is an accredited member of that culture, and a welcome one.

## JOHN WAIN

## Along the Tightrope*

What distinguishes this essay by John Wain (1925–    ) is its common-sense temperateness, which indeed the metaphor of the title (developed in the last paragraph) demonstrates. It appeared in a volume of essays by young—or comparatively young—British novelists, poets, and critics, who have been dubbed (in the fashion of the journalist trying to keep pace with "the new") the "Angry Young Men." In fact, the book's editor, Tom Maschler, points out that it is "a collection of separate positions"; that, while some of the contributors may be angry, none is exclusively so; and that not all of them are young. They are contemporaries, but they are also "in the tradition"; and their principal claim to distinction may well be that (especially in their novels) they have made what they can of a present set of conditions in terms of its resemblances to past occurrences. Wain's prose (as does his position) contrasts vividly with the open, pugnacious, even violent extraversion of the final essay in this collection.

> The world is only the mirror of ourselves. If it's something to make one puke, why then puke, me lads, it's your own sick mugs you're looking at!—HENRY MILLER

*T*he writer's subject-matter, the thing all literature is *about*, can be indicated very simply: it is about what it is like to be a human being. Everybody has his own view of what constitutes humanity, and this view determines his actions and attitudes; if he is an artist, it determines what kind of art he produces. Authors fall into two categories, broadly

* The spelling in this selection has been Americanized by the editor.

speaking: those whose concern with humanity is analytical and enquiring, and those who are out to *recommend* something positive. The first type stands back from humanity and asks, "What is it?" The second type runs forward, pointing and beckoning the rest to follow.

But this simple division, though useful as a preliminary, is really an over-simplification, because every author combines both types, the difference being in how the two are mixed. They all analyze and investigate, and they all—even if they aren't fully conscious of it—have something to recommend. The artist's function is always to *humanize* the society he is living in, to assert the importance of humanity in the teeth of whatever is currently trying to annihilate that importance. In the Middle Ages, his task was to assert the importance of humanity in the teeth of a religious orthodoxy, to declare that there could be and ought to be such a thing as life here and now as well as life hereafter. Today, the adversary is the machine; having surrounded ourselves with mechanisms that are miracles of precision and refinement, we have become so lost in contemplation of them that all our thinking has become mechanistic. Our ambition is to become machines—then we shall be certain of the very best of everything. This worship of the machine is a far worse tyranny than the Church, even at its most megalomaniac, ever dreamed up; it is worse to the precise degree that the television screen is more pervasive than the pulpit, the loudspeaker louder than the human voice, the aeroplane faster than the horse. This means that the job of humanizing our environment has to be taken more seriously than ever. *And he that is not with us is against us.*

But an author, whether he is going to preach to humanity or merely investigate it, has first to get himself into some intelligible relationship with the bulk of his fellow-creatures. Here is the first problem; let me indicate it with a quotation. It is always helpful to see how these things have been formulated by other people. Let us take that passage in Christopher Isherwood's *Lions and Shadows,* where the narrator goes to the seaside. He begins, you may remember, by indulging in a masochistic loathing-spree as he contemplates the English on holiday. At last, however, the reflection breaks in:

But beneath all my note-taking, my would-be scientific detachment, my hatred, my disgust, there was the old sense of exclusion, the familiar grudging envy. For, however I might sneer, these people *were* evidently enjoying themselves in their own mysterious fashion, and why was it so mysterious to me? Weren't they of my own blood, my own caste? Why couldn't I—the would-be novelist, the professional observer—understand them? Why didn't I know—not coldly, from the outside, but intuitively, sympathetically, from within—what it was that made them perform their grave ritual of pleasure; putting on blazers and flannels in the morning, plus-fours or white trousers in the afternoon, dinner jackets in the evening; playing tennis, golf, bridge; dancing, without a smile, the foxtrot, the tango, the blues; smoking their pipes, reading the newspapers, organizing a sing-song, distributing prizes after a fancy-dress ball? True, I wasn't alone in my isolation. People like my friends and myself, I thought, are to be found in little groups in all the larger towns; we form a proudly self-sufficient, consciously declassed minority. We have our jokes, we amuse each other enormously; we are glad, we say, that we are different. But are we really glad? Does anybody ever feel sincerely pleased at the prospect of remaining in permanent opposition, a social misfit, for the rest of his life? I knew, at any rate, that I myself didn't. I wanted—however much I might try to persuade myself, in moments of arrogance, to the contrary—to find some place, no matter how humble, in the scheme of society. Until I do that, I told myself, my writing will never be any good; no amount of talent or technique will redeem it; it will remain a greenhouse product; something, at best, for the connoisseur and the clique.

There we have the problem. And stating it in someone else's words is already a kind of comfort; it brings the sense that the difficulty is universal; if others have overcome it, it may be possible to learn from them how to succeed in one's turn; if they have all failed, one will either uniquely succeed, or fail in excellent company. There are many statements I might have quoted, but I chose Isherwood's because I find it, in tone and terms of reference, immensely sympathetic. Especially that bit about not wanting to be a greenhouse writer, admired by "the connoisseur and the clique." How one agrees! Better *no* reputation than the kind of reputation that accretes and clings to a Corvo, a Firbank, a Lautréamont even!

No, indeed, one doesn't want to stay in permanent opposition. But there is one thing worse—permanent conformity. No age in human history was ever so acceptable, so free of cankers and evils, that its more clear-sighted inhabitants could afford to string along with it *all* the time. A mechanical conformity, a mechanical rebelliousness, are both useless. The first has few temptations for an artist, the second many; especially as most artists are the type who fall easily into a pattern of unconventionality and defiance in childhood, and then tend to follow this pattern for sixty years after it has ceased to correspond to a genuine situation. How many an ageing genius, thundering defiance at the world, is in reality compensating himself for the mindless rigors of some loathsome little boarding-school back in 1912. On the other hand, the advice that is sometimes given to artists, that they should get on with their work and let society look after itself, is based on a lack of understanding of what their work *is*. What is needed, not just in artists, but in everyone who hopes to be more than a mere worker or mere drone in the hive, is a sense of touch. As I was making notes for this essay I heard a broadcast in which P. M. S. Blackett, the English scientist who is most widely accepted as spokesman for his calling, was being questioned about his views in general; several attempts were made to pin him down on the question of the scientific responsibility for extinction weapons; finally, asked point-blank whether or not a scientist was free to refuse to hand over the results of his research to irresponsible politicians and soldiers, he virtually threw up the whole subject in despair, with the words, "No one is free, in a closely integrated society like ours." This is certainly true, and an artist who claims to have *no* relationship with the society he lives in is claiming a freedom which he does not possess; even if he is a mystic, whose wants are limited to a prayer-mat and a begging bowl, it was probably some flaw in his relationship with society in general that drove him to adopt that position in the first place.

An artist, then, will have some position *vis-à-vis* the rest of the world whether he wants it or not—even if it is the sterile and undeveloping attitude of "permanent opposition"—and his work, again whether he wishes it or not, will reflect his views on the matter. So it is in order for him to marshal his thoughts, from time to time, about what could broadly be called "social" issues. The chief danger is that he may be pushed too often into the rôle of social prophet. The public, at the moment, is in an alarmingly eager mood.

*Signs are taken for wonders. "We would see a sign!"* The minute any kind of artist attracts attention, he is treated as a spokesman for his generation, his nation, his class, and what not. We have all seen, and deplored, the absurd results of the wide-spread journalistic habit of making *Lucky Jim* a symbol for anything that happened to be going about in search of a symbol. In all the mountains of print that have heaped up around that novel, there has been hardly a word of intelligent criticism. The overriding impulse, now more than ever, is to use any kind of articulate person—articulate with pen, with brush, with chisel, with musical notes—as a witch-doctor. The individual artist, who knows that his art is not merely another page of Hansard, is unwilling to have this rôle thrust on him; he veers away from it; so the solution is to find half a dozen or so who have some points of resemblance, then proclaim a Trend or a Movement. The latest of these fatuities is the Angry Young Man business; a phrase, I believe, originally applied to Mr. Woodrow Wyatt, a politician, and subsequently extended far enough to include on the one hand a handful of poets, dramatists and novelists, and on the other such figures as Mr. Colin Wilson and the late James Dean, both of whom belong to the active rather than comtemplative life; they symbolize, in their own persons, the thing the others are supposed to be talking about. As a journalistic stunt, this will pass; the artist has merely to recognize, as one more fact about the world he is living in, that he has to be his own interpreter as well as the original provider of things to be interpreted; the journalists have abrogated their function; the task of comment, which in a better age he could have left to them, is now passed back to him again.

So one begins the process of trying to weigh up the society one is living in, and to find some coherent attitude towards it. And the first thing that stands out, to my mind, is the curious nature of the changes we are living through. Everyone always speaks of the twentieth century as an epoch of rapid change, so rapid as to be without parallel; old people, interviewed by the local press on their ninetieth birthdays, are always asked what changes they have seen, and always give the appropriate answer, the one that is expected of them; nothing, wherever they look, is what it was, or where it was, when they were young.

But when we look at this change in all its proliferation of detail, the most striking thing is not its extent, its completeness, but its lumpy and patchy quality. This lumpiness is observable both spatially (rapid change going on in one quarter, complete standstill in another) and temporally (curious stoppings and startings over a period of years). I find this most clearly illustrated when I consider the grown-ups' talk of "the future" when I was a small boy. The generation of my parents had been brought up in a world that did not seem to them to be changing much (though I think they were wrong), and had, after 1914, been plunged into a mill-race of change from which they saw no prospect of ever emerging. They naturally assumed that every process of which they had seen the beginning would continue at the same pace. Take one detail: church attendance, for instance. Before 1914, if a tradesman wanted the custom of solid citizens, he had to turn up at church, and see to it that his family turned up with him; a doctor or solicitor who wanted to establish his practice couldn't afford to be known as a Freethinker; his place was at morning service with the rest of the respectable world. So the churches were always full. Then came the war, and a general untying of this kind of social corsetry; the churches attracted one in ten of their previous congregations, mostly older people. So, to my parents, it seemed natural to expect that when this remnant died off, nobody would go to church at all, and organized religion would be at a standstill. In fact, of course, the level has remained about where it was; all that had happened was that social pressure was relaxed, so that the only people who attended church were those who wanted to; if these were mainly the older people, that too was natural. In other words, an initial violent change was followed by a long period of stability. And this has happened in countless other spheres. Aviation, for instance. In 1930, when I was five, my elders took it for granted that in twenty years' time "everyone would have his own aeroplane—like cars today." For some years *Punch* had been publishing cartoons about traffic jams in the air, policemen on point-duty suspended from balloons, and so forth. And what happened? Long before I came of age, private aviation was as extinct as private charity.

In the field of politics it was the same. Most middle-aged people, when I was a boy, lived in continual expectation of a revolution, organized by "the Reds." (It was this fear of "Reds," of course, that led our governing class to extend so warm a welcome to those sterling anti-Reds, Hitler and Mussolini, and thus involve us in the second war—and how easily we have forgiven them!) This fear was natural; they had seen 1916, both in Russia and, small-scale but near at hand, in Ireland; and they expected, once again, that the process, having started, would continue at about the same speed. Every strike, every hunger-march, was the work of the "Reds," who were already hiding under the beds of old women of both sexes, ready to cut their throats. And here we are, nearly three decades further on, and the English working class have never been less Red in their history; all they are interested in is wringing higher and higher wages out of the bankrupt industries that employ them, with never a thought of altering the social structure in any way.

In fact, of course, what appeared to be the very rapid and sweeping changes brought about by the first world war had been well under way for some time. What the war did was to shake the fabric or ordinary convention so much that the new ideas were let loose. There was no longer any need to *épater le bourgeois*, because the bourgeois, in the pre-1914 sense of the word, no longer existed. So the immediate effect was that developments which had been carried on offstage, where the "average man" couldn't see them, came onstage. Very little was actually initiated in this period; in the arts, the real starting-point is in the years immediately before the shooting started. The "new" literature of the twenties was mainly produced by men like Lawrence, Joyce, Wyndham Lewis, Pound and Eliot, who had got quite firmly started before the war. By contrast, a writer like Aldous Huxley, who was accepted by millions as a symbol of modernity, was only superficially an innovator. The ferment of ideas that many people associate with his work was in fact the *vulgarization* of a process that had been going on, at the centers of discussion, for half a lifetime previously. Consider this sentence, describing the intellectual atmosphere at Oxford: "There may have been too much restlessness and desire for change, there certainly was a tendency to treat everything as an open question, which led to a general sense of insecurity in matters of opinion." When does that date from? The 1920's? No, the 1860's (*Life and Letters of Mandell Creighton,* 1913, chap. 3). And what is true of writing holds equally well for everything else. Mr. David Sylvester, in a recent article (*Twentieth Century,* March 1957) has it this way:

It seems to me that the twenty-five years or thereabouts leading up to the 1914 war were a time of astonishing creative ferment in almost every field. It was not only fine art that made a great leap of the imagination during this time. The foundations of modern logic and analytical philosophy were laid at this time by Frege, Russell and others, as were the foundations of psycho-analytic investigation by Freud and his colleagues. What has happened since in these fields might be just as aptly described as a specialized development of those initial discoveries as the art of the last forty years could be described as a specialized development of the discoveries of Cézanne and Monet and Gauguin and Rodin. And this even applies to the physical sciences. The invention or discovery of the aeroplane, of wireless telegraphy, of Röntgen rays, of the principles of atomic physics—these too belong to the time of Cézanne and early Picasso.

With this tremendous leap, our century took off into space; and to people living in the twenties, it seemed that the changes must go on. In fact, I sometimes think that my generation, those who came of age immediately after the second war, were the first to grasp clearly that this was simply not happening. Where were all the things my parents and their friends used to prophesy when I was a nipper? Nowhere, it seemed, except in the pages of early Wells, mouldering on the shelves. Strangest of all was the attitude of people who had been young in the twenties, and were now getting into middle age. In their youth, it had seemed that the rigid crust of conventional life was cracking from top to bottom; a few more holes punched in it, and it would be nothing but a heap of crumbs. And behold! everything had somehow drifted back into something like the old shape; things like marriage, and private property, and war, and the division of the world into nations, and the Church, and the public schools—there they all were, the same as ever! To such people, the twentieth century must seem like one long tragic swindle. It isn't a new situation; an exactly parallel sequence of events happened in the lifetime of Wordsworth; he had just that glimpse of a new world, with

> France standing on the top of golden hours,
> And human nature seeming born again.

That's the trouble with new starts. Human nature is always seeming born again, and always growing up into much the same kind of shape as it always had.

Not that anyone of my age has had to face the problem of disillusionment. About the first fact we learnt about the world we were living in was that there aren't any new starts. From the age of ten, I inhabited a world in which everyone knew that a war was coming—i.e., that the War to End War had done nothing of the kind. The twenties had been an enormous gate, opening on to nothing special. One hardly knew whether to be glad or sorry that one hadn't been among the people who trooped through that gate, hearts beating high, and later had to adjust to the ordinariness of what they found. On the principle that to travel hopefully is better than to arrive, one should, I suppose, be sorry. Still, it can't be helped. What we have to cope with is this sense of being arrested in mid-air. Our whole society is suffering from a sensation very much like the one you get if you brace yourself to jump down ten stairs and then find it was only one. And this calls into being a special kind of intellectual nuisance: the crusading modernist, who is prepared to jump down ten stairs even if he has to dig a pit to do it. There he is, out of sight below ground-level in his pit, but his voice can be heard continually, making the same querulous demand to the rest of us to get our spades and do some digging.

In short, the position is difficult because of the slowness of change, not its speed. The surface of life has altered very quickly, but the inner core was re-structured in about 1912, and until the next major step forward—which may not be for a century or two, if ever—it is unlikely to alter much. Journalists don't realize this because they think that things like television, artificial satellites and cars with no clutches are signs of change—are, indeed, changes in themselves. But of course the only change worth taking any notice of is a change in character. If a man appears wearing a new suit, his baby daughter may think he has changed, but his wife and friends know that he hasn't.

This is what we have to get used to; this living with key ideas that are not new, that have already been absorbed—however incompletely —into the bloodstream of the community. Whenever we look up a date, we find ourselves staggered by the mere length of time all these "modern" ideas have been going. For instance, one of the last of the really "basic" books, the ones that put forward ideas which have since been accepted by *everyone,* was Freud's *Psychopathology of Everyday Life.* And Freud tells us in the preface that he established the basic idea in an essay, "On the Psychic Mechanism of Forgetfulness," in 1898. In short, the whole thing is a nineteenth-century discovery; another instance, among thousands, of the fact that we are still living in the era created by those incredible frockcoated, bewhiskered giants.

In one way, the task of those of us who pick up the main burden now, in the fifties, is harder than it was for our predecessors. In the recent past, it was enough—or, at any rate, it was widely felt to be enough—if you were "modern"; that is, if you welcomed the new ideas with a certain enthusiasm, and with whatever degree of misunderstanding and clumsiness. Auden's poems, with their hotch-potch mixing-in of every up-to-date idea, are the perfect document of "modernism"; all the better as a document in that they have, after all, a certain quality that sets them apart from the merely rubbishy. As I say, you could get by. And you could also get by in the forties, without doing much more than be portentous and solemn. The war made genuinely constructive thought impossible, and at the same time created a demand for an acceptable substitute; as a result, the forties were the heyday of charlatanism. We are still plagued by some of the reputations that were first made in those slap-happy days, though the Great Healer is, I am happy to say, beginning to do his work.

But it is the present generation who are really brought face to face with these key ideas of our society; who can't, at this distance of time, get by on mere enthusiastic acceptance; who have to keep their heads.

What do I mean, in detail, by "keeping our heads"? In the first place, a rejection of wholesale thinking and block attitudes. If a mechanical rebelliousness is futile, it is also true that an uncritical "acceptance" of the age one lives in is not so much culpable as impossible. How *can* anyone say that he accepts, or rejects, the twentieth century *en bloc?* It is too full of unresolved muddles for that. Not only have the forces of change acted patchily, leaving inert areas (e.g. the physical sciences have changed out of recognition, while the civil law has remained in the nineteenth century; we still cannot get rid of the death penalty or revolutionize the prison system); not only that, but the various eddies of modern thought have lost touch with one another. To take one example and let it stand for a thousand, consider our attitude to "nature"; using the word, here, to mean the opposite of "man-made" or "artificial." In one way, the twentieth century is great on Nature. The dominant science in our grandfathers' day was biology, and the metaphors on which they based all their thinking were derived from that study. Thus the metaphor of evolution colored political and historical thinking and has survived unchanged in most academic disciplines till today. The dominant science of our time is psychology; it, too, has its leading metaphors, which have passed into popular thought, the most influential being the idea of repression and the uncovering of successive layers of consciousness, so that the layman's picture of the psychiatrist is of Peer Gynt contemplating his onion. And behind this lies the archetypal modern belief: it is unwise to tamper with Nature; the instinctual forces will go forward with a bull-like rush, and you must either stand out of the way or be gored. D. H. Lawrence, with his notion of the hidden springs of power, is the typical twentieth-century prophet; he saw this power as surging up from below the reach of the conscious mind, which could hamper but not command it. It is not too much to say that this belief, revolutionary when Lawrence first formulated it, has now taken unchallenged possession of the collective mind; virtually *everybody* agrees with it. So far, we are for Nature. And just as the mind must peel off its layers, so must the body. Let the sun shine for thirty minutes —even the watery sun of England—and every patch of grass is covered with nearly-naked figures, rapt, worshipping, mystically intent on soaking up the holy rays. *Nature!* Dive into the sea, roast in the sun, let your impulses grow up straight rather than tortuously—for grow they will, in some guise. Up to this point, it would seem that all of us, in our civilization, were unanimous in this at least. Until one looked round more widely.

Until one noticed, for instance, the kind of medical science we put our faith in. The chemists' shops, thronged all day with seekers after well-being—well-being in the shape of palliatives to ease symptoms; our medical laboratories where "research" is directed to the frontal attack of these same symptoms. These places are reared and supported by the energy of an idea, and that idea is in flat contradiction of the worship of a beneficent Nature. Its theoretical basis is that Nature, too weak and faulty to defend herself, is open to the assaults of hostile bacteria, which can only be combated by training a specially ferocious brand of antibiotics, like ferrets, to hunt them down. So the new wonder-drugs succeed each other at intervals of a few months; a new one is tried, it gobbles up the bacteria, the symptoms vanish, a victory is proclaimed in military metaphor ("such-and-such a disease is *conquered*"), and Nature is properly in her place. But of course, before the ink is dry on the newspapers that celebrate this victory the evil bacteria have gone home and put on a new uniform, to reappear as something else—a new set of symptoms to be isolated and attacked. On with the job!—train a new cageful of ferrets! There's no nonsense here about Nature and her benevolence. If a man is ill, the answer is to pump him full of some chemical concoction whose job is to get in there and *work*. The same thing is seen in the now fashionable "check-up." Every few weeks one reads in the newspaper that some politician has gone into a nursing-home "for a check-up." If he is an American statesman, the findings will be made public; if an Englishman, they will be reticently concealed; but in either case the same thing has happened. A lung man has looked at his lungs, a liver man at his liver, a nose-and-throat man at his nose and throat, and so on. The more important he is, the more specialists he has. If he is as important as Mr. Eisenhower, he can have a left knee-cap specialist to examine his left knee-cap, and a right knee-cap man for his right, if he wants to. These specialists have their own dynamic metaphor; they are detectives, and all the parts of the man's body are suspects, which have to be questioned, examined, weighed, and—if faulty—immediately chastised, i.e. set upon by the appropriate ferrets. Nature, in this context, is far from the numinously authoritative figure she assumes elsewhere. At worst she is an enemy, at best an erring child to be scolded and corrected.

Let this stand as an emblem of the difficulties of a man who wishes to reject, or accept, the age we live in. Here we have this hotch-potch of conflicting ideas about Nature; the distinguishing mark of the twentieth-century man, if he has one at all, is his willingness to hold these contradictory ideas simultaneously in his head. He trusts in Nature when he sun-bathes, or talks about the evils of "repression" (thought of, in this connection, as a kind of super-constipation); he mistrusts and fears her when he goes round to his doctor for a shot of penicillin. The confusion repeats itself in many other spheres; over materials, for instance. It is cheaper to make a thing out of plastics than out of wood or leather, so the more expensive craftsman makes a point of using natural materials, and "artificial," in Elizabethan English a term of praise, comes to mean something cheap and nasty. Then we get the motor-car with its metal instrument panel painted to imitate the grain of wood. Lip-service to Nature, just as the electric light bulb set in a plastic imitation of a candle-stick is lip-service to age and primitive simplicity.

The word "primitive," having at last cropped up, points to the area in which this confusion is a special concern of the artist. Primitivism, which is the artistic equivalent of sun-bathing and psycho-analysis, has dominated the arts for a long time now; the abandonment of metre and rhyme in poetry, which had set in by 1914, echoed the discovery, by visual artists, of the merits of rock-painting and native sculpture. But the drive towards the primitive was set in motion, and directed, by a sophisticated impulse to find new techniques to match the altered demands of the *Zeitgeist*—an impulse which was sufficient in itself to keep modern art at a wide remove from the *genuinely* primitive; in other words, the electric-light candle again, but this time as an artistic and intellectual necessity rather than a mere whim. (But the whim *derives* from the necessity; it corresponds to something real, after all.) In music, the technical discoveries of the previous three centuries were largely thrown away, and the new music repeated the blend of self-conscious technique and highly engineered "freedom." But I have said enough, for a topic which was introduced only as an example. How can one accept or reject?—the only course is to keep one's head.

This keeping one's head may seem too trivial to be erected into a serious ideal, but there are epochs in which it is the hardest thing one can do, and at the same time the most valuable. Historical parallels are misleading, and if I say that the present age seems to have some affinities with the period 1660–1700, I don't mean that we can use that or any other period as the basis for forecast. But that, like this, was a time of assessment and digestion; terribly destructive strife was a recent memory; clear thinking, rather than originality, was what counted. One fact that tends to confirm my belief in the accuracy of this assessment is the anger shown by many middle-aged people when they hear it. Some of the most scathing rejoinders that, as a critic, I have provoked, have been when, in no spirit of contention, I have remarked that the task of the immediate future seemed to me one of consolidation. On one such occasion, Mr. Pritchett, amid much speculation about the cultural effects of free education and what-not, said sniffily that he "could imagine a brighter future for literature." So can I; I was not saying that my diagnosis was bright, merely that it was accurate. These people always assume that to say an era of experiment has ended is to imply that it has come to nothing. Whereas the problem of what to do with a mass of new material can be as urgent, and as challenging, as the problem of how to accumulate it in the first place.

According to my brief, I am supposed to say something, in this essay, about my own work and how it arises from the way I view things. The task is the simpler because so little of it has, at the moment of writing, been published, and not very much of that little has attracted any attention. My first novel, *Hurry on Down,* has been assimilated to the Angry Young Man business; my poems have been taken as evidence of the new literary conservatism and traditionalism; my criticism is supposed to show the new "Redbrick" academicism, as opposed to the old fruity, porty academicism that has long been familiar. None of these assessments is anything but a caricature, though the caricature itself offers valuable evidence as to the nature of the group mind.[1]

All artists who do not see themselves as mere entertainers are engaged in grappling with the problems that face the society they live in. And the artist cannot grapple with a problem, in his art, unless it is one that has got into his own life. He can indicate it, in an objective, critical way, by writing articles and so forth; but art is an affair of the whole man, and the whole man cannot respond to anything that has not been lived out. Hence "Look in thy heart, and write" is still the primary adage, though it doesn't mean that all a writer has to do is gush and have "sincerity," i.e. wear his heart on his sleeve. An artist can only have one principle: to treat whatever seems to him to present itself insistently for treatment, in the bit of life lived by him, in the corner of history and geography he inhabits. Thus, when I wrote *Hurry on Down,* the main problem which had presented itself in my own existence was the young man's problem of how to adapt himself to "life," in the sense of an order external to himself, already there when he appeared on the scene, and not necessarily disposed to welcome him; the whole being complicated by the fact that in our civilization there is an unhealed split between the educational system and the assumptions that actually underlie daily life. We spend a good deal of money, both publicly and as individuals, on having the young taught to appreciate the masterpieces of literature and art; we maintain professors to lecture to them on philosophy and other high-flying subjects; and then we turn them out into a world that has no use for these things, a world whose operative maxim is "Don't respect or consider anything except material powers and possessions." The shock of this meeting is always a painful one, and the best work any teacher can do is to make it more painful, rather than cushion it. I myself had an exceptionally sheltered life, in this respect; I went straight from one university where I was learning to another where I was teaching; but this only exacerbated the sense of guilt I felt about the whole thing. So naturally I wrote a novel about a man who had been given the educational treatment and then pitchforked out into the world; adding for good measure, and for realism's sake, another cluster of problems which concerned the

---

[1] For an "assessment" which neatly gathers all these strands into one, cf. Stephen Spender in *Gemini,* vol. 1, no. 1, p. 5: "The undergraduates and instructors [sic] at the Redbrick Universities are fully aware of this [i.e. the "urbanity" of "the senior universities"], and like to draw a distinction between their scholarship, their critical awareness, their intellectual intensity, and the Oxford-Cambridge softness and lack of any but genteel standards. Of course, this is a false dramatization. The real contrast today is between the Oxford-Cambridge assumption of collective superiority which to some extent atrophies the existence of each undergraduate and absorbs everything into its kind of classiness: and the emphasis on squalor in writers like Kingsley Amis, John Wain, John Osborne, etc., which is the opposite side of the same medal of what is perhaps basically English class-consciousness." I invite the reader to meditate on the style, as well as the substance, of this passage.

disappearance of the old-style *bourgeoisie,* among whom the hero was supposed to have been brought up. (He was widely taken by reviewers to be the typical scholarship boy, but that notion was derived not from the book, but from the surrounding air.) A top-dressing of emotional problems about women, and the thing was complete. When the mixture was stirred up and cooked, the central thing that emerged was a moral point—something to do with the nature of goodness— but nobody, except myself, saw this, so there is no point in bringing it up now. In outline, the book was quite conventional; its starting-point might have been that scene in *Antic Hay* where Gumbril, having thrown up his job as a schoolmaster, comes home and confronts his father.

"Well, well," said Gumbril Senior, sitting down again, "I must say I'm not surprised. I'm only surprised that you stood it, not being a born pedagogue, for as long as you did. What ever induced you to think of turning usher I can't imagine."

. . . "What else was there for me to do?" asked Gumbril Junior, pulling up a chair towards the fire. "You gave me a pedagogue's education and washed your hands of me."

Thirty years separate *Antic Hay* and *Hurry on Down,* but the situation of the young man has not changed; he must still set out from that starting-point: "You gave me a pedagogue's education and washed your hands of me." Because *any* liberal education, in the world we have moved into, is "a pedagogue's education"; its only direct application must be in perpetuating itself, by handing the same material on to another generation. It cannot turn outwards into the world at large, because the world rejects it. This, in short, was the situation that had met me in my own life, and accordingly this was what I wrote about. I followed it up with a novel that was meant to be constructive, and to attack fashionable despair and nihilism; the man decides to commit suicide on the first page, and on the last he looks back and wonders how he could have been so misguided; life intervenes and teaches him the necessary lessons. The failure of this book was so spectacular that I can only assume that everyone found it literally unreadable; certainly very few of the comments it received were any use to me, because they all seemed to be by people who had not read further than the first ten pages: e.g. one journalist quite recently attacked the book as "hysterical," because it gave a picture of contemporary young manhood as seedy, despairing, self-lacerating, etc.: he should have made it clear that he was taking the first chapter and letting it stand for the whole, a procedure which, if generally adopted, would revolutionize criticism. There is nothing one can do about this, except admit that the book failed to reach an audience, and write it off.

With regard to the future, all I can do is to go on trying to tackle the problems of contemporary life as they confront me personally: "tackle" them by seeking to give them adequate literary expression, rather than "solve" them. A writer makes his books out of his ignorance and folly, as much as out of his knowledge and wisdom; *King Lear* is as much about what Shakespeare didn't know as about what he did— and all the more human for that. As far as novels are concerned, I suppose I shall try to grasp these problems in clusters, rather than singly. Problems don't occur in isolation, they occur in the context of other problems. For instance, I have completed a novel (*The Contenders*), to be published in 1958, which tries to tackle the problem of (a) material ambition as a corrupting power, (b) rivalry as ditto, (c) whether personal relationships or "work" in the Carlylean sense is the better foundation for a life, (d) the metropolitan versus the provincial virtues, i.e. "being in touch" versus "sturdy independence." I have tried not to write the book as an arid thesis, but to allow all these issues to spring naturally from the interplay of theme and character and to attract towards themselves any other issues which may be thrown up *en route*. The novel is a useful form for this kind of treatment because it lends itself to the slow unfolding of a cluster of themes; it gives both writer and reader time to turn round in; Lawrence meant something of this kind, I suppose, when he said that if *Hamlet* had been a novel it wouldn't have been so mysterious. More clarification in detail could have been provided. Other forms, notably poetry, strike me as useful in dealing with emotional and moral problems at the point of crisis. The kind of short, compressed poem that I write, at any rate, is meant to present its subject-matter with the immediacy of the sudden shocks you get in life. The short story, too, can work in something like the same way by picking the moment when a thing comes to the boil and relying on suggestion to convey what lies before and after. However, there are many kinds of poem and story, and I don't want to sound unwilling to try, at any time, something quite different from what I have sketched here. At any rate, the basic equipment of any artist is (i) an interest in the technical details of his art, (ii) a willingness to respond to the life about him—what Dr. Leavis calls "a reverent openness to experience"; and this twofold equipment I hope and believe that I have; the rest is largely a matter of luck.

Having spoken of "luck," I must put in a qualification, otherwise I shall have the straw-in-the-hair, manna-from-heaven brigade thinking I am coming round to their side. In the arts (as, perhaps, in life?) "luck" comes to those who put themselves in the way of it; the bird of inspiration will perch on your shoulder all the more readily if your shoulder is dusted and held in the most favorable position. That is the importance of (i) above: an interest in the technical side of one's art. You can't love the soul of literature without loving her body. At the moment of writing (though this may not apply when this comes to be printed), the technical problem most insistently present to my mind is that of tragi-comedy. In my first two novels, I made a fairly rough-and-ready attempt at the presentation of serious issues through the medium of very broad comedy, not to say outright farce. There was no attempt at delicate shading from one mood to another; on the contrary, it was the violent juxtaposition that made the effect, as far as I was concerned. The justification of this method, I thought, was its realism; "life" is, notoriously, like that, always mingling the grotesquely comic with the sombre or even tragic. I am not sorry I made these two attempts, but in future I want to achieve more of a compound, rather than a mixture, of elements; I still think that the novel, to get in a wide enough sweep of life, needs comic as well as sombre ingredients, but I find myself increasingly inclined to doubt whether art can afford to imitate life as directly as that; because our raw experience comes to us in unsorted lots, doesn't mean that when we come to interpret it imaginatively we should still keep it in the same jumble. Of course the need for tragi-comedy has always been recognized; you could extract a good enough working program from Dr. Johnson's words:

Shakespeare's plays are not in the rigorous and critical sense either tragedies or comedies, but compositions of a distinct kind; exhibiting the real state of sublunary nature, which partakes of good and evil, joy and sorrow, mingled with endless variety of proportion and innumerable modes of combination; and expressing the course of the world, in which the loss of one is the gain of another; in which, at the same time, the reveller is hasting to his wine, and the mourner burying his friend; in which the malignity of one is sometimes defeated by the frolick of another; and many mischiefs and many benefits are done and hindered without design.

I cannot think of any resounding peroration to finish with; but I do know that the best hope for a significant and valuable literature is that those who have chosen writing as a profession should *do their best*—should think of their work as serious, and not be afraid to seem in earnest about it. One of the plagues of modern life is that a literary man has a certain status; it is worth the trouble to acquire a reputation as a writer if your aims are social or even pecuniary; such a reputation can be used as an instrument in the furthering of all sorts of ambitions which have nothing to do with literature, nothing to do with the state of our civilization, nothing to do with anything except the writer's own personal advancement. At the moment, the literary world is organized very conveniently for such people; the smart magazines, which should be playing an important part in the dissemination of ideas, are too often used simply as a stage on which the latest candidate for public attention can display his bag of tricks. The trouble with this is not merely that people become materially successful who don't deserve to; that doesn't matter, and will in any case always happen; "getting on" isn't important. The danger is that when *every* book is reviewed by some charlatan whose only concern is to leave the reader with an impression of *his* cleverness, *his* personality, *his* graceful style, when *every* magazine is edited by someone whose object is to keep intact the network of social and political relationships that permitted his own rise to power, in short, when every genuine object is submerged in a general grabbing for plums and security—then the intellectual life of the country will be at a standstill. The only hope is that people—ordinary, non-writing people —will not stand for it; that the *flâneur* who tries to get by on "style" and "wit" will be sharply challenged to produce his credentials; that the critic who never risks a personal judgment, but merely hands on the valuations that are current in his circle, will be needled into speaking for himself once in a while. And perhaps finally—but this, I admit, is Utopian—it will become conventional to measure a man's worth by his solid achievement instead of his slickness and showmanship.

All this matters because civilized life depends on a certain amount of discrimination, which provides the climate in which excellence can be seen and encouraged. And this is what a man of creative talent has the right to demand of the society he lives in; it is a *right*, not a luxury. Imaginative work is difficult, exhausting, always lonely and frequently agonizing; I do not see how any society can have the face to ask an artist to undergo the ordeal of creation unless it is prepared to meet him half-way by making the effort of discrimination. That is why I have so hammered this point about keeping one's head, about having balance and critical awareness. The present phase of history finds Western mankind in the position of an inexpert tightrope walker, who has launched himself with a slithering rush, and now finds himself halted, with a sea of upturned faces below him, and the second half of his journey to go. *That* is why we cannot afford charlatanism; it is also why the young must continue to ignore their elders who jeer at them for being cautious, for dealing in half-measures, for not having "passion" or being "committed." Some of my generation have fallen for this claptrap and taken in their turn to advocating a blind rush along the rest of the tightrope. I believe we must have the nerve to go on step by step; and that means having the courage to say No to our fools, however influential and important they may be.

*NORMAN MAILER*

# The White Negro

Norman Mailer (1923–    ) claims to have written the first "American existentialist novel" (*Barbary Shore*, 1951). The following essay is an attempt to define what he thinks being both

American and "existentialist" was in the years following World
War II. It is powerfully and urgently and truculently written. If
it has value, it is by way of its indicating the *emotional* difference
in the impact each of the world wars has had upon us. Many of
the feelings of people who exist in a marginal society (a deprived
society, which is discriminated against) are here brought together.
The essay is pre-eminently antirational; it attacks all types of
thought and discourse which Mailer regards as having a rational
base. He comes up with a declaration of passion, anger, irrationality;
the major test is the experiencing of life as against the formulation
of plans for explaining and describing it.

*Our search for the rebels of the generation led us to the hipster. The
hipster is an* enfant terrible *turned inside out. In character with his
time, he is trying to get back at the conformists by lying low . . . You
can't interview a hipster because his main goal is to keep out of a
society which, he thinks, is trying to make everyone over in its own
image. He takes marijuana because it supplies him with experiences
that can't be shared with "squares." He may affect a broad-brimmed
hat or a zoot suit, but usually he prefers to skulk unmarked. The hipster
may be a jazz musician; he is rarely an artist, almost never a writer.
He may earn his living as a petty criminal, a hobo, a carnival roustabout
or a free-lance moving man in Greenwich Village, but some hipsters
have found a safe refuge in the upper income brackets as television
comics or movie actors. (The late James Dean, for one, was a hipster
hero.) . . . It is tempting to describe the hipster in psychiatric terms
as infantile, but the style of his infantilism is a sign of the times. He
does not try to enforce his will on others, Napoleon-fashion, but contents
himself with a magical omnipotence never disproved because never
tested. . . . As the only extreme nonconformist of his generation, he
exercises a powerful if underground appeal for conformists, through
newspaper accounts of his delinquencies, his structureless jazz, and his
emotive grunt words.*
    —"Born 1930: The Unlost Generation" by Caroline Bird
        *Harper's Bazaar*, Feb. 1957

*P*robably, we will never be able to determine the psychic havoc
of the concentration camps and the atom bomb upon the unconscious
mind of almost everyone alive in these years. For the first time in
civilized history, perhaps for the first time in all of history, we have
been forced to live with the suppressed knowledge that the smallest facets
of our personality or the most minor projection of our ideas, or indeed
the absence of ideas and the absence of personality could mean equally
well that we might still be doomed to die as a cipher in some vast
statistical operation in which our teeth would be counted, and our hair
would be saved, but our death itself would be unknown, unhonored,
and unremarked, a death which could not follow with dignity as a
possible consequence to serious actions we had chosen, but rather a

death by *deus ex machina* in a gas chamber or a radioactive city; and so if in the midst of civilization—that civilization founded upon the Faustian urge to dominate nature by mastering time, mastering the links of social cause and effect—in the middle of an economic civilization founded upon the confidence that time could indeed be subjected to our will, our psyche was subjected itself to the intolerable anxiety that death being causeless, life was causeless as well, and time deprived of cause and effect had come to a stop.

The Second World War presented a mirror to the human condition which blinded anyone who looked into it. For if tens of millions were killed in concentration camps out of the inexorable agonies and contractions of super-states founded upon the always insoluble contradictions of injustice, one was then obliged also to see that no matter how crippled and perverted an image of man was the society he had created, it was nonetheless his creation, his collective creation (at least his collective creation from the past) and if society was so murderous, then who could ignore the most hideous of questions about his own nature?

Worse. One could hardly maintain the courage to be individual, to speak with one's own voice, for the years in which one could complacently accept oneself as part of an elite by being a radical were forever gone. A man knew that when he dissented, he gave a note upon his life which could be called in any year of overt crisis. No wonder then that these have been the years of conformity and depression. A stench of fear has come out of every pore of American life, and we suffer from a collective failure of nerve. The only courage, with rare exceptions, that we have been witness to, has been the isolated courage of isolated people.

## II

It is on this bleak scene that a phenomenon has appeared: the American existentialist—the hipster, the man who knows that if our collective condition is to live with instant death by atomic war, relatively quick death by the State as *l'univers concentrationnaire,* or with a slow death by conformity with every creative and rebellious instinct stifled (at what damage to the mind and the heart and the liver and the nerves no research foundation for cancer will discover in a hurry), if the fate of twentieth century man is to live with death from adolescence to premature senescence, why then the only life-giving answer is to accept the terms of death, to live with death as immediate danger, to divorce oneself from society, to exist without roots, to set out on that uncharted journey into the rebellious imperatives of the self. In short, whether the life is criminal or not, the decision is to encourage the psychopath in oneself, to explore that domain of experience where security is boredom and therefore sickness, and one exists in the present, in that enormous present which is without past or future, memory or planned intention, the life where a man must go until he is beat, where he must gamble with his energies through all those small or large crises of courage and unforeseen situations which beset his day, where he must be with it or doomed not to swing. The unstated essence of Hip, its psychopathic brilliance, quivers with the knowledge that new kinds of victories increase one's power for new kinds of perception; and defeats, the wrong kind of defeats, attack the body and imprison one's energy until one is jailed in the prison air of other people's habits, other people's defeats, boredom, quiet desperation, and muted icy self-destroying rage. One is Hip or one is Square (the alternative which each new generation coming into American life is beginning to feel), one is a rebel or one conforms, one is a frontiersman in the Wild West of American night life, or else a Square cell, trapped in the totalitarian tissues of American society, doomed willy-nilly to conform if one is to succeed.

A totalitarian society makes enormous demands on the courage of men, and a partially totalitarian society makes even greater demands for the general anxiety is greater. Indeed if one is to be a man, almost any kind of unconventional action often takes disproportionate courage. So it is no accident that the source of Hip is the Negro for he has been living on the margin between totalitarianism and democracy for two centuries. But the presence of Hip as a working philosophy in the sub-worlds of American life is probably due to jazz, and its knife-like entrance into culture, its subtle but so penetrating influence on an avant-garde generation—that post-war generation of adventurers who (some consciously, some by osmosis) had absorbed the lessons of dis-illusionment and disgust of the Twenties, the Depression, and the War. Sharing a collective disbelief in the words of men who had too much money and controlled too many things, they knew almost as powerful a disbelief in the socially monolithic ideas of the single mate, the solid family and the respectable love life. If the intellectual antecedents of this generation can be traced to such separate influences as D. H. Law-rence, Henry Miller, and Wilhelm Reich, the viable philosophy of Hemingway fits most of their facts: in a bad world, as he was to say over and over again (while taking time out from his parvenu snobbery and dedicated gourmandise), in a bad world there is no love nor mercy nor charity nor justice unless a man can keep his courage, and this indeed fitted some of the facts. What fitted the need of the adventurer even more precisely was Hemingway's categorical imperative that what made him feel good became therefore The Good.

So no wonder that in certain cities of America, in New York of course, and New Orleans, in Chicago and San Francisco and Los Angeles, in such American cities as Paris and Mexico, D.F., this particular part of a generation was attracted to what the Negro had to offer. In such places as Greenwich Village, a ménage-a-trois was completed—the bo-hemian and the juvenile delinquent came face-to-face with the Negro, and the hipster was a fact in American life. If marijuana was the wed-ding ring, the child was the language of Hip for its argot gave expres-sion to abstract states of feeling which all could share, at least all who were Hip. And in this wedding of the white and the black it was the Negro who brought the cultural dowry. Any Negro who wishes to live must live with danger from his first day, and no experience can ever be casual to him, no Negro can saunter down a street with any real certainty that violence will not visit him on his walk. The cameos of security for the average white: mother and the home, job and the family, are not even a mockery to millions of Negroes; they are impossible. The Negro has the simplest of alternatives: live a life of constant humility or ever-threatening danger. In such a pass where paranoia is as vital to survival as blood, the Negro had stayed alive and begun to grow by following the need of his body where he could. Knowing in the cells of his existence that life was war, nothing but war, the Negro (all exceptions admitted) could rarely afford the sophisticated inhibitions of civilization, and so he kept for his survival the art of the primitive, he lived in the enormous present, he subsisted for his Saturday night kicks, relinquishing the pleasures of the mind for the more obligatory pleasures of the body, and in his music he gave voice to the character and quality of his existence, to his rage and the infinite variations of joy, lust, languor, growl, cramp, pinch, scream and despair of his orgasm. For jazz is orgasm, it is the music of orgasm, good orgasm and bad, and so it spoke across a nation, it had the communication of art even where it was watered, perverted, corrupted, and almost killed, it spoke in no matter what laundered popular way of instantaneous existential states to which some whites could respond, it was indeed a communication by art because it said, "I feel this, and now you do too."

So there was a new breed of adventurers, urban adventurers who drifted out at night looking for action with a black man's code to fit their facts. The hipster had absorbed the existentialist synapses of the Negro, and for practical purposes could be considered a white Negro.

To be an existentialist, one must be able to feel oneself—one must know one's desires, one's rages, one's anguish, one must be aware of the character of one's frustration and know what would satisfy it. The over-civilized man can be an existentialist only if it is chic, and deserts it quickly for the next chic. To be a real existentialist (Sartre admittedly to the contrary) one must be religious, one must have one's sense of the "purpose"—whatever the purpose may be—but a life which is directed by one's faith in the necessity of action is a life committed to the notion that the substratum of existence is the search, the end meaningful but mysterious; it is impossible to live such a life unless one's emotions provide their profound conviction. Only the French, alienated beyond alienation from their unconscious could welcome an existential philosophy without ever feeling it at all; indeed only a Frenchman by declaring that the unconscious did not exist could then proceed to explore the delicate involutions of consciousness, the microscopically sensuous and all but ineffable *frissons* of mental becoming, in order finally to create the theology of atheism and so submit that in a world of absurdities the existential absurdity is most coherent.

In the dialogue between the atheist and the mystic, the atheist is on the side of life, rational life, undialectical life—since he conceives of death as emptiness, he can, no matter how weary or despairing, wish for nothing but more life; his pride is that he does not transpose his weakness and spiritual fatigue into a romantic longing for death, for such appreciation of death is then all too capable of being elaborated by his imagination into a universe of meaningful structure and moral orchestration.

Yet this masculine argument can mean very little for the mystic. The mystic can accept the atheist's description of his weakness, he can agree that his mysticism was a response to despair. And yet . . . and yet his argument is that he, the mystic, is the one finally who has chosen to live with death, and so death is his experience and not the atheist's, and the atheist by eschewing the limitless dimensions of profound despair has rendered himself incapable to judge the experience. The real argument which the mystic must always advance is the very intensity of his private vision—his argument depends from the vision precisely because what was felt in the vision is so extraordinary that no rational argument, no hypotheses of "oceanic feelings" and certainly no skeptical reductions can explain away what has become for him the reality more real than the reality of closely reasoned logic. His inner experience of the possibilities within death is his logic. So, too, for the existentialist. And the psychopath. And the saint and the bullfighter and the lover. The common denominator for all of them is their burning consciousness of the present, exactly that incandescent consciousness which the possibilities within death has opened for them. There is a depth of desperation to the condition which enables one to remain in life only by engaging death, but the reward is their knowledge that what is happening at each instant of the electric present is good or bad for them, good or bad for their cause, their love, their action, their need.

It is this knowledge which provides the curious community of feeling in the world of the hipster, a muted cool religious revival to be sure, but the element which is exciting, disturbing, nightmarish perhaps, is that incompatibles have come to bed, the inner life and the violent life, the orgy and the dream of love, the desire to murder and the desire to create, a dialectical conception of existence with a lust for power, a dark, romantic, and yet undeniably dynamic view of existence for it sees every man and woman as moving individually through each moment of life forward into growth or backward into death.

### III

It may be fruitful to consider the hipster a philosophical psychopath, a man interested not only in the dangerous imperatives of his psychopathy but in codifying, at least for himself, the suppositions on which his inner universe is constructed. By this premise the hipster is a psychopath, and yet not a psychopath but the negation of the psychopath for he possesses the narcissistic detachment of the philosopher, that absorption in the recessive nuances of one's own motive which is so alien to the unreasoning drive of the psychopath. In this country where new millions of psychopaths are developed each year, stamped with the mint of our contradictory popular culture (where sex is sin and yet sex is paradise), it is as if there has been room already for the development of the antithetical psychopath who extrapolates from his own condition, from the inner certainty that his rebellion is just, a radical vision of the universe which thus separates him from the general ignorance, reactionary prejudice, and self-doubt of the more conventional psychopath. Having converted his unconscious experience into much conscious knowledge, the hipster has shifted the focus of his desire from immediate gratification toward that wider passion for future power which is the mark of civilized man. Yet with an irreducible difference. For Hip is the sophistication of the wise primitive in a giant jungle, and so its appeal is still beyond the civilized man. If there are ten million Americans who are more or less psychopathic (and the figure is most modest), there are probably not more than one hundred thousand men and women who consciously see themselves as hipsters, but their importance is that they are an elite with the potential ruthlessness of an elite, and a language most adolescents can understand instinctively for the hipster's intense view of existence matches their experience and their desire to rebel.

Before one can say more about the hipster, there is obviously much to be said about the psychic state of the psychopath—or, clinically, the psychopathic personality. Now, for reasons which may be more curious than the similarity of the words, even many people with a psychoanalytical orientation often confuse the psychopath with the psychotic. Yet the terms are polar. The psychotic is legally insane, the psychopath is not; the psychotic is almost always incapable of discharging in physical acts the rage of his frustration, while the psychopath at his extreme is virtually as incapable of restraining his violence. The psychotic lives in so misty a world that what is happening at each moment of his life is not very real to him whereas the psychopath seldom knows any reality greater than the face, the voice, the being of the particular people among whom he may find himself at any moment. Sheldon and Eleanor Glueck describe him as follows:

The psychopath . . . can be distinguished from the person sliding into or clambering out of a "true psychotic" state by the long tough persistence of his anti-social attitude and behaviour and the absence of hallucinations, delusions, manic flight of ideas, confusion, disorientation, and other dramatic signs of psychosis.

The late Robert Lindner, one of the few experts on the subject, in his book *Rebel Without a Cause—The Hypnoanalysis of a Criminal Psychopath* presented part of his definition in this way:

. . . the psychopath is a rebel without a cause, an agitator without a slogan, a revolutionary without a program: in other words, his rebelliousness is aimed to achieve goals satisfactory to himself alone; he is incapable of exertions for the sake of others. All his efforts, hidden under no matter what disguise, represent investments designed to satisfy his immediate wishes and desires . . . The psychopath, like the child, cannot delay the pleasures of gratification; and this trait is one of his underlying, universal characteristics. He cannot wait upon erotic gratification which convention demands should be preceded by the chase before the kill: he must rape. He cannot wait upon the development of prestige in society: his egoistic ambitions lead him to leap into headlines by daring performances. Like a red thread the predominance of this mechanism for immediate satisfaction runs through the history of every psychopath. It explains not only his behaviour but also the violent nature of his acts.

Yet even Lindner who was the most imaginative and most sympathetic of the psychoanalysts who have studied the psychopathic personality was not ready to project himself into the essential sympathy—which is that the psychopath may indeed be the perverted and dangerous front-runner of a new kind of personality which could become the central expression of human nature before the twentieth century is over. For the psychopath is better adapted to dominate those mutually contradictory inhibitions upon violence and love which civilization has exacted of us, and if it be remembered that not every psychopath is an extreme case, and that the condition of psychopathy is present in a host of people including many politicians, professional soldiers, newspaper columnists, entertainers, artists, jazz musicians, call-girls, promiscuous homosexuals and half the executives of Hollywood, television, and advertising, it can be seen that there are aspects of psychopathy which already exert considerable cultural influence.

What characterizes almost every psychopath and part-psychopath is that they are trying to create a new nervous system for themselves. Generally we are obliged to act with a nervous system which has been formed from infancy, and which carries in the style of its circuits the very contradictions of our parents and our early milieu. Therefore, we are obliged, most of us, to meet the tempo of the present and the future with reflexes and rhythms which come from the past. It is not only the "dead weight of the institutions of the past" but indeed the inefficient and often antiquated nervous circuits of the past which strangle our potentiality for responding to new possibilities which might be exciting for our individual growth.

Through most of modern history, "sublimation" was possible: at the expense of expressing only a small portion of oneself, that small portion could be expressed intensely. But sublimation depends on a reasonable tempo to history. If the collective life of a generation has moved too quickly, the "past" by which particular men and women of that generation may function is not, let us say, thirty years old, but relatively a hundred or two hundred years old. And so the nervous system is overstressed beyond the possibility of such compromises as sublimation, especially since the stable middle-class values so prerequisite to sublimation have been virtually destroyed in our time, at least as nourishing values free of confusion or doubt. In such a crisis of accelerated historical tempo and deteriorated values, neurosis tends to be replaced by psychopathy, and the success of psychoanalysis (which even ten years ago gave promise of becoming a direct major force) diminishes because of its inbuilt and characteristic incapacity to handle patients more complex, more experienced, or more adventurous than the analyst himself. In practice, psychoanalysis has by now become all too often no more than a psychic blood-letting. The patient is not so much changed as aged, and the infantile fantasies which he is encouraged to express are condemned to exhaust themselves against the analyst's non-responsive reactions. The result for all too many patients is a diminution, a "tranquilizing" of their most interesting qualities and vices. The patient is indeed not so much altered as worn out—less bad, less good, less bright, less willful, less destructive, less creative. He is thus able to conform to that contradictory and unbearable society which first created his neurosis. He can conform to what he loathes because he no longer has the passion to feel loathing so intensely.

The psychopath is notoriously difficult to analyze because the fundamental decision of his nature is to try to live the infantile fantasy, and in this decision (given the dreary alternative of psychoanalysis) there may be a certain instinctive wisdom. For there is a dialectic to changing one's nature, the dialectic which underlies all psychoanalytic method: it is the knowledge that if one is to change one's habits, one must go back to the source of their creation, and so the psychopath exploring backward along the road of the homosexual, the orgiast, the drug-addict, the rapist, the robber and the murderer seeks to find those violent parallels to the violent and often hopeless contradictions he knew as an infant and as a child. For if he has the courage to meet the parallel situation at the moment when he is ready, then he has a chance to act as he has never acted before, and in satisfying the frustration—if he can succeed —he may then pass by symbolic substitute through the locks of incest. In thus giving expression to the buried infant in himself, he can lessen the tension of those infantile desires and so free himself to remake a bit of his nervous system. Like the neurotic he is looking for the opportunity to grow up a second time, but the psychopath knows instinctively that to express a forbidden impulse actively is far more beneficial to him than merely to confess the desire in the safety of a doctor's room. The psychopath is ordinately ambitious, too ambitious ever to trade his warped brilliant conception of his possible victories in life for the grim if peaceful attrition of the analyst's couch. So his associational journey into the past is lived out in the theatre of the present, and he exists for those charged situations where his senses are so alive that he can be aware actively (as the analysand is aware passively) of what his habits are, and how he can change them. The strength of the psychopath is that he knows (where most of us can only guess) what is good for him and what is bad for him at exactly those instants when an old crippling habit has become so attacked by experience that the potentiality exists to change it, to replace a negative and empty fear with an outward action, even if—and here I obey the logic of the extreme psychopath—even if the fear is of himself, and the action is to murder. The psychopath murders—if he has the courage—out of the necessity to purge his violence, for if he cannot empty his hatred then he cannot love, his being is frozen with implacable self-hatred for his cowardice. (It can of course be suggested that it takes little courage for two strong eighteen-year-old hoodlums, let us say, to beat in the brains of a candy-store keeper, and indeed the act—even by the logic of the psychopath—is not likely to prove very therapeutic for the victim is not an immediate equal. Still, courage of a sort is necessary, for one murders not only a weak fifty-year-old man but an institution as well, one violates private property, one enters into a new relation with the police and introduces a dangerous element into one's life. The hoodlum is therefore daring the unknown, and so no matter how brutal the act, it is not altogether cowardly.)

At bottom, the drama of the psychopath is that he seeks love. Not love as the search for a mate, but love as the search for an orgasm more apocalyptic than the one which preceded it. Orgasm is his therapy —he knows at the seed of his being that good orgasm opens his possibilities and bad orgasm imprisons him. But in this search, the psychopath becomes an embodiment of the extreme contradictions of the society which formed his character, and the apocalyptic orgasm often remains as remote as the Holy Grail, for there are clusters and nests and ambushes of violence in his own necessities and in the imperatives and retaliations of the men and women among whom he lives his life, so that even as he drains his hatred in one act or another, so the conditions of his life create it anew in him until the drama of his movements bears a sardonic resemblance to the frog who climbed a few feet in the well only to drop back again.

Yet there is this to be said for the search after the good orgasm: when one lives in a civilized world, and still can enjoy none of the cultural nectar of such a world because the paradoxes on which civilization is built demands that there remain a cultureless and alienated bottom of exploitable human material, then the logic of becoming a sexual outlaw (if one's psychological roots are bedded in the bottom) is that one has at least a running competitive chance to be physically healthy so long as one stays alive. It is therefore no accident that psychopathy is most prevalent with the Negro. Hated from outside and therefore hating himself, the Negro was forced into the position of exploring all those moral wildernesses of civilized life which the Square automatically condemns as delinquent or evil or immature or morbid or self-destructive or corrupt. (Actually the terms have equal weight. Depending on the telescope of the cultural clique from which the Square surveys the universe, "evil" or "immature" are equally strong terms of condemnation.) But the Negro, not being privileged to gratify his self-esteem with the heady satisfactions of categorical condemnation, chose to move instead in that other direction where all situations are equally valid, and in the worst of perversion, promiscuity, pimpery, drug addiction, rape, razor-slash, bottle-break, what-have-you, the Negro discovered and elaborated a morality of the bottom, an ethical differentiation between the good and the bad in every human activity from the go-getter pimp (as opposed to the lazy one) to the relatively dependable pusher or prostitute. Add to this, the cunning of their language, the abstract ambiguous alternatives in which from the danger of their oppression they learned to speak ("Well, now, man, like I'm looking for a cat to turn me on . . ."), add even more the profound sensitivity of the Negro jazzman who was the cultural mentor of a people, and it is not too difficult to believe that the language of Hip which evolved was an artful language, tested and shaped by an intense experience and therefore different in kind from white slang, as different as the special obscenity of the soldier which in its emphasis upon "ass" as the soul and "shit" as circumstance, was able to express the existential states of the enlisted man. What makes Hip a special language is that it cannot really be taught—if one shares none of the experiences of elation and exhaustion which it is equipped to describe, then it seems merely arch or vulgar or irritating. It is a pictorial language, but pictorial like non-objective art, imbued with the dialectic of small but intense change, a language for the microcosm, in this case, man, for it takes the immediate experiences of any passing man and magnifies the dynamic of his movements, not specifically but abstractly so that he is seen more as a vector in a network of forces than as a static character in a crystallized field. (Which, latter, is the practical view of the snob.) For example, there is real difficulty in trying to find a Hip substitute for "stubborn." The best possibility I can come up with is: "That cat will never come off his groove, dad." But groove implies movement, narrow movement but motion nonetheless. There is really no way to describe someone who does not move at all. Even a creep does move—if at a pace exasperatingly more slow than the pace of the cool cats.

## IV

Like children, hipsters are fighting for the sweet, and their language is a set of subtle indications of their success or failure in the competition for pleasure. Unstated but obvious is the social sense that there is not nearly enough sweet for everyone. And so the sweet goes only to the victor, the best, the most, the man who knows the most about how to find his energy and how not to lose it. The emphasis is on energy because the psychopath and the hipster are nothing without it since they do not have the protection of a position or a class to rely on when they have overextended themselves. So the language of Hip is a language of energy, how it is found, how it is lost.

But let us see. I have jotted down perhaps a dozen words, the Hip perhaps most in use and most likely to last with the minimum of variation. The words are man, go, put down, make, beat, cool, swing, with it, crazy, dig, flip, creep, hip, square. They serve a variety of purposes, and the nuance of the voice uses the nuance of the situation to convey the subtle contextual difference. If the hipster moves through his night and through his life on a constant search with glimpses of Mecca in many a turn of his experience (Mecca being the apocalyptic orgasm) and if everyone in the civilized world is at least in some small degree a sexual cripple the hipster lives with the knowledge of how he is sexually crippled and where he is sexually alive, and the faces of experience which life presents to him each day are engaged, dismissed or avoided as his need directs and his lifemanship makes possible. For life is a contest between people in which the victor generally recuperates quickly and the loser takes long to mend, a perpetual competition of colliding explorers in which one must grow or else pay more for remaining the same (pay in sickness, or depression, or anguish for the lost opportunity) but pay or grow.

Therefore one finds words like go, and make it, and with it, and swing: "Go" with its sense that after hours or days or months or years of monotony, boredom, and depression one has finally had one's chance, one has amassed enough energy to meet an exciting opportunity with all one's present talents for the flip (up or down) and so one is ready to go, ready to gamble. Movement is always to be preferred to inaction. In motion a man has a chance, his body is warm, his instincts are quick, and when the crisis comes, whether of love or violence, he can make it, he can win, he can release a little more energy for himself since he hates himself a little less, he can make a little better nervous system, make it a little more possible to go again, to go faster next time and so make more and thus find more people with whom he can swing. For to swing is to communicate, is to convey the rhythms of one's own being to a lover, a friend, or an audience, and—equally necessary— be able to feel the rhythms of their response. To swing with the rhythms of another is to enrich oneself—the conception of the learning process as dug by Hip is that one cannot really learn until one contains within oneself the implicit rhythm of the subject or the person. As an example, I remember once hearing a Negro friend have an intellectual discussion at a party for half an hour with a white girl who was a few years out of college. The Negro literally could not read or write, but he had an extraordinary ear and a fine sense of mimicry. So as the girl spoke, he would detect the particular formal uncertainties in her argument, and in a pleasant (if slightly Southern) English accent, he would respond to one or another facet of her doubts. When she would finish what she felt was a particularly well-articulated idea, he would smile privately and say, "Other-direction . . . do you really believe in that?"

"Well . . . No," the girl would stammer, "now that you get down to it, there is something disgusting about it to me," and she would be off again for five more minutes.

Of course the Negro was not learning anything about the merits and demerits of the argument, but he was learning a great deal about a type of girl he had never met before, and that was what he wanted. Being unable to read or write, he could hardly be interested in ideas nearly as much as in lifemanship, and so he eschewed any attempt to obey the precision or lack of precision in the girl's language, and instead sensed her character (and the values of her social type) by swinging with the nuances of her voice.

So to swing is to be able to learn, and by learning take a step toward making it, toward creating. What is to be created is not nearly so important as the hipster's belief that when he really makes it, he will be able to turn his hand to anything, even to self-discipline. What he must do before that is find his courage at the moment of violence, or equally make it in the act of love, find a little more of himself, create a little more between his woman and himself, or indeed between his mate and himself (since many hipsters are bisexual), but paramount, imperative, is the necessity to make it because in making it, one is making the new habit, unearthing the new talent which the old frustration denied.

Whereas if you goof (the ugliest word in Hip), if you lapse back into being a frightened stupid child, or if you flip, if you lose your control, reveal the buried weaker more feminine part of your nature, then it is more difficult to swing the next time, your ear is less alive, your bad and energy-wasting habits are further confirmed, you are farther away from being with it. But to be with it is to have grace, is to be closer to the secrets of that inner unconscious life which will nourish you if you can hear it, for you are then nearer to that God which every hipster believes is located in the senses of his body, that trapped, mutilated and nonetheless megalomaniacal God who is It, who is energy, life, sex, force, the Yoga's *prana*, the Reichian's orgone, Lawrence's "blood," Hemingway's "good," the Shavian life-force; "It"; God; not the God of the churches but the unachievable whisper of mystery within the sex, the paradise of limitless energy and perception just beyond the next wave of the next orgasm.

To which a cool cat might reply, "Crazy, man!"

Because, after all, what I have offered above is an hypothesis, no more, and there is not the hipster alive who is not absorbed in his own tumultuous hypotheses. Mine is interesting, mine is way out (on the avenue of the mystery along the road to "It") but still I am just one cat in a world of cool cats, and everything interesting is crazy, or at least so the Squares who do not know how to swing would say.

(And yet crazy is also the self-protective irony of the hipster. Living with questions and not with answers, he is so different in his isolation and in the far reach of his imagination from almost everyone with whom he deals in the outer world of the Square, and meets generally so much enmity, competition, and hatred in the world of Hip, that his isolation is always in danger of turning upon itself, and leaving him indeed just that, crazy.)

If, however, you agree with my hypothesis, if you as a cat are way out too, and we are in the same groove (the universe now being glimpsed as a series of ever-extending radii from the center) why then you say simply, "I dig," because neither knowledge nor imagination comes easily, it is buried in the pain of one's forgotten experience, and so one must work to find it, one must occasionally exhaust oneself by digging into the self in order to perceive the outside. And indeed it is essential to dig the most, for if you do not dig you lose your superiority over the Square, and so you are less likely to be cool (to be in control of a situation because you have swung where the Square has not, or because you have allowed to come to consciousness a pain, a guilt, a shame or a desire which the other has not had the courage to face). To be cool is to be equipped, and if you are equipped it is more difficult for the next cat who comes along to put you down. And of course one can hardly afford to be put down too often, or one is beat, one has lost one's confidence, one has lost one's will, one is impotent in the world of action and so closer to the demeaning flip of becoming a queer, or indeed closer to dying, and therefore it is even more difficult to recover enough energy to try to make it again, because once a cat is beat he has nothing to give, and no one is interested any longer in making it with him. This is the terror of the hipster—to be beat—because once the sweet of sex has deserted him, he still cannot give up the search. It is not granted to the hipster to grow old gracefully—he has been captured too early by the oldest dream of power, the gold fountain of Ponce de Leon, the fountain of youth where the gold is in the orgasm.

To be beat is therefore a flip, it is a situation beyond one's experience, impossible to anticipate—which indeed in the circular vocabulary of Hip is still another meaning for flip, but then I have given just a few of the connotations of these words. Like most primitive vocabularies each word is a prime symbol and serves a dozen or a hundred functions of communication in the instinctive dialectic through which the hipster perceives his experience, that dialectic of the instantaneous differentials of existence in which one is forever moving forward into more or retreating into less.

## V

It is impossible to conceive a new philosophy until one creates a new language, but a new popular language (while it must implicitly contain a new philosophy) does not necessarily present its philosophy overtly. It can be asked then what really is unique in the life-view of Hip which raises its argot above the passing verbal whimsies of the bohemian or the lumpenproletariat.

The answer would be in the psychopathic element of Hip which has almost no interest in viewing human nature, or better, in judging human nature, from a set of standards conceived a priori to the experience, standards inherited from the past. Since Hip sees every answer as posing immediately a new alternative, a new question, its emphasis is on complexity rather than simplicity (such complexity that its language without the illumination of the voice and the articulation of the face and body remains hopelessly incommunicative). Given its emphasis on complexity, Hip abdicates from any conventional moral responsibility because it would argue that the results of our actions are unforeseeable, and so we cannot know if we do good or bad, we cannot even know (in the Joycean sense of the good and the bad) whether unforeseeable, and so we cannot know if we do good or bad, we cannot be certain that we have given them energy, and indeed if we could, there would still be no idea of what ultimately they would do with it.

Therefore, men are not seen as good or bad (that they are good-and-bad is taken for granted) but rather each man is glimpsed as a collection of possibilities, some more possible than others (the view of character implicit in Hip) and some humans are considered more capable than others of reaching more possibilities within themselves in less time, provided, and this is the dynamic, provided the particular character can swing at the right time. And here arises the sense of context which differentiates Hip from a Square view of character. Hip sees the context as generally dominating the man, dominating him because his character is less significant than the context in which he must function. Since it is arbitrarily five times more demanding of one's energy to accomplish even an inconsequential action in an unfavorable context than a favorable one, man is then not only his character but his context, since the success or failure of an action in a given context reacts upon the character and therefore affects what the character will be in the next context. What dominates both character and context is the energy available at the moment of intense context.

Character being thus seen as perpetually ambivalent and dynamic enters then into an absolute relativity where there are no truths other than the isolated truths of what each observer feels at each instant of his existence. To take a perhaps unjustified metaphysical extrapolation, it is as if the universe which has usually existed conceptually as a Fact (even if the Fact were Berkeley's God) but a Fact which it was the aim of all science and philosophy to reveal, becomes instead a changing reality whose laws are remade at each instant by everything living, but most particularly man, man raised to a neo-medieval summit where the truth is not what one has felt yesterday or what one expects to feel tomorrow but rather truth is no more nor less than what one feels at each instant in the perpetual climax of the present.

What is consequent therefore is the divorce of man from his values, the liberation of the self from the Super-Ego of society. The only Hip morality (but of course it is an ever-present morality) is to do what one feels whenever and wherever it is possible, and—this is how the war of the Hip and the Square begins—to be engaged in one primal battle: to open the limits of the possible for oneself, for oneself alone because that is one's need. Yet in widening the arena of the possible, one widens it reciprocally for others as well, so that the nihilistic fulfillment of each man's desire contains its antithesis of human cooperation.

If the ethic reduces to Know Thyself and Be Thyself, what makes it radically different from Socratic moderation with its stern conservative respect for the experience of the past, is that the Hip ethic is immoderation, child-like in its adoration of the present (and indeed to respect the past means that one must also respect such ugly consequences of the past as the collective murders of the State). It is this adoration of the present which contains the affirmation of Hip, because its ultimate logic surpasses even the unforgettable solution of the Marquis de Sade to sex, private property, and the family, that all men and women have absolute but temporary rights over the bodies of all other men and women—the nihilism of Hip proposes as its final tendency that every social restraint and category be removed, and the affirmation implicit in the proposal is that man would then prove to be more creative than murderous and so would not destroy himself. Which is exactly what separates Hip from the authoritarian philosophies which now appeal to the conservative and liberal temper—what haunts the middle of the Twentieth Century is that faith in man has been lost, and the appeal of authority has been that it would restrain us from ourselves. Hip, which would return us to ourselves, at no matter what price in individual violence, is the affirmation of the barbarian for it requires a primitive passion about human nature to believe that individual acts of violence are always to be preferred to the collective violence of the State; it takes literal faith in the creative possibilities of the human being to envisage acts of violence as the catharsis which prepares growth.

Whether the hipster's desire for absolute sexual freedom contains any genuinely radical conception of a different world is of course another matter, and it is possible, since the hipster lives with his hatred, that many of them are the material for an elite of storm troopers ready to follow the first truly magnetic leader whose view of mass murder is phrased in a language which reaches their emotions. But given the desperation of his condition as a psychic outlaw, the hipster is equally a candidate for the most reactionary and most radical of movements, and so it is just as possible that many hipsters will come—if the crisis deepens—to a radical comprehension of the horror of society, for even as the radical has had his incommunicable dissent confirmed in his experience by precisely the frustration, the denied opportunities, and the bitter years which his ideas have cost him, so the sexual adventurer deflected from his goal by the implacable animosity of a society constructed to deny the sexual radical as well, may yet come to an equally bitter comprehension of the slow relentless inhumanity of the conservative power which controls him from without and from within. And in being so controlled, denied, and starved into the attrition of conformity, indeed the hipster may come to see that his condition is no more than an exaggeration of the human condition, and if he would be free, then everyone must be free. Yes, this is possible too, for the heart of Hip is its emphasis upon courage at the moment of crisis, and it is pleasant to think that courage contains within itself (as the explanation of its existence) some glimpse of the necessity of life to become more than it has been.

It is obviously not very possible to speculate with sharp focus on the future of the hipster. Certain possibilities must be evident, however, and the most central is that the organic growth of Hip depends on whether the Negro emerges as a dominating force in American life. Since the Negro knows more about the ugliness and danger of life than the White, it is probable that if the Negro can win his equality, he will possess a potential superiority, a superiority so feared that the fear itself has become the underground drama of domestic politics. Like all conservative political fear it is the fear of unforeseeable consequences, for the Negro's equality would tear a profound shift into the psychology, the sexuality, and the moral imagination of every White alive.

With this possible emergence of the Negro, Hip may erupt as a psychically armed rebellion whose sexual impetus may rebound against the anti-sexual foundation of every organized power in America, and bring into the air such animosities, antipathies, and new conflicts of interest that the mean empty hypocrisies of mass conformity will no longer work. A time of violence, new hysteria, confusion and rebellion will then be likely to replace the time of conformity. At that time, if the liberal should prove realistic in his belief that there is peaceful room for every tendency in American life, then Hip would end by being absorbed as a colorful figure in the tapestry. But if this is not the reality, and the economic, the social, the psychological, and finally the moral crises accompanying the rise of the Negro should prove insupportable, then a time is coming when every political guide post will be gone, and millions of liberals will be faced with political dilemmas they have so far succeeded in evading, and with a view of human nature they do not wish to accept. To take the desegregation of the schools in the South as an example, it is quite likely that the reactionary sees the reality more closely than the liberal when he argues that the deeper issue is not desegregation but miscegenation. (As a radical I am of course facing in the opposite direction from the White Citizen's Councils—obviously I believe it is the absolute human right of the Negro to mate with the White, and matings there will undoubtedly be, for there will be Negro high school boys brave enough to chance their lives.) But for the average liberal whose mind has been dulled by the committee-ish cant of the professional liberal, miscegenation is not an issue because he has been told that the Negro does not desire it. So, when it comes, miscegenation will be a terror, comparable perhaps to the derangement of the American Communists when the icons to Stalin came tumbling down. The average American Communist held to the myth of Stalin for reasons which had little to do with the political evidence and everything to do with their psychic necessities. In this sense it is equally a psychic necessity for the liberal to believe that the Negro and even the reactionary Southern White are eventually and fundamentally people like himself, capable of becoming good liberals too if only they can be reached by good liberal reason. What the liberal cannot bear to admit is the hatred beneath the skin of a society so unjust that the amount of collective violence buried in the people is perhaps incapable of being contained, and therefore if one wants a better world one does well to hold one's breath, for a worse world is bound to come first, and the dilemma may well be this: given such hatred, it must either vent itself nihilistically or become turned into the cold murderous liquidations of the totalitarian state.

# VI

No matter what its horrors the Twentieth Century is a vastly exciting century for its tendency is to reduce all of life to its ultimate alternatives. One can well wonder if the last war of them all will be between the blacks and the whites, or between the women and the men, or between the beautiful and ugly, the pillagers and managers, or the rebels and the regulators. Which of course is carrying speculation beyond the point where speculation is still serious, and yet despair at the monotony and bleakness of the future have become so engrained in the radical temper that the radical is in danger of abdicating from all imagination. What a man feels is the impulse for his creative effort, and if an alien but nonetheless passionate instinct about the meaning of life has come so unexpectedly from a virtually illiterate people, come out of the most intense conditions of exploitation, cruelty, violence, frustration, and lust, and yet has succeeded as an instinct in keeping this tortured people alive, then it is perhaps possible that the Negro holds more of the tail of the expanding elephant of truth than the radical, and if this is so, the radical humanist could do worse than to brood upon the phenomenon. For if a revolutionary time should come again, there would be a crucial difference if someone had already delineated a neo-Marxian calculus aimed at comprehending every circuit and process of society from ukase to kiss as the communications of human energy—a calculus capable of translating the economic relations of man into his psychological relations and then back again, his productive relations thereby embracing his sexual relations as well, until the crises of capitalism in the Twentieth Century would yet be understood as the unconscious adaptations of a society to solve its economic imbalance at the expense of a new mass psychological imbalance. It is almost beyond the imagination to conceive of a work in which the drama of human energy is engaged, and a theory of its social currents and dissipations, its imprisonments, expressions, and tragic wastes are fitted into some gigantic synthesis of human action where the body of Marxist thought, and particularly the epic grandeur of *Das Kapital* (that first of the major *psychologies* to approach the mystery of social cruelty so simply and practically as to say that we are a collective body of humans whose life-energy is wasted, displaced, and procedurally stolen as it passes from one of us to another)—where particularly the epic grandeur of *Das Kapital* would find its place in an even more God-like view of human justice and injustice, in some more excruciating vision of those intimate and institutional processes which lead to our creations and disasters, our growth, our attrition, and our rebellion.

# INDEX